"Leclerc and Peterson affirm our sinned-against brokenness and our hope of full redemption! Their prophetic voices are poignant and provocative in providing alternative theological perspectives that take survivors' experiences and needs well into account. Although a work of theology, there are so many pastoral implications that offer brilliant helps to our everyday dilemmas of grief-stricken, abandoned, and abused parishioners. There is a balm in Gilead for those on the back side of the cross."

—Rondy Smith
Founder and CEO, Rest Stop Ministries

"Contemporary social movements are raising a level of awareness to the suffering of victims in ways that were previously without precedent. Yet, part of what I see taking place in these movements is a society attempting to grapple with victimization in the absence of a theology that adequately addresses very complex issues. . . . This book offers the kind of creative, astute, and well-timed theology so needed for such a time as this."

—Timothy R. Gaines
Trevecca Nazarene University

"There are very few resources that help us understand how trauma can have an impact on the *spiritual* life and experience of a survivor. . . . This book helps bridge this gap. I have woven some of this book's theology into my practice with clients. I have heard more than once 'Why haven't I ever heard this before?' The insights offered by the authors will help pastors, clinicians, and survivors themselves work toward healing and wholeness."

—Julie Schmidt
LCSW

"This book will be important for educators and pastors; it will be timely for Christians everywhere. More narrowly, Leclerc and Peterson's emphasis meets a pronounced need in Wesleyan circles, in which language of atonement and holiness focuses on freedom from sin but may leave out those who have experienced unwilling violation. Instead of perceiving the atonement primarily as freeing people from guilt, this book takes seriously that the cross represents hope and redemption for those sinned against."

—Kara Lyons-Pardue
Point Loma Nazarene University

"This volume is a valuable, potent theological contribution to the growing body of literature focusing on the experiences, wisdom, and theological protest of the 'sinned against,' dismantling the focus of traditional atonement theologies and giving voice to so many of us who are survivors of violence."

—Elaine A. Heath
Author of *Healing the Wounds of Sexual Abuse: Reading the Bible with Survivors*

"Graphic and heartbreaking yet hopeful, practical help for the church striving to be God's incarnate presence to those who have suffered unspeakable cruelty and abuse at the hands of others—a thoughtful exposition of atonement theories, forgiveness, and encouragement. As a hospital chaplain, this book has helped me transcend my own weak 'but God is good' conclusions and come to sound biblical answers inspiring healing and hope—for myself and those I serve."

—Karla S. Sampson
Hospital chaplain

"Who is God for the godforsaken? Leclerc and Peterson bring us in for an unflinching look at the abandoned God on the cross. We listen for what the atonement has to tell us about freedom—not only for sinners but for those who have been sinned against. It is a journey from death to life. This book has powerful resonance for those walking alongside victims of modern slavery and abuse, and powerful hope for the victims themselves."

—Jennifer Roemhildt Tunehag
Director of Global Church Engagement, World Freedom Network

"Leclerc and Peterson offer a rich and deep theological and psychological perspective on the meaning of the atonement for the sinned against. Rarely is theology done with such great practical psychological insight and sophistication. This is not pop theology or psychology, but it is immediately practical; something that I as a psychotherapist and a pastor can immediately put to use. All those who care for the 'sinned against' should read this book."

—Brad D. Strawn
Fuller Theological Seminary

The Back Side of the Cross

The Back Side of the Cross

An Atonement Theology
for the Abused and Abandoned

Diane Leclerc and Brent Peterson

Foreword by
Lynn Bohecker

CASCADE *Books* · Eugene, Oregon

THE BACK SIDE OF THE CROSS
An Atonement Theology for the Abused and Abandoned

Copyright © 2022 Diane Leclerc and Brent Peterson. All rights reserved. Except for brief quotations in critical publications or reviews, no part of this book may be reproduced in any manner without prior written permission from the publisher. Write: Permissions, Wipf and Stock Publishers, 199 W. 8th Ave., Suite 3, Eugene, OR 97401.

Cascade Books
An Imprint of Wipf and Stock Publishers
199 W. 8th Ave., Suite 3
Eugene, OR 97401

www.wipfandstock.com

PAPERBACK ISBN: 978-1-6667-3171-2
HARDCOVER ISBN: 978-1-6667-2446-2
EBOOK ISBN: 978-1-6667-2447-9

Cataloguing-in-Publication data:

Names: Leclerc, Diane, author. | Peterson, Brent, author. | Lynn Bohecker, foreword.

Title: The back side of the cross : an atonement theology for the abused and abandoned / Diane Leclerc and Brent Peterson; foreword by Lynn Bohecker.

Description: Eugene, OR: Cascade Books, 2022 | Includes bibliographical references and index.

Identifiers: ISBN 978-1-6667-3171-2 (paperback) | ISBN 978-1-6667-2446-2 (hardcover) | ISBN 978-1-6667-2447-9 (ebook)

Subjects: LCSH: Salvation—Christianity. | Sin. | Victims—Religious life. | Jesus Christ—Crucifixion.

Classification: BT715 B25 2022 (paperback) | BT715 (ebook)

VERSION NUMBER 062722

We would like to dedicate this book to all who have suffered at the back side of the cross, including our own students and parishioners who have stood there.

And to Floyd E. Cunningham. Dad, because of your dark night of the mind, heart, and soul I can see pain where many may not. I do not believe your depression was a gift from God, but it was a gift to me. May you continue, truly, to rest in peace.

Contents

Permissions | ix
Foreword | xi
　—By Lynn Bohecker, PhD, LMFT
Preface | xv
Acknowledgments | xvii
The Authors | xix

PART 1: **A Back-Sided Theology of the Cross**

CHAPTER 1
To Theodicy and Beyond | 3

CHAPTER 2
The Other Side of Sin | 21

CHAPTER 3
Toward Saving the Conventional Cross | 39

CHAPTER 4
The Cross as Converted Symbol | 66

CHAPTER 5
Violence and Scapegoating | 78

CHAPTER 6
Child Abandonment | 101

CHAPTER 7
The Sexual Abuse of Jesus | 116

CHAPTER 8
Forgiving God | 131

CHAPTER 9
Resurrection for the Sinned-Against | 145

CHAPTER 10
Forgiveness from the Back Side | 165
 —By Diane Leclerc, PhD and Julie Schmidt, LCSW

PART 2: **Pastoral Resources**

CHAPTER 11
Standing in the Gap of Nurture: The Minister as Child Advocate | 201
 —By Aisling Zweigle

CHAPTER 12
Sorrow in the Saving: Lament as Faith | 215
 —By John W. Nielson

CHAPTER 13
Re-Envisioning the Table: Eucharist as Therapeutic Healing | 230

Bibliography | 247

Permissions

Scripture quotations labeled NIV are from the Holy Bible, New International Version. Copyright © 1973, 1978, 1984, 2011 by Biblica, Inc. Used by permission of Zondervan. All rights reserved worldwide.

Des Pres, Terrance. *The Survivor: An Anatomy of Life in the Death Camps*. Oxford: Oxford University Press, 1976. Excerpt used with permission.

Girard, René. *Sacrifice*. Translated by Matthew Pattillo and David Dawson. East Lansing, MI: Michigan State University Press, 2011. Excerpt used with permission.

Hall, Terese A. "Spiritual Effects of Childhood Sexual Abuse in Christian Women." *Journal of Psychology and Theology* 23 (1995) 129–34. Excerpt used with permission.

Mjaaland, Marius Timmann. "The Fractured Unity of God: Lament as a Challenge to the Very Nature of God." In *Evoking Lament*, edited by Eva Harasta and Brian Brock, 99–117. New York: T. & T. Clark International, 2009. Excerpt used with permission.

Nightbirde. (Aka: Marczewski, Jane.) Blog: "God is on the Bathroom Floor." Excerpt used with permission.

Soelle, Dorothee. *Suffering*. Philadelphia: Fortress, 1975. Excerpt used with permission.

Wiegman, Issac. "Divine Forgiveness and Mercy in Evolutionary Perspective." In *Connecting Faith and Science: Philosophical and Theological Inquiries*, edited by Matthew Nelson Hill and Wm. Curtis Holtzen, 183–214. Claremont, CA: Claremont, 2017. Excerpt used with permission.

Wiesenthal, Simon. *The Sunflower: On the Possibilities and Limits of Forgiveness*. New York: Schocken, 1976. Excerpt used with permission.

Foreword

By
Lynn Bohecker

This book serves an extremely useful purpose by showing that Christ has something to offer those who have been sinned against. Dominant themes in Christianity emphasize our sinful nature and highlight the necessity of confession of sin for salvation. These teachings can bring great relief and assurance of sins forgiven for those who have done harm to others. However, the church has not done well at articulating, or even understanding, how to help people who have been victimized. People who are hurting in this way are often invisible in our midst, and we are unaware of their emotional and spiritual needs.

Those who have been harmed by the sins of others have historically been silenced. Silenced by their abusers, silenced by those to whom they thought they could turn, and silenced by society as a whole. Few want to hear of their horrors, their pain, and their suffering. Some may not be aware of the damaging effect that being harmed by another is having on their lives. Some are aware of the impact, but do not know what to do about it. Many are unable to move on after they have been harmed by another, after surviving being the recipient of someone else's sins. These survivors often experience unwanted psychological symptoms such as anxiety, avoidance, sleep problems, and the reliving of the event. In essence, their whole perspective of the world shifts dramatically, and many are unable to get out of this ongoing living nightmare. Emotional healing comes from untangling myths about the harmful events, expressing their hurts, understanding their innocence, and speaking the truth of their experiences. In psychotherapy survivors are taught and encouraged to harness calm, work through their memories, and re-engage in life.

The "Me Too" movement started in order to empower women who have survived sexual harassment and sexual assault through solidarity and strength in numbers to break their silence and profess their experience only by saying "Me Too." "Black Lives Matter" is an international movement that also involves speaking out against violence and systemic racism towards African Americans. More and more people are coming forward, breaking the societal norms of silence by increasing conversations of the experiences of harm by the sins of others. Even with movements such as the two examples provided here, not much has changed so far. The adage that people should not talk about religion, politics, or money in polite company should be amended to include not initiating conversations of victimization, abuse, and oppression; the *norm of silence* that comes after experiences that fall into these categories is so ubiquitous that it does not even need to be mentioned, doubling the censorship.

Herein lies a problem, a dialectic. People who have been harmed by the sins of others need to speak about it to be healed, and no one is willing to listen and hear. This is akin to the philosophical thought experiment of the tree falling in the forest—does it make a sound if no one is around to hear it? The metaphysics of this issue relates similarly to the possibility of unperceived existence. And so, can something exist without being recognized? Did the harmful experience really happen if there is no witness to the event, and no one else to tell in order to validate it? The first important lesson for people who are ministering to those who have been harmed is to actively listen. Many pastors have been trained in listening skills, but it is possible that they do not really hear what goes beyond their experience, or the way they see reality. Theologians are trained to look for the broad strokes of human existence, but can float so far above the clouds that their thoughts do not touch the individual human. Caregivers, like pastors, need to know how to respond to abuse stories in a way that demonstrates they have really heard. People who have been harmed by others often feel hopeless. Pastors, then, can offer hope, but not in the way hope is offered to repentant sinners. An extremely useful purpose of this book is to provide a way to reach those who need a different perspective of hope. *The Back Side of the Cross* is a timely book for theologians, pastors, and even survivors, offering hope and healing for the sinned-against.

This is a theology book, first and foremost. Its methodology is to take the reality of abuse and abandonment as an extremely relevant source for theological reflection. It addresses theologies of theodicy, hamartiology, atonement, and Christology; and it proposes a juxtaposition between liberation and protest theology that moves in the direction of a new type of theology (that blends content and method) called "back-side theology." (This is explained thoroughly in chapter 1.) The purpose of this type of theology moves directly to practical implications. While this is not a book written as a "how-to" manual (its theology is too deep for such a depiction), it nonetheless offers important and foundational insights that are easily applied to real situations, real people, and hopefully for real healing.

Thus, for pastors, the content of the book could be an essential and practical guide when working with the sinned-against. It shows that the atonement of Christ has powerful potential to speak to those who have been wronged, especially those who have been abused and abandoned, and who wonder if they are included in the expanse of God's grace. The pastor will broaden her or his perspective, and grow in their ability to empathize with those on the "back side."

This book is well suited for academic settings as a theological textbook and could be of much interest in the fields of psychology, counseling, and social work. In sum, the authors present an extensive atonement theology from a new and different perspective, as well as very practical help that can reach those who need assurance of something new out of their suffering. It is theologically rigorous and thorough, but also trauma-informed. But there is one other audience who may benefit. It is important to address them directly.

For those who have been sinned against, the message here is that you can experience hope and healing. You, and everyone else who reads this book, may also experience uncomfortable emotions and memories. One way to address this is to be up front about the content, and to announce a "trigger warning." While I as a trained psychotherapist believe it is worth the journey through the book, it will most likely be a very difficult read for some who are on their path toward healing. Thus, some reminders and suggestions are in order: Try to keep yourself feeling safe and well. To facilitate your wellness, you may wish to make a list of activities you enjoy or that calm you. Before you begin to read a section, and after you finish, you may wish to spend some time involved in those activities. It may be helpful for you to rate your level of discomfort, distress, anxiety, or fear on a rating scale of 0–10, similar to the physical pain scale you may be asked when visiting a physician or dentist; you can also rate your emotional level in the same way.

When you experience discomfort, take a moment to rate yourself. Try not to read past when it becomes overwhelming as that may make you feel worse. Do not read this book when you are very upset or feel rushed. If you feel upset by something you have read or something you have thought of, or felt while reading, the best thing to do is to talk to an understanding and supportive person. If that is not possible, stop reading and do an activity you enjoy. Self-care is of the utmost importance for you.

Again, I want to let you know that *The Back Side of the Cross* is worth it. While what it covers is deep and wide, it is written with compassion and true empathy. This book deals with the meaning of suffering in a way that those who have been abused and abandoned can find solidarity and understanding in. In the area of abuse survivor literature, theological depth is sometimes put aside to meet immediate needs. Academic theology often theorizes to the extent that it flies far above real human experience. This book is therefore unique in offering theological depth, practical help, and potential for healing.

Preface

What has the cross traditionally symbolized? In Christian theology from its beginning, there has been a long history that has analyzed the doctrine of sin and the doctrine of the atonement from the perspective of the sinner only. As such, the problem of sin and the promise of salvation emphasize the importance of the repentance and faith of sinners and God's justification in response. This is the dominant theme in Christian preaching and teaching in the context of the church. But is there more to say? The primary question of this book is this: if the cross has always been portrayed as the means of salvation for sinners, does it have anything to say to those who have been sinned-against? We affirm that the atonement of Christ has powerful potential to speak to those who have been wronged, especially to those who have been abused and abandoned, who we imagine as cowering at the back side of the cross wondering if they are included.

This has been a question that Diane Leclerc has been pondering for the last thirty-plus years. She is a survivor of sexual abuse by a church member when she was a teenager. Besides her own personal struggle, her roles as pastor, professor, and theologian have driven her to make sense of abuse in the Christian context; encountering other survivors among her parishioners and students has only strengthened the sense of urgency through the years to find better "answers" for those who suffer. Ironically, the church for so many has been a place that has caused more woundedness and little healing. Despite concrete statistics about the high incidence of abuse that have broken into a general conscious awareness in society, the church has often ignored or callously minimized the issue in its midst. Worse yet, scandals of abuse in the church by its leaders have gone public to an embarrassing number and degree, despite attempts to cover up and hide them. What is not as public is that the statistics about the prevalence of various forms of abuse are not less for Christians. One in four women, and one in six men will be sexually abused in her/his lifetime—inside and outside the church—not to mention the myriad of other forms of abuse and oppression, from childhood and elderly neglect to violent abuse due to racism, sexism, classism, and ableism. It is impossible to name all the ways people wound people severely. Victims of all kinds are in the church. But we never look them in the eye and ask about their stories. Especially in light of the shame surrounding sexual abuse in particular, the church postures itself to deny that such things occur. We refuse to be hospitable to those who experience suffering of all kinds because we do not want to think through what it might say about God, or about us. In the meantime, these victims sit through our worship services and congregational gatherings in search of a theology that does not leave them on the side of the road, and for real caring people to help bind up their wounds. This disparity between the hope of the Christian gospel and the apathy of so many Christians around such issues led Diane to start a group for abuse victims *inside* the church. One of the most fruitful exercises was to write out what they wanted their fellow congregants to know about how hard it was for them to be there.

Abuse and abandonment are not new issues, but they have only more recently become fodder for theological reflection. Brent Peterson has been a long-term listener and advocate. He was deeply affected by one book in particular: *The Other Side of Sin: Woundedness from the Perspective of the Sinned-Against,* which is a compilation of chapters edited by Andrew Sung Park and Susan L. Nelson, published in 2001. He began teaching the book in his upper-division theology courses. The students' responses gave him great pause, and a sense of urgency to find theological "answers" to aid those who were suffering so deeply. This was coupled with an awakening that many in the church have been ignored. Brent also had a long-standing and deep passion for the recovery of lament in the life of the church. It was at this juncture that Diane and Brent began talking through the theology of the cross, and how it could be reinterpreted for the sinned-against. These conversations—that never seemed finished—turned into a book that has taken several years to complete. It is by no means the final word on the subject. Far from it. There is so much more work to do to respond to the suffering of abuse victims with theological integrity. We hope here to offer a substantial contribution.

Acknowledgments

This book would not have been written without incredible support from a wide variety of people. So many have encouraged our efforts by tenaciously believing in the project. Our colleagues in the College of Theology and Christian Ministry at Northwest Nazarene University have cheered us around every lap of what turned out to be a very long marathon. We are also on staff at the same church, and have appreciated the care and interest of those at College Church of the Nazarene in Nampa, Idaho.

Diane is very thankful to everyone through the years who has shared her/his story of heartache around issues of abuse with her, especially the College Church Survivors Group, and countless students at the university. I hold each account as priceless china in my hands. I am thankful for family and for so many dear friends who have helped me persevere in life in general, who also seemed to know when to ask, and *not* to ask, how the book was coming. And I especially want to thank my own professional counselors who have helped me discover the freedom I have found, especially one of my first, Judy Paul, and my last, Dr. Barbara Ottenhoff. Where would I be personally without you?

Brent would like to thank Dr. Ruth Duck, who first opened his eyes in graduate school to the lost gift of lament in the church and the great need to care for the sinned-against. I am also thankful for the work and conversations with Dr. Andrew Sung Park, whose writing has been illuminating. I am also thankful to the many students and parishioners who have had the courage to share their journey of pain and abuse, that were too often silenced either by shame or false guilt or were simply ignored. I am thankful to my colleague, Diane, as we have journeyed together on this hard but important conversation. Finally, I thank my wife and children, who have been a constant source of encouragement and joy.

We offer now to you, the reader, what feels like a very sacrificial offering. May God make these words helpful to those who seek to care for those at the back side of the cross, and healing for those who stand there. You do not stand alone.

The Authors

Diane Leclerc is Professor of Historical Theology at Northwest Nazarene University, where she has taught for over twenty years. Her expertise is in the areas of Patristic Studies, the theology of John Wesley, and the nineteenth-century Holiness Movement. She has also written and spoken broadly in the areas of feminism, pastoral theology, disability studies, and extensively on the theology of holiness (her denomination's key theological tenant). She is past president of the Wesleyan Theological Society. Her keen interest in writing for those who have been abused comes out of her own personal experiences of abuse, and her extensive work with women in pastoral settings. She is an ordained elder, with over thirty years of pastoral ministry experience. She has been lead pastor of two congregations, and presently serves as an associate pastor in addition to her full-time teaching position.

Brent Peterson is Dean of the College of Theology and Christian Ministries and Professor of Theology at Northwest Nazarene University. His primary areas of expertise are ecclesiology, Wesleyan theology, Christology, and sacramental/ liturgical theology. He is a leading voice in the Wesleyan tradition on the sacraments, and is a member of the North American Academy of Liturgy in the Eucharist Seminar. He is a convener for the Worship Seminar for the Oxford Institute for Methodist Theological Studies. He also founded the Wesleyan Liturgical Society as a branch of the Wesleyan Theological Society. He is an ordained elder and has over twenty years of pastoral ministry experience, and presently serves as an associate pastor in addition to his roles as professor and dean.

The Contributors

John Nielson is Assistant Professor of Practical Theology at Eastern Nazarene College, and serves as their music director as well. He is an ordained elder with over thirty years of pastoral ministry experience, most recently in Upper Marlboro, Maryland, where he served for twenty-four years. He received his Doctor of Ministry degree from Nazarene Theological Seminary in 2013. His dissertation was *Developing Practices of Corporate Lament for the Local Parish*. It includes an extensive list of pastoral resources for those seeking to incorporate communal lament into their worship services and other ministry contexts.

Julie Schmidt is a Licensed Clinical Social Worker. She is trained in therapies to address trauma including Eye Movement Desensitization and Reprocessing, Trauma Focused Cognitive Behavioral Therapy, and Psychomotor Therapy. She has worked in the mental health field for fifteen years with adults, teens, and children. She is currently employed at St. Luke's Regional Medical Center (Boise, ID) as part of the Children's Behavioral Health team. She has also spoken about trauma response in the church, and has led a small group for abuse victims in her congregation.

Aisling Zweigle is an ordained elder who presently serves as Family Life Pastor for Tenth Church (Missionary Alliance) in Vancouver, British Columbia. She has served as an associate pastor in a wide variety of churches, and as an early childhood educator with children from around the world. She also served as a missionary and child advocate overseas in Manila, Philippines. She is certified in early childhood education, and has a Master of Arts in Religious Education, with an emphasis in holistic child development and trauma-informed care.

PART 1

A Back-Sided Theology of the Cross

I have had cancer three times now, and I have barely passed thirty . . . I spent three months propped against the wall. On nights that I could not sleep, I laid in the tub like an insect, staring at my reflection in the shower knob. I vomited until I was hollow. I rolled up under my robe on the tile. The bathroom floor became my place to hide, where I could scream and be ugly; where I could sob and spit and eventually doze off, happy to be asleep, even with my head on the toilet . . .

I am God's downstairs neighbor, banging on the ceiling with a broomstick. I show up at His door every day. Sometimes with songs, sometimes with curses. Sometimes apologies, gifts, questions, demands. Sometimes I use my key under the mat to let myself in. Other times, I sulk outside until He opens the door to me Himself. I have called Him a cheat and a liar, and I meant it. I have told Him I wanted to die, and I meant it. Tears have become the only prayer I know. Prayers roll over my nostrils and drip down my forearms. They fall to the ground as I reach for Him. These are the prayers I repeat night and day; sunrise, sunset . . .

Even on days when I'm not so sick, sometimes I go lay on the [bath] mat in the afternoon light to listen for Him. I know it sounds crazy, and I can't really explain it, but God is in there—even now. I have heard it said that some people can't see God because they won't look low enough, and it's true. Look lower. God is on the bathroom floor.[1]

—Nightbirde

---

1. Nightbirde, "God is on the Bathroom Floor."

CHAPTER 1

To Theodicy and Beyond

Everybody in the block had typhus ... [I]t came to Belsen Bergen [concentration camp] in its most violent, most painful, deadliest form. The diarrhea caused by it became uncontrollable. It flooded the bottom of the cages, dripping through the cracks into the faces of the women lying in the cages below, and mixed with blood, pus and urine, formed a slimy, fetid mud on the floor of the barracks...[1]

Urine and excreta poured down the prisoners' legs, and by nightfall the excrement which had frozen to our limbs, gave off its stench. We were really no longer human beings in the accepted sense. Not even animals, but putrefying corpses moving on two legs...[2]

The location was slippery and unlighted. Of the thirty men on this assignment (to clean the latrines], an average of ten fell into the pit in the course of each night's work. The others were not allowed to pull the victims out. When the work was done

---

1. Perl, *I Was a Doctor in Auschwitz*, 171.
2. Weiss, *Journey Through Hell*, 211.

and the pit empty, then and then only were they permitted to remove the corpses . . .[3]

The men could not bring themselves to obey this devilish order [to drink out of the toilet bowls]; they only pretended to drink. But the block-fuehrers had reckoned with that; they forced the men's heads deep into the bowls until their faces were covered with excrement. At this the victims almost went out of their minds—that was why their screams had sounded so demented.[4]

What a horrific place to start a book! What unbearable scenes of human cruelty that invade our imagination from reading only the few paragraphs above. We obviously decided to start with such a disturbing depiction of Holocaust horror. But not without reason. This is a book about suffering. In particular, it is a book about suffering at the hands of others. It begins with this question: does the cross of Christ have anything to say to the "sinned-against"? In the history of theological reflection, theology has done well to explain how the cross helps sinners. Such theories fall under the category of the atonement. But we believe that forgiving sinners is only part of the potency of the crucifixion and resurrection of Jesus. There are those at the "back side" of the cross who need something else. Those who have been abused and abandoned look on, and wonder if the cross has anything to say to them.

An unfortunate but necessary aspect of this book, then, is that before we can talk about the nature of the healing available in the cross of Christ, a heavy dose of the dreadfulness of suffering must be swallowed. And so scenes like the one described above, which happened in the course of human history in our relatively recent past, can also serve us metaphorically here, if you will: to fully empathize with the type of human experiences addressed in the following chapters, we must fall into the pits with those who have been forsaken and left to die. To offer Christian hope (no matter how potentially helpful) *without* true empathy is often hollow, empty, and void. Sufferers hear only platitudes when we speak to them from the safety and comfort "above" them. "Survivors do not bear witness to guilt, neither theirs

3. Weinstock, *Beyond the Last Path*, 157–58.
4. Szalet, *Experiment "E,"* 42.

nor ours, but to objective conditions of evil. In the literature of survival we find an image of things so grim, so heartbreaking, so starkly unbearable, that inevitably the survivor's scream begins to be our own."[5] Seeking to be cruciform, we strive here to write from "below" and huddle with the rejected at the "back side" of the cross.[6] In a sincere attempt to find genuine empathy, we seek first to sit with those terrorized and paralyzed. We take a cue from David Blumenthal (who has written an intriguing book that juxtaposes victims of the Holocaust and victims of sexual abuse). He writes:

> One of the paths of our life [should be] walking with the victim—beyond endurance, into suffering that cannot be told—as best we can. One tack in our lives is to confront what we would rather avoid, with as much courage as we can muster . . . as an act of solidarity; not in guilt, but as an act of remembrance. We must do this in our texts, in our deeds, in our commitments.[7]

This book will not be an "easy read," for it will take suffering and sufferers seriously, as an attempt at such solidarity.

To put it even more directly, important in this introduction is a note on "tone" as related to our ultimate intentions. We believe that appropriate language and voice will be crucial to our task. "A curious fact about language . . . is that to write about terrible things in a neutral tone, or with descriptions barren of subjective response tends to generate the irony so virulent as to end in cynicism or despair. On the other hand, to allow feeling much play when speaking of atrocity is to border on hysteria and reduce the agony of millions to a moment of self-indulgence," Terrance De Pres warns.[8] What we hope is that this will be a thoroughly theological work that seeks its groundedness in the experience of real suffering—subjective enough to remain existentially relevant, but not so subjective that we impose a type of forced voyeurism of the writers' personal angst (or experiences) onto the readers. The subject matter evokes enough angst on its own. The same author that cautions us about tone in the quote above, also reminds us that an appropriate response does, in fact, *necessarily* enter the realm of the sacred. De Pres continues by suggesting that a "religious vocabulary" will help balance our voices with hope in the midst of such atrocious suffering. "Only a

---

5. Des Pres, *Survivor*, 49.

6. We use the *back side* of the cross metaphorically to point to experiences of innocent suffering that still cover the abused with deep shame—experiences that have been imposed on the sufferers by another and carry the extra weight of humiliation that in effect degrades and dehumanizes them; also as in a person's backside.

7. Blumenthal, *Facing the Abusing God*, 54.

8. De Pres, *Survivor*, vi.

language of Ultimate Concern can be adequate to facts such as these."[9] We will attempt to make theological generalizations delicately. While doing so with appropriate care and humility, we do want to make bold moves about how the life and death and resurrection of Jesus the Christ are more than relevant to the subject matter, indeed to the objectified subjects themselves who have been sinned against.

Theodicy as Rational Defense

We want to make something very clear at the start. Whatever this book is, it is not a *theodicy*. Theodicy deals with religious questions about the nature of suffering. The ultimate quest of the type of theology called theodicy, which is often more philosophical in method and character, is to "justify God" in light of the brutalities of human existence. The theological question, also known as "the problem of evil," is how two seemingly absolute characteristics of the Judeo-Christian God—omnipotence and goodness (love)—can coexist under the conditions of a world where evil and suffering run rampant through the streets of human experience. How can God be all-powerful and not use that power to end senseless suffering? How can God be good and all-loving and allow such suffering in the first place? Theodicies often deconstruct, or at least redefine, God's power or God's goodness, or give reasons why suffering is somehow beneficial for humanity, either individually or as a whole, either in the present or in the future. Again, their goal is to defend God, to get God off the hook through theoretical gymnastics. Defending God creates another burden on victims who have already taken on responsibility for their trauma. In a sense, theodicy is an odd type of apologetics (most often defined as a defense of Christian truth). Whatever this book is, it is not a defense of God. We are after very different kinds of apologies.

"How do we cope with insurmountable obstacles that are thrown our way, with events causing such terrible pain that we cannot seem to go on? Are we supposed to suffer in silence, to endure and accept this deplorable plight without complaint?" asks Claudia Welz.[10] We would like to emphatically state that the answer to this question will not come through rational theodicies that are humming a very different tune than the song-cries of lament that arise from the abyss of unspeakable pain. De Pres writes, "An agony so massive should not be, indeed cannot be, reduced to a bit of datum

---

9. De Pres, *Survivor*, vi.
10. Welz, "Trust and Lament," 118.

in a theory."[11] Rational theodicies "seem out of place to people who are helplessly watching their lives fall apart. Crying, wailing, mute horror [from those who suffer]. Who would want to impose regulations and restrictions on such spontaneous responses?" Welz rightly asks.[12]

Theodicies can suppress, through these kinds of theoretical abstractions, the natural reactions of sufferers, who experience suffering as the bitter taste of meaningless pain, who are hardly interested in theoretical anythings. Theodicies force them to ingest what should be expelled and rejected—rational answers to absurd situations. Further, "Even after moments of terror and paralysis," Welz continues, "when the question of how life can continue slowly starts to rise, it is still difficult to decide what exactly should or should not be done."[13] Indeed, pain increases when the realization comes that sometimes, in some situations, there is nothing to be *done*, if doing means fixing. Sometimes, in some situations, the only option is screaming that resolves into a "courage to [continue to] be."[14] Theodicies in effect mute cries of lament, let alone cries of protest, complaint, or accusation precisely because they try to explain the relation of God to suffering in wholly inadequate ways. Theodicies try to make sense of the senseless. Marius Timmann Mjaaland states, "While often carried out with the best of intentions, dealing with the problem in the abstract suppresses the contradictions of suffering, replacing them instead with rational discourse."[15] While most often presented like a defense in a courtroom, some theodical images are not even very rational. At their worst, Christian theodicies paint pictures of God as either vicious or emaciated, and humans as either vile or limitless—all Picassoesque distortions of theological reality. Their misguidedness is particularly keen when we consider *victims*. Dorothee Soelle writes: "There have been innumerable religious attempts to explain suffering. The difficulty lies less in the existential interpretation that people give to their pain than in the later theological systemization, which has no use for suffering that hasn't been named and pigeonholed. Thus, for example . . . [what] is systematized [is often] the proposition that all pain comes from God."[16]

It is admittedly difficult to preserve a proper view of God in the face of innocent suffering. The force of the question that theodicy seeks to answer superimposes itself on biblical interpretation and biblical theology

---

11. De Pres, *Survivor*, vii.
12. Welz, "Trust and Lament," 118.
13. Welz, "Trust and Lament," 118.
14. A phrase used by Paul Tillich in his famously titled book, *Courage to Be*.
15. Mjaaland, "Fractured Unity of God," 101.
16. Soelle, *Suffering*, 20.

particularly. The fact is that the question of theodicy is a relatively new adventure in theological study. "The assumption that there is something called the problem of evil which creates a discourse called 'theodicy' occurred at the same time that modern atheism came into being. The creation of 'the' problem of evil is a correlative of the creation of a god that, it was presumed, could be known separate from a community of people at worship . . . The problem with the problem of evil is that the issue presupposes that the question of God's existence can be separated from God's character."[17] The Bible, wholly expressive of multiple worshipping communities, is not interested in finding an answer. The closest we come is found in the book of Job, and in Jesus' short reflections on the man born blind. The temptation is great to look for a systematic and satisfying resolution in Scripture itself. But "for the early Christians, suffering and evil . . . did not have to be 'explained.' Rather, what was required was the means to go on if the evil could not be 'explained.' Indeed, it was crucial that such suffering or evil not be 'explained'—that is, it was important not to provide theoretical accounts of why such evil needed to be in order that certain good results occur, since such an explanation would undercut the necessity of the community capable of absorbing the suffering."[18] Said succinctly, the question "why" was not their concern; more important is the imperative question "how"—how would they endure the suffering and persecution they faced?

As a theoretical problem, the problem of evil creates the best defense for atheism, because it is simply unanswerable logically. Many Christians have "lost faith" in the face of inexplicable suffering. One victim expressed that she grew up with faith "but my faith was not big enough to hold the life I experienced."[19] It is not logically tenable to hold on to the idea that an all-powerful and all-loving God can allow innocent suffering. And so, the easiest way to answer the question is to modify God's power or God's love. Process theology represents a reinterpretation of God's power or sovereignty. It, in effect, reaches the conclusion that God does not do anything about suffering because God can't.[20] God's love, which never overrides human free will for any reason, renders God "impotent" to interfere by direct action. God can only woo us to make the most of the circumstances in which we find ourselves. Logically, there must be an opposite possibility, namely, that God is not all-loving or good. This is best reflected in what is known as protest theology (which will be discussed further below). This

---

17. Hauerwas, *Naming the Silences*, 41–42.
18. Hauerwas, *Naming the Silences*, 49.
19. Said by a client in therapy for trauma.
20. See Oord, *God Can't*.

theology puts "God on trial" and questions God's goodness. And so, one way to solve the problem of evil is to deconstruct what is believed about God in the traditional form, as a means of defending some configuration of the existence of some kind of a god. Again, the problem of evil is often used as a defense for atheism.

Theodicy as Religious Sadomasochism

Such a defense for atheism is ironically pushed along by some of the places where Christian thought has wandered, because of the kind of God some theologies have created; there are Christian forms of God not deemed worthy of worship by detractors. Perhaps some of the most damaging ideas have arisen "unconsciously"—by which we mean ideas about God that were not intended to directly answer theodicy, but ones that are now used in such a manner. It is certainly beyond our scope here to give an account of the interpretation of suffering in different eras and movements throughout Christian history. We can assert that there have been times when the focus was on the love of God, and God's presence with the sufferer (such as in medieval Catholic mysticism). At other points, the problem of evil is solved by insisting that there is no such thing as innocent suffering; the emphasis is on the idea that all pain, affliction, and suffering, indeed all evil done to human beings, comes directly from the hand of a sovereign God because we deserve it. "The God who produces suffering and causes affliction becomes the glorious theme of a theology that directs our attention to the God who demands the impossible and tortures" us when those demands are not met.[21] Intensely dangerous and destructive themes come during the Reformation that are still used today. Listen to the following words:

> [We are] miserable sinners, conceived and born in guilt and sin, prone to iniquity, and incapable of any good work, and . . . in our depravity we make no end of transgressing thy commandments.
>
> [We] confess, as is indeed true, that we are unworthy to lift up our eyes unto heaven and appear in thy presence, and we ought not to presume to hope that thou wilt listen to our prayers if thou takest account of the things we lay before thee.
>
> And surely, O Lord, from the very chastisements which thou has inflicted upon us, we know that for the justest causes thy wrath is kindled against us; for, seeing Thou art a just Judge, thou afflictest not thy people when not offending. Therefore, beaten with thy stripes, we acknowledge that we have provoked

21. Soelle, *Suffering*, 22.

> thy anger against us: and even now we see thy hand stretched forth for our punishment. The swords which thou art wont to use in inflicting vengeance are now drawn, and those with which though threatenest sinners and wicked men we see ready to smite. But though thou mightest take much severer punishment upon us than before, and thus inflict blows an hundredfold more numerous, and though disasters only less dreadful than those with which thou didst formerly chastise the sins of thy people Israel, should overtake us, we confess that we are worthy of them, and have merited them by our crimes.
>
> Scriptures teach us that Pestilence, War, and other calamities of this kind are chastisements of God, which he inflicts on our sins.[22]

Dorothee Soelle calls this theological sadism, which "schools people in thought patterns that regard sadistic behavior as normal, in which one worships, honors, and loves a Being whose radicality, intentionality, and greatest sharpness is that he slays. The ultimate conclusion of theological sadism is worshipping the executioner."[23] In an attempt to maintain God's sovereignty, this theology pushes God's power to a frightening degree. But it does "solve" the problem of evil. Why is there suffering in the world? Because everyone is guilty, no one is innocent, and God brings all suffering as a form of "justifiable" punishment. The result is an affirmation of a sadistic god, that requires a certain amount of denial or suppression of this reality.

The affirmation of a sadistic God also traditionally requires a parallel masochism on our part that comes in the form of passive submission to all suffering as God's will. The most subtle form of this is the belief that God causes suffering "for our good." Such a position is rampant in popular Christianity today. "Suffering is there to break our pride, demonstrate our powerlessness, exploit our dependency. Affliction has the intention of bringing us back to God who only becomes great when he makes us small. In that case affliction is seen as unavoidable . . . Suffering is understood to be a test, sent by God, that we are required to pass," Soelle writes. God forces something upon us without our consent, until we break. In her opinion on this point, "Theologians have an intolerable passion for explaining and speaking when silence would be appropriate."[24]

A crucial, but often overlooked outcome of a Christian masochistic view is that a position of demanded submission and acquiescence of one's suffering as God's will make resistance to suffering inappropriate and thus

---

22. Calvin, "Forms of Prayer for the Church," 100, 107, 108.
23. Soelle, *Suffering*, 28.
24. Soelle, *Suffering*, 19.

impossible to express. The sexual connotation here stands as a vivid analogy, as God forces suffering upon us. In light of this conclusion, it makes sense to say that religion is an "opioid of the people" that keeps them under control. Taking all suffering as from God's hand prevents working against the reasons and conditions that allow suffering to continue. Soelle makes this interesting observation: "Whoever deals with his personal suffering only in the way our society has taught him—through illusion, minimization, suppression, apathy—will deal with societal suffering in the same way."[25] Sadomasochistic theology washes over any sense of injustice. All justice comes from God, and all must be accepted. It solves the problem of evil, but at what cost?

Beyond Theodicy

Giving theodical answers, then, is not an act of solidarity with those who suffer. It often estranges victims from us, and from their own confounding experiences. It is precisely traditional theodicy that should not be done in the presence of such sufferers. Most precisely, justifying God can be a slap in the face, a cold and stale litany of the wrong kind, to those who carry survivor's pain, or even survivor's "guilt." Marius Timmann Mjaaland states, "Rather than actually addressing the problem, [theodicy] keeps us at an abstract level and simply papers over the horrific abyss that appears horrific precisely because suffering is experienced as abandonment by God, or even the result of divine hatred."[26] But that is exactly what theodicy does, because as long as God is justified, freed from responsibility for neglecting the abused's needs—or as long as their agony, misery, and tragedies are easily explained away by denying their absurdity (by insisting they have some greater and benevolent purpose)—there is no place for the expression of genuine anger specifically directed toward God. Mjaaland concurs: "The thesis of a theodicy becomes a *prosthesis* which *replaces* a break or fracture within suffering. And at times it becomes a prohibition against the objectionable idea that one might level accusations at God because of injustices, suffering, and evil (or due to God's absence)."[27] Perhaps the need to defend God comes most from those for whom God does not need to be defended. Defending God becomes a means of defending one's own acts of contribution to the systemic issues that perpetuate victimization. Victims need something else.

---

25. Soelle, *Suffering*, 4.
26. Mjaaland, "Fractured Unity of God," 101.
27. Mjaaland, "Fractured Unity of God," 100–101.

Again, we begin with the presupposition that defending God through reasonable argument does nothing for the sufferer. This is not to say that we abandon all theological reflection in the name of mystery or for the purpose of "taking a moment of silence." This too is an inadequate type of theodicy because appeals to mystery still attempt to protect God's justifiability. With fear and trembling, we boldly acknowledge that finding an answer to the problem of evil—or put differently, protecting God's innocence—is not the goal of this project. (We may even be bold enough to suggest that it is not a helpful goal in any context, theological, existential, or otherwise.) What we do seek here is help for the sufferer, and deeper understanding on the part of bystanders. And yet there are theological questions around the periphery of theodicy that are worth serious reflection if we truly want to help. We will not avoid the "why" question, because it is a visceral response to pain and suffering. But we will not answer it in the typical fashion of a rational theodicy, and certainly not by asserting that suffering is punishment for sin.

Victimization and Back Side Theology

We want to assert that some traditional theories of the atonement are masked theodicies. We want to change the question. What we want to ask is whether the cross of Christ has anything to say to those, not who sin, but who have been *sinned against*. This may seem like a false dichotomy that denies "all have sinned." This is not our point. By invoking the category of the sinned-against, we acknowledge that there is innocent suffering everywhere we turn—suffering that is not a direct consequence of one's own sin, but that is inflicted by the hands of another person. The cross's efficacy for the sinner has been dominant throughout Christian history. We want to press, does the symbol that stands at the center of all of Christian faith address the *victims* of the actions of those who sin? Christianity has done very well at providing various "atonement theories" that explain in great detail how Jesus' death brings forgiveness and salvation to sinners. Indeed, it seems that this has not only been their primary focus, but their singular focus. In order to explicitly subvert this tradition, we ask boldly: what would an understanding of the atonement for the *sinned-against* look like?

We first confess we have a problem. The label "sinned-against" represents a person who is faceless, nameless, placeless. She embodies these X-less realities experientially. We know she is there, but for the most part theology and theologians have only seen her shadow. For the most part, we fail to see or acknowledge *her* pain at all, except in the abstract. In the abstract, we can feel pity or be socially concerned for situations in our neighborhoods or across the world that oppress her; but to us *she* is literally "no one" in particular, and it is more than easy to ignore "no one." This is the sentence of every abused victim on the face of the earth: obscurity. We obscure her through theological generalizations. Instead we want her to exist in our imaginations as we write every single word of this book (imagining that such imagining gives more credibility and integrity to our writing). But even this heartfelt "gesture" objectifies *her*. We will *use her* in this theological endeavor to bring this or that situation to light. But we will not bring light to her, no matter how pure or passionate our intentions may be. Unless we board a plane, or walk across the street to find her reality, we perpetuate her X-lessness and her nonbeing. Theological generalizations often do nothing for real people. But certainly not all theologies lead to such nonaction, do they?

For this reason and others, what we seek to write is definitely a type of "liberation" theology since all liberation theologies are driven by a call to action. Liberation theology is contextualized theology that names groups that stand in need of some type of emancipation—but if it only names the need, it has failed; liberation theology is intended to be a catalyst for actual change. Soelle (writing as a German liberation theologian of the generation that came after the era of the Holocaust), strongly reminds us how imperative change is:

> The issue we face today, in my view, is not about the necessity and possibility of eliminating misery but about the persons through whom this process is carried out. *Who* is working on the abolition of the social conditions which of necessity produce suffering? Surely not those who are free from suffering. Surely not those who are incapable of suffering, who at the same time have lost the ability to perceive the suffering of others. Neither is it those who are so thoroughly destroyed through continual suffering that they can respond only in helpless or aggressive attempts to flee. Only those who themselves are suffering will work for the abolition of conditions under which people are exposed to senseless, patently unnecessary suffering, such as hunger, oppression, or torture. Are we going to ally ourselves with them—or are we going to remain on the other side of the barrier?[28]

As liberation theology is often labeled, ours will join theologies from the "underside," on the side of those in pain. As a liberation theology we will start with the situation of suffering, and ultimately affirm the solidarity of God with the sufferer. It is certainly our aim as writers of this book that

28. Soelle, *Suffering*, 2–3.

real change can occur; there are structures and forces to be overturned. But it is not always easy to find such forces because they are so suppressed by a society unwilling to acknowledge the issues we want to expose to light.

As a liberation theology, this book is concerned with the rights and freedoms of certain groups. But rather than being a contextualized theology that has a specific *face* or an obvious *place*—African, African American, Asian, Latina(o), feminist, womanist, etc.—the groups we will address are clusters that are most often unidentifiable on an empirical level. They are not groups based on race, gender, or even socio-economic factors (although these may indeed be very influential). What we want to develop is something related to, but different than theology from the "underside."

We want to write a theology from the "back side," from the "back side of the cross," which symbolizes for us a place of shame based on unspeakable experiences. We will write specifically about victims of violence, neglect or abandonment, and abuse. They are oppressed "groups" based solely on shared experiences that are peculiarly alienating and dehumanizing, and most often hidden and unspoken.

Victims of violence, neglect, and abuse come in all shapes and sizes. Victims are of various ethnicities, young and old, male and female, trans or not. There are no identifying features on which to base our proclivity to categorize, other than common horrible experiences. And yet victims too stand in need of liberation—often desperately. Liberation from what?, we might ask. Here too, the answer is not obvious, as in observable. Certainly some are literally held captive and need to be freed, such as victims of the sex trade and human trafficking. Others' "captivity" is more psychological, even spiritual. All victims need liberation in some way, in the sense of being freed from a disempowering and dehumanizing woundedness, that may be presently happening or that happened years earlier. According to psychiatrist Leonard Shengold, victims of childhood abuse and neglect have been *de-souled*. "Soul murder is neither a diagnosis nor a condition. It is a dramatic term for circumstances that eventuate in crime—the deliberate attempt to eradicate or compromise the separate identity of another person. The victims of soul murder remain in large part possessed by another, their souls in bondage to someone else."[29] All victims need the liberation of being rehumanized and re-dignified.

But there is also a "back sidedness" of the liberation for those who experience victimization that makes its "freedom" unique. Whereas liberation for women of color, for example, identifies evil done against such women that needs to be resisted so that they may find "liberation" and indeed *celebrate*

---

29. Shengold, *Soul Murder*, 2.

their identity as women of color, liberation for the victim is different. There is no underlying common identity to celebrate. The only commonality that might unite victims is their apparent vulnerability—which can never be celebrated. In fact, it is common to blame the victim for such vulnerability, and to subsequently ascribe some kind of guilt to them personally. For this reason and others, unfortunately the experiences of abuse, pain, and suffering are kept hidden and secret, and the damaged are left alone. It is hard to find commonality, let alone community, when what might bind them is a shared sense of the horror of what they have endured. In such "back sidedness" victims are often covered in a silent shame all their own.

We have discovered that for survivors of sexual abuse in particular, the very act of telling their story has often been liberating, and brings them out of a suffocating isolation. Often the perpetrator threatens, manipulates, and intimidates to such a degree that the victim is terrorized by fear of what the abuser will do if they break their silence. This is incredibly confounding if the abused are children at the time of the abuse. Often healing begins when those victimized begin to tell their story and share their experiences with compassionate listeners. The perpetrators' threats are disempowered. But after the story is told, it often goes that survivors can slip back into hiding. Wearing the badge of "survivor" openly can be much more difficult than in the case of other liberationist groups. Unless there is some obvious physical impairment as a result of victimization, the reality they live in is often not perceived. It is an internal branding that victims endure. It is a wounding that can bring the commonality necessary for a shared call for liberation, but it is too often a wounding borne in seclusion. There is a "back sidedness" to their experiences, a facelessness and anonymity that runs along the "underside" call for freedom common to all liberation theology. Being silent and unseen has kept them safe. It is an incredible act of bravery to step into the light of being known. Unfortunately, we can easily avert our ears from their unique kind of painful cry as well as our eyes from their shadowy figures. Particularly in American culture, we tend to neglect, if not altogether ignore, the "sick" and wounded who live in an air of tragedy. They remind us of our own mortality and immorality, a fact we would much rather deny or at least forget. If they sense this, and they do, why in the world would they increase their vulnerability to further harm by identifying themselves?

Back side theology is also a type of "protest" theology. Back side theology could be seen, methodologically, as a blending of protest and liberation theologies. Protest theology is also known as Jewish protest theology or Holocaust theology. In its most popular form, it is expressed by persons such as Elie Wiesel in books such as *Night*.[30] Protest theology rejects theodicies, focuses on the existential experience of God's abandonment, and is open to the possibility of God's guilt. Our back side theology will start with the situation of suffering, but, unlike liberation theology, it will not presume God's solidarity with the sufferer if such a presumption denies or cuts short the experience of God's abandonment so palatable for those who suffer from various forms of evil, or prevents cries of protest. Allowing persons to feel abandoned by God is key; they should not be argued out of it. Many chapters below will sound like protest.

And yet, back side theology parts ways with Holocaust protest theology in that God's solidarity with the abandoned is ultimately maintained *precisely* as Jesus, who is God, experiences Godforsakenness. At the center of a "back side atonement" then is Christ's cry of agony: "My God, my God, why have you forsaken me." This cry of course, comes from Psalm 22. Old Testament scholar Stephen Riley offers these reflections.

> In Psalm 22, the psalmist, like someone ripping off a band-aid, forces us to consider the ways we are surrounded by events and issues that feel like "bulls of Bashan," "wild dogs or horned oxen," or "companies of evildoers." We are forced to think about the way these things make "our bones feel out of joint," "our hearts melt like wax," or "our tongues stick to the roofs of our mouths." When we stop to consider them, it is no wonder that we feel abandoned. We wonder why it seems there is no rescue, no respite, no hope in some situations. Unfortunately, many feel that they cannot utter the words of the Psalmist. They may have been taught that as a person of faith they should not question God or feel rejected by God. This leads to a sense of failure in faith or isolation because the "common sense" of our community is that it is not acceptable to feel overwhelmed or forsaken. However, the good news for us is that in the wisdom of the biblical canon and the church, laments like Psalm 22 have been included in our regular worship and, most specifically, in one of our highest holy days, Good Friday.[31]

30. A Hungarian-born Jewish-American writer, professor, political activist, Nobel laureate, and Holocaust survivor, Elie Wiesel was the author of fifty-seven books, including *Night*, a work based on his experiences as a prisoner in the Auschwitz, Buna, and Buchenwald concentration camps. Wiesel's 1979 play *The Trial of God* is about a trial in which God is the defendant, and is reportedly based on events that Wiesel himself witnessed as a teenager in Auschwitz. Over the course of the trial, a number of arguments are made, both for and against God's guilt. Wiesel's theological stance, illustrated through the intuitive possibilities of literature, is a theology of existentialist protest, which neither denies God nor accepts theodicies.

31. Riley, "Psalm 22."

Back side theology, particularly regarding the atonement, allows for protests against God for allowing the atrocities of victimization. Again, these protests must not be short-circuited, or short-lived. But ultimately, though strangely, we may also find solace in the violent victimization of Christ on the cross, who endured the fullest extent of human cruelty, not "in our place" but by our side, in full solidarity with the abandoned.

Definitions and Extensions

Further definitions will be useful at this point, as we further fine-tune our intended "audience." First, victimization implies "affliction" at the hand of others. Affliction, according to Simone Weil, can be distinguished from other forms of suffering.[32] She suggests that affliction has three essential dimensions: physical, psychological, and social. There have been recent studies that have scientifically connected the three. We now know that it is not uncommon for nonphysical trauma to cause physical pain (alongside the more obvious fact that physical pain can cause psychological and emotional turmoil, especially if physical pain is chronic).[33] The social dimension comes from the experience of alienation. There is a loneliness in suffering in general, as others withdraw from those who suffer, at times to the point of ostracism. And there is a sense of isolation that comes from the reality that every experience of suffering is unique. Certainly abuse elicits social, as well as physical and psychological, consequences.

The suffering of affliction in victimization can be characterized by both a sense of powerlessness and a sense of meaninglessness. Being in a powerless position implies that there is nothing anyone can do to change the circumstances or the effects of their situation. Such a sense of helplessness and incapacity can lead to despair of the deadliest kind.[34] There is the experience, sometimes literally, of entrapment, subjugation, and subjection. Victims, again, need liberation in various forms. Walking in tandem with powerlessness is a profound sense of the meaninglessness much suffering presents. This is exacerbated by the absurdity of abuse. It simply should not be. One can, even at a young age, experience a bewilderment when suffering comes at the hands of another. There is no good reason to justify it, thus rendering it truly and intensely meaningless. And so, definitively, the abused are among the afflicted.

---

32. Weil, *Waiting for God*, 117.
33. See Van der Kolk, *Body Keeps the Score*.
34. See Kierkegaard, *Sickness Unto Death*.

Victimization also includes violence. By violence, we agree with J. Denny Weaver when he writes, "I am using 'violence' to mean harm or damage . . . Violence as harm or damage includes physical harm or injury to bodily integrity. And it incorporates a range of acts and conditions that include damage to a person's dignity or self-esteem. Abuse comes in psychological and sociological as well as physical forms."[35] Weaver extends his definition of violence to include *all* forms of abuse. Obviously a singular incident of physical violence includes psychological and emotional damage, and trauma from which to recover. Habitual domestic abuse intensifies the trauma and can lengthen the recovery.

One type of violence and abuse comes in the form of religious or *spiritual* abuse. According to the National Association for Christian Recovery, there are many types of spiritual abuse.[36] In one sense, all abuse can affect a victim's spirituality. The internal fracturing that results from violence and abuse certainly includes one's soul or spirit. This can cause a deep dysfunctioning in how to relate to God. But more specifically, religious or spiritual abuse can be identified when the place of abuse is a religious organization, or done by a spiritual leader or authority figure. Sexual abuse scandals in both Catholic and Protestant churches are becoming more well-known, as are their devastating effects on the victims. Spiritual abuse can happen when spiritual truths or biblical texts are used to do harm or to manipulate people into dysfunctional thoughts or behaviors. This type of coercive control often damages its victims' ability to relate well to God, as a God of love. It introduces a grace-less contingency into persons' relationships with God, emphasizing that they must work hard enough to gain God's approval. One damaging effect is a unique type of obsessive compulsive disorder known as scrupulosity. A person obsessively attends to spiritual disciplines repetitively to a damaging degree. Recovery from all types of consequences of spiritual abuse is especially difficult. How does one heal spiritually when his or her Christian faith has become toxic to them? Truly spiritual abuse is a form of violence.

Another form of violence is sexual abuse. There are effects of sexual victimization, in particular, that follow different psychological and spiritual tributaries than physical abuse alone. We will attempt to be broad in our definitions of violence and abuse, but will deal with sexual abuse on its own. While we will present chapters on violence, abandonment, and sexual abuse as separate treatments, we are not implying that there is not significant overlap and mingling results in the hearts and lives of victims. The point

---

35. Weaver, *Nonviolent Atonement*, 8.
36. See the National Association for Christian Recovery's website.

is to move to a comprehensive realization of the nature of affliction of the sinned-against.

What comes next are chapters in Part 1 that are theological in nature. Attention will be given to the theological relevance of the victimized, and the cross's relationship to them. Traditional theories of the atonement are reconstructed, and new theories presented. Particular reflection will be given to the experiences of Christ as a victim of violence, abandonment, and abuse and to his woundedness as a source of empathy and healing. Part 2 is intended to move toward the practical implications of "back side theology," particularly for the church and her priests and pastors. In Part 2, the practices such as the pastoral care of children, liturgical lament, and holy sacraments will be opened and explored as guidance to be used by the church that is willing to change its salvation narrative to one of radical inclusion. Hopefully in its gestalt, the theological and practical reflections of this book will lead to our most uncompromising claim: to the hidden need for the outrageous opportunity of forgiving God—an act born out of honest desperation, but one that can lead to a new kind of emancipation, mending, and healing for those abused and abandoned.

It is important as we proceed to be explicit about language. First, we use the word *victim* in these pages. Some reflection is necessary on the word, for at least one obvious reason: using the word *victim* can indeed reify, even concretize victimization. And so, here at the beginning we want to make it clear that by utilizing the word *victim* we in no way want to keep victims in a place of victimization. Some literature, particularly around the issues of sexual abuse, prefers to use the term *survivor* to identify victims of such abuse. Utilizing survivor language is intended to highlight that as a person seeks recovery and healing, they are therefore no longer a "victim" (which implies powerlessness). "Survivor" when applied to abuse explicitly suggests that the person has lived through the victimization and is now on another path. (Survivor in Holocaust literature refers to anyone who came out alive.) We are very sensitive to these concerns of labeling experiences. We will return to them when victimization is again discussed in relation to the atonement. Indeed this very project is intended to facilitate means toward healing, and resists any hint of perpetuating victimization even in our use of language. But not all are on the path of recovery. Some have never shared their story. Some remain perpetually or cyclically victimized. And so, we employ the word *victim* not to demean the person, or to remove hope of healing, but to keep before us that some remain silent or silenced, and countless are still enduring pain at the hands of others.

Secondly, since much of the content of the book is about the atonement, we stand in a bit of a dilemma. Atonement theology often needs to distinguish between the persons of the Trinity in order to explain who experiences what during Christ's crucifixion. Traditional language is easiest. It is easy to say, for example, that the Father abandons the Son. And yet, using "Father" language in a book about victims of abuse would be, to put it bluntly, *re-traumatizing* for some who have suffered at the hands of fathers or father figures in their lives. To do so would betray the very essence of our subject matter, since so many of the abused and abandoned find "male," and male familial language, can be extremely problematic when applied to God.

There have been many options proposed in efforts to avoid gendering God in the last few decades. Some have suggested God as "Source" or God as "Creator." But here we can lose the personal nature of God by using source, or restrict the multiple functions of the first person of the Trinity to a creator role only. And so, throughout this book, especially in chapters 5 and 6, we have chosen to identify "the Father" as "the First Person." By choosing this term, we hope to emphasize the *personal nature* of God. We have attempted to be trinitarianly precise, but at times we may obscure some important nuances unintentionally. Sometime our language will be bulky. This may necessitate a close reading, and so we encourage the reader to carefully distinguish the persons of the Trinity throughout the conversation. We ask you to join us in honoring some of the victimized in this way.

CHAPTER 2

The Other Side of Sin

It was a beautiful spring day. The daily chores and work of the day almost were enough to distract me from the worry over my husband. While any soldier's wife learns to deal with the loneliness, fear, and uncertainty, each day requires strength and energy to keep life as normal as possible. My body was tired, sore, and dirty from the day's work. One of my favorite times of the day was my afternoon bath to wash away not only the dirt from my body, but also the fear and stress that also seemed to layer itself upon my frame. This day was like all others.

After my bath, I was working on supper when a knock came at my door. I was so alone in my thoughts it startled and caused me to jump. Was it someone with bad news about my husband? Was it a stranger at the door? No, it was a servant from the palace. He was kind but very inquisitive, asking many questions about my family. I told him my name and connections, the name of my father and my husband. It was an abrupt conversation and seemed to be over before it began. After the servant left, I pondered the reason for such a visit. It did make me think of my father who had only passed away five years earlier. He and my grandfather were connected to the king as advisors. I did miss him and his words of hope, comfort, and promise. It also was both wonderful and hard to speak the name of my husband. When he is absent from my thoughts, the moments move quicker and I can ignore my pain over his battles and my fear for his safe return. Yet I trust that God will be faithful to me, as I remain faithful to God.

It was only a matter of hours when another knock came and startled me again. While I was still nervous to answer, I wondered if this knock was connected to the previous one. It was. I opened the door. I opened the door and everything changed. I opened the door and my life took a direction that caused great pain, anger, fear, torment. It was this same servant from the palace, but this time there was a host of other servants in accord. The servant mentioned that I was receiving a high honor. "The king would like to meet you." I was a bit shocked. I had thought the king would be with my husband at the battle. Despite my grandfather's association, and my husband's loyalty to him, I had only seen the king from a distance at a parade in the city square, though I can see his palace from the river behind my home. The head servant did not miss a beat and slowly announced that these fellow servants would help prepare me to properly meet the king. They came with perfume, oils, and the finest fabrics to wear. While it felt nice to be pampered, I could not help asking myself, why would the king would want to see me? Could he have bad news about my husband? Certainly a low ranking army official would bring a tragic report, not the king himself.

Before I knew it, we were on our way to the palace. I closed the door of my home behind me as we left. Little did I know how much would begin to close around me. At the palace, and after pleasantries with the king, it became obvious what his intentions really were. He told me that he had seen me bathe and my beauty enchanted him. His words were clearly meant to manipulate. He could not get me out of his head. He had to admire and adore one of God's most beautiful creatures. While his words attempted to flatter, they actually made me feel guilty and dirty, and ashamed. Perhaps this was all my fault. I should have taken more care to bathe out of plain sight lines. I should have been more careful.

What was I to do? Certainly he knew I was married. I had told the servant explicitly that my husband was in the king's army fighting the king's war. Was this a test by God? Was our king not God's anointed? Who was I to say no to the king? I felt despair. I really had no choice. But perhaps if I allowed this to happen, God would prompt the king to help bring my husband home. All I could do was disembody my mind as I endured it. You do not resist the king. And I understood that although he set me up and in essence raped me, I could be severely punished as an adulterer. He was beyond such laws. It also became obvious that after the king was done he wanted little to do with me. He sent me on my way. Someone opened the palace doors as I left, and then closed them behind me.

I opened the door to my own home, where now I felt almost as an alien. I felt all alone. I felt like I had betrayed my husband. I felt ashamed. I felt broken. I felt this was my fault. Had I been faithful to God? Would God punish my husband for my behavior? Guilt, sadness, fear and lots of tears through a desperate and despairing night. I bathed again, of course, but not outside. It didn't help the anguish no matter how hard I tried to scrub it off. The haunting memory of that night persisted like a sliver in my mind for several weeks. As hard I tried to pretend it never happened, the shame was faithful to remind me.

It was nearly five weeks later when I started to not feel well. The nausea would not go away. I tried to ignore this unpleasantness, but it seemed I just could not overcome it, and a sense of foreboding began to rise. Oh no. Could it be? Finally, I began to ask around, and one night I opened the door as a nursemaid came to my home. This opened door would also be a door that closed off what I thought would be my future. After asking me several questions and looking me over, this nursemaid knew my ailment. I dreaded for her to say it, for it would make it real. "You are pregnant," she said in a cold and steely tone. While I could understand each word individually in that sentence, I wanted to scream in denial at their meaning. I was in shock. She gave me the first of many looks I would receive from people, a look of condescension, disapproval, and disgust. This nursemaid also knew very well that my husband, as was hers, was away fighting in the king's war. She told me of some things I needed to do for the pregnancy and then simply left me in what felt like utter isolation. After a few days the reality begin to sink in and I knew I had to tell the king. I found a way to get a message to him, a very short message. "I am pregnant." What confusion when I heard nothing from the king. Had he received the news? Was he ignoring his child in my womb? Certainly his silence testified to the fact that he would place the blame and shame on me for what he had done. I couldn't breathe. I could be killed. I was in a gehenna.

It was thirteen days later when I received another knock at the door. Would this be the king's reply? Would he desire to abandon me and kill me and my child to erase the rape that I had caused? Instead, my worst nightmare. It was a messenger from the army. I knew immediately in his eyes that he was informing me of my husband's death. I dropped to the floor sobbing uncontrollably. While this messenger was doing his duty, informing me on the heroic loss of my husband in battle, all I could feel was shame. Something came over me that sensed that my husband had died somehow because of my sin. Still dripping with shame, I began to feel rage as well. This king had violated me, and I was the one to suffer this excruciating loss. At some point the messenger left and I found enough strength to close the door. It was now a door that would never open again to the figure of my husband.

A month transpired after the news of my husband's death. I felt as if the mourning would never end. In the middle of the day another knock. I was very tempted at this point never to open the door again, but I mustered the willpower to open it.

I opened the door to another part of my journey that forever closed the door on any happiness. It was the same servant who came asking questions. He informed me that the king was very sorry for the death of my husband and was inviting me to come and live in the palace. I would not be coming as a stranger, but as both the mother of his child and his wife. A knife ripped my gut. During the month I feared desperately for me and my child's future. How on earth would we survive? I continued to expect death to come at some point soon. And now? To be invited to the place that had started the horrific series of events? The rage returned. But I had no choice. What else could I do? It was a matter of life and death.

The door to the king's palace was opened for me, as before, but this time as his wife. I wish I could say that my pain, shame, humiliation, fear, and despair-mixed-with-rage remained in my small home, but it navigated its way into the palace and came with me. I eventually just felt dread and dead. It was several months later that I actually learned the reason for my dear husband Uriah's death. It was at the hands of this second husband, the king. I learned the entire plot was a way for the king to hide the lie of "our" adultery. This child inside me was a physical bodily reminder of "our" fornication. So, now I was married to the king, who had violated me and had my husband killed. I felt lost and trapped. A prophet had confronted the king. God was greatly displeased with all that he had done, I was told. This was the reason for King David's sorrow and repentance. His offer to me after? To appease his conscience? The prophet affirmed that God had taken away the king's sin, yet there still was a price. My son would die. He did. I now live in quiet desperation in the palace with the knowledge that the king killed Uriah. And God killed my child as punishment. If only I had been more careful about bathing, and had never opened that door.[1]

---

1. A paraphrase of the events of 2 Samuel 11 and 12.

Perspectives are often about power. For far too often, as Christianity has told this story about Bathsheba, it has been basically about David. David's sin, David's conquest, David's guilt, David's sorrow, David's pain, David's confession, and God's forgiveness of David. When this story of David is told, Christians are encouraged to confess the ways they have sinned against God, seek God's forgiveness, find healing, and be restored to God. All of this is, of course, the gospel. But it is only part of the gospel. How do the Bathshebas, then and now, find healing and solace? When the dominant narrative is to free sinners from guilt, the only soteriological option provided for people is to confess their sins. And yet, is confession of sin what Bathsheba needed? Some would say yes. Bathsheba was an adulterer. But this take on the narrative ignores the issues of power, abuse, and the abuse of power. It ignores the context of the powerlessness of women, even women with some social stature, in the days of David. Did Bathsheba need to confess, or did she need a place to scream, cry, and seek justice? Rather than approaching God with penitence, perhaps she could have approached God with an angry lament. "God, how could you let this happen?" "God, do you care about my pain?" "Why am I losing a child because the king took advantage of me?" Again, some may resist this interpretation and say "well, it was her choice to go to the palace"; "She was also complicit." To be complicit necessarily implies the power of choice. But did she have a choice?

It is curious that some have a difficult time allowing anyone to simply be a victim. The church has often neglected to pay attention to those who have been victims of sin. There has been little liturgical space for victims of sin to find healing, let alone theological reflection on victimization. Elaine Heath asks, "How many women and men are walking among us today bearing the wounds of sexual abuse, alienated from the God who longs to heal them, not knowing the power of the gospel because pastors and church members have not learned to read the Bible with survivors . . . ? Could it be that one of the reasons the church is failing to evangelize people today is that we are not taking seriously the pervasive reality of sexual abuse and its consequences for survivors—that we are not offering them the good news they need to hear?"[2] One key theologian who works with these issues is Andrew Sung Park, particularly in his books *The Other Side of Sin*, *The Wounded Heart*, and *From Hurt to Healing*.[3]

---

2. Heath, *We Are the Least of These*, 5–6.

3. Park and Nelson, eds., *Other Side of Sin*; Park, *Wounded Heart of God*; and *From Hurt to Healing*.

Salvation for the Sinned-Against

Andrew Sung Park rightly notes that in Christian theology there has been a long history that has analyzed the doctrine of sin, or hamartiology, from the perspective of the sinner only. As such, the problem of sin and the promise of salvation emphasize the importance of the confession of sin—the prayer of repentance to God, reconciliation with God, justification by faith in God, and sanctification in God. The need of the sinner is a strictly "vertical" need. And yet, there has been little analysis and discussion for the oppressed, the victims of sinners.[4] While the doctrine of sin, following Augustine and Luther, is most often expressed as some form of a self curved in upon itself, as pride and self-centeredness,[5] Park seriously questions to what extent the doctrine of salvation itself can be myopically and ironically self-centered on behalf of the powerful oppressor. Too often there is a unilateral perspective that neglects the victim. Park argues that the idea of justification by faith has

---

4. Park, *Wounded Heart of God*, 72–73.

5. Diane Leclerc and other feminist thinkers have challenged the dominant theological stance that equates sin with pride. See Leclerc, *Singleness of Heart*. Also see Saiving, "Human Situation." Although Saiving does not make reference to Kierkegaard in her article, her conclusions are very similar to his. In *Sickness Unto Death*, Søren Kierkegaard expands his existential anthropology by explicating his doctrine of sin. The quest of the person is to become a self in Kierkegaard's scheme. His concept of self is that of a synthesis, of a relation that integrates the individual's internal polarities. These polarities include finitude/infinitude and possibility/necessity. It is impossible for the individual to negotiate these unless he or she is related to the One that is greater than the self. "The self cannot attain and remain in equilibrium and rest by itself, but only by relating itself to the Power which constituted the whole relation." Selfhood is attained only through Christian faith. But the individual who lacks such faith is in despair, "the sickness unto death." This despair, or sin, can be manifested in two ways: there are *two* ways of failing to be a true self. There is the despair of trying to be a self by oneself, which Kierkegaard names the "manly" form of despair. There is also the opposite despair, the despair of not willing to be a self at all, which he names the "womanly" form of despair. Man attempts to overcome the anxiety of selfhood by forcing the poles of infinitude and possibility. Woman, on the other hand, relinquishes herself to the poles of finitude and necessity. Woman, according to Kierkegaard, gives herself away, thus losing her true self. The man, in contrast, defiantly attempts to maintain himself independently and egotistically, despairingly determined to be himself. But again, woman attempts to be rid of herself by losing herself in another. "Defiance" and "weakness" are Kierkegaard's final labels for the masculine and feminine forms of despair, respectively. See Kierkegaard, *Sickness Unto Death*, 144. Working closely with the Danish text, Sylvia Walsh interprets a key passage in Kierkegaard: "In abandoning or throwing herself altogether into that which she devotes herself, woman tends to have a sense of self only in and through the object of her devotion. When the object is taken away, her self is also lost. Her despair, consequently, lies in not willing to be herself, that is, in not having any separate or independent self-identity." Walsh, "On 'Feminine' and 'Masculine' Forms of Despair," 124.

too often focused on the change of juridical/legal status before God, while not affecting our sinful nature. For some parts of Christianity, the language of being "clothed in Christ's righteousness" implicitly affirms that persons are simply covered by Christ, while little actual healing ever occurs. Christian theology has named this as "imputed righteousness." In other words, God considers persons righteous through Jesus Christ, but does not make persons righteous—as in an actual change in character, even nature. Yet in those traditions that do affirm imparted righteousness and the process of sanctification, there is still most often the limited focus on the sinner.

Moreover, the strong emphasis of more Reformed traditions on the power of original sin and the important theological maxim that "we are saved by grace through faith, through no work of our own," has often led Christians to a resignation that persons have no power over sin, and that sin is inevitable *and* necessary.[6] As such, this can lead to a dangerous corollary: when sin occurs, persons are not fully responsible for their sin because there is a deeper cause beyond their control. The only recourse then is the confession of sin and the removal of guilt by a God who has some other means to be "satisfied." Another unfortunate corollary is that it tends to lead to very individualistic conceptions of Christian faith. This further exacerbates the sense of marginalization for the oppressed. More Wesleyan–Arminian traditions may focus on the need for sanctification, but it still can be interpreted as a very individualistic process.

Park argues that a deeper and truer understanding of the doctrine of justification goes beyond simply being justified before God in a legal change of status (which can lead to antinomianism), and even beyond the sanctification of the individual (which can lead to the danger of self-righteous judgmentalism); a genuine understanding of salvation must include the willingness to care about the wronged. The Christian gospel aims far higher than "Jesus and me" and my own reconciliation. Rather, the Christian gospel encompasses a cosmic redemption and reconciliation of all things. Within this broader imagination of redemption, persons become aware that their relationship to God is intricately tied to their treatment of others. Furthermore, justification admonishes not simply concern for my own personal eternal destination, but demands the communal task of seeking justice and healing for victims now.[7] The problem persists that too often in the church the only confessions given liturgical space are for oppressors to confess their sins to God alone.

---

6. Reinhold Niebuhr argues that sin cannot be necessary, even if it is inevitable. Niebuhr, *Nature and Destiny of Man*, 251–60.

7. Park, *Wounded Heart*, 97.

The Third Party

In the Old Testament, if one commits deeds of sins, there will be punishment, there will be consequences, but there is the possibility of forgiveness through some type of atonement (or sacrifice). There are two parties: YAHWEH, the almighty Holy Other, and sinners. To a degree this is not bad theo-logic. However, it is incomplete. Walter Brueggemann suggests that the Old Testament also speaks about the third party of the sinned-against.[8]

In the Exodus narrative three parties shape the cast. Pharaoh, YAHWEH, and the Israelites led by Moses. Pharaoh is the ruthless leader, who violates, abuses, and objectifies the people of God. Pharaoh is the power of chaos, the power that undoes creation, and clearly the sinner. YAHWEH is the one true God there to challenge Pharaoh's claim of "divinity." YAHWEH comes on the scene after hearing the cries of the Israelites. Yet in the exodus narrative, the suffering and bondage of the Israelites in Egypt is not a result of sin. One mistake made with the Old Testament narrative is to read backwards and to assume the bondage of the Israelites in Egypt is a form of punishment or exile. What the Israelites need in Egypt is not the confession of their sin, but a redeemer to save them. They need an intervening advocate. Brueggemann notes that Israel initiates their deliverance with their strong and persistent cry. Often in the discourse with Moses, YAHWEH refers to this lament and responds, "I have heard the cry of my people."

While this book will later deal specifically with the healing available through worshipful laments, it is crucial here especially to celebrate God's invitation to come, to those who have been sinned against, the victims. It was not only appropriate for the Israelites to cry out in Egypt, it would have been appropriate for Bathsheba to cry out in anger and pain against God, as a woman who represents unanimity with all who have ever suffered at the hands of others.

As stated above, the church has not created the appropriate liturgical space or theological solidarity for those who have been sinned against. The causes of this are many. Wide and deep are its rationalizing litanies. It seems beyond coincidence that often those with liturgical and theological power are complicit with oppressors who wish to keep the cries of the needy, and the guilt of their victimizing sin, at bay; and thus, they can craft liturgies or theological arguments only for the powerful. Or more likely, liturgists and theologians are unaware of those at the back side of the cross. They appropriately rehearse the familiar tunes of justification and forgiveness for sinners. This is still part of the gospel. It would not be appropriate to reject

---

8. See Brueggemann, "Shrill Voice of the Wounded."

the reality that *all* have sinned and fallen short of God's glory. All stand in need of forgiveness. And yet, this in no way justifies someone's oppression and victimization of any kind on others in the name of some universal accountability and punishment. God does not inflict us on others to bring about divine justice. Therefore, our preaching, singing, and imagination must create space for those who suffer wounds that need healing at no fault of their own.

Lament

While more space will be given to the meaning and practice of lament later (chapter 13), some beginning reflections are important here. It is noteworthy that by category, laments are the largest number of psalms in the Psalter. Psalm 22 contains the lament Jesus cries from the cross as the one who has been forsaken. A lament is not pious whining. A lament is a stirring cry, where God is asked to be a better God, indeed, where God is held accountable. Most laments have three groups present: the speaker, God, and the enemy. In many laments, God's silence or inaction is seen as a failure of God to protect and preserve the faithful servant. As mentioned earlier in chapter 1, theodicy, which aims at justifying God, is cross-purposed from true lament. In many ways, laments are anti-theodicies. While theodicies attempt to get God off the hook, laments place the blame and culpability directly on God. Laments hold God accountable. Yet the problem lies in that most Christian expressions of worship exclude lament, and call only for happy praise. This is why so many persons who suffer, who grieve, who feel pain for an infinite number of reasons feel out of place during Sunday morning communal worship. If Christians fail to follow the model of the Psalter and only offer expressions of praise without any space for lament, such praise can become hollow and ring false in the ears of the abused.

It is crucial here to recognize that laments are never expressions of doubt in God, but are based ultimately on trust and hope. Expressing anger with God certainly affirms God's existence. Not only that, nearly every lament psalm resolves into proclamation of God's faithfulness in the past, and hope for God's renewed activity in the future. Lamenters do not cry out to whom they believe to be an impotent God unable to respond.

Nowhere is the power of lament seen as clearly in the Old Testament than in the figure of Job. A strong thread within the Old Testament affirms that if one lives a righteous life, all will go well, and a blessed life will result. There is a common assertion that "if you live inside the moral order willed by God, you will benefit from God's blessings."⁹ This is the primary logic found most clearly in the wisdom literature of Psalms and Proverbs, and of which the book of Job is a part. Certainly this is not completely false, in that living in faithfulness to God has great benefit, and living poorly in sin can have negative consequences. The problem comes in making an equal equation of cause and effect that leads to the wrong conclusion that if one suffers it is the direct result of some sin or conscious lack. This is where Job's friends end up. The book of Job is a tremendous gift, too often ignored by Christians, that addresses the issue of what happens when *righteous* people suffer. The question is sometimes posed as "why do bad things happen to good people?" As one follows the narrative of Job, after all the loss, pain, and destruction he endured, Job's wife and friends serve as faithful evangelists of the too simplistic formulas that could be gleaned from a shallow interpretation of Psalms and Proverbs. Clearly Job has sinned, they say. This is why terrible things happen to him. Job is being punished. Yet Job refuses to accept this "friendly" pronouncement, and chooses instead to lament.

In Job's great lament, he asks God to be present, to show up and give account for the unjust hardship and suffering he has experienced. In many ways, Job initiates an assault upon God's character, whom Job declares to be morally indifferent and unreliable. Of course we know that God shows up in the famous "whirlwind speech" of Job 38. God reminds Job that God is God, and Job is not. Through some of the most powerful poetry in all of Scripture, God invites Job to gaze upon the power, beauty, and even destruction of nature that God has called into being. In God's second speech, God declares that God's justice is within God's freedom. And yet, God does not answer the ultimate question of *why* Job has suffered. In many ways God's answer disregards and leaves unsatisfied the issue of Job's rage. What seems to matter is that in the end God affirms that Job has been found righteous and thus stands "vindicated" in a sense, and that the suffering Job experienced was not a result of sin in Job's life. Furthermore, and very importantly, Job is praised for refusing to accept that his victimization was God's punishment.

What is fascinating about all of this is that God never speaks to Job about the wager Satan has placed in the courtroom of God. God ultimately does provide what Job most desperately needs—not an answer to "why" this has happened—but the very presence of God in the midst of his pain. It is the presence and compassion of God that de-absolutizes the notion that all of life's circumstances are based on a system of reward and punishment of one's deeds. Unfortunately, the message of the book of Job is still missed or

---

9. Brueggemann, "Shrill Voice of the Wounded," 25.

forgotten. Even some Christians remain convinced that suffering in every circumstance implies the guilt of the sufferer.

Han

In recent years, one helpful source for theology has been the Asian context, and particularly the Korean concept of han.[10] It is theorized that this cultural idea arose through Korea's history, which records invasions and wars dating back to at least the sixteenth century, including most recently, of course, the Korean War, where the country and its people were literally ripped apart. This has brought a type of cultural consciousness deeply shared by its people. Minjung[11] theologian Suh Nam-dong describes han as the "feeling of unresolved resentment against injustices suffered, a sense of helplessness because of the overwhelming odds against one, and a feeling of acute pain in one's guts and bowels, making the whole body writhe and squirm, and an obstinate urge to take revenge . . . all these combined."[12] Kevin Considine concurs:

> Han is not identical with the English term suffering. Suffering is too thin to account for the full complexity of woundedness. Han points to the interconnected levels of woundedness in human beings, their communities, and all of creation. Han is a festering wound and frozen energy in need of unraveling. The question is not if it will unravel, but when and how it will unravel and what the consequences will be.[13]

Andrew Sung Park is the foremost Christian theologian on the subject of han today. Park provides one of his most important contributions to the subject by illuminating the Asian concept of han for Western audiences. He writes:

> Han is the collapsed anguish of the heart due to psychosomatic, social, economic, political, and cultural repression and oppression. When internal and external forces cause our suffering to

---

10. For precise definitions of han, see for example Chan Hee Son, *Haan of Minjung Theology*.

11. Minjung theology is a theology originating in 1970s Korea. *Minjung* literally means "of the people," and minjung theology could be considered a type of liberation theology in Korea, with Marxist overtones, as it seeks social justice for ostracized and poor Koreans.

12. Yoo, *Korean Pentecostalism*, 221.

13. Considine, "Han and Salvation," 87. Also see Considine's full-length work, *Salvation and the Sinned-Against*.

reach a critical point, it collapses to a singularity of agony. The collapsed sadness, bitterness, rage, and hopelessness become the vortex of our agony, overwhelming our conscious and unconscious modes of thinking. In other words, han is the physical, mental, and spiritual response to a terrible wrong done to a person. It elicits a warped depth of pain, a visceral physical response, an intense rending of the soul, and a sense of helplessness.[14]

Park applies the concept of han beyond the Korean context to express the anguish of sufferers of all types of victimization. Since it has no English equivalent, simple definitions fail. But beyond trying to technically define it, it still speaks to a depth of human experience that goes beyond mere words. It is existentially understood by those who have been sinned against, and especially by those whose victimization has been repeated or continuous. This somewhat unique cultural consciousness accessible in the Asian context, if it is applied more broadly, can help the church consider a more robust soteriology, as Park does. How are victims of others' sin to find healing? Han "accentuates the meaning of salvation by including the healing of victims in the notion of salvation."[15] Han is the experience of the powerless, the marginalized, the helpless, and the voiceless.[16] Perhaps equally important to its characterization as anguish, han also carries the connotation of a deep longing or hope for healing. "The positive unraveling of han can lead to psychological, emotional, spiritual, and physical healing; the creation of a nurturing and constructive community; and the strength for positive resistance, protest, and action to confront and change unjust political and social systems."[17]

Paying attention to han can also help the church to recognize the communal and tangled web of relationships. Although it is often forgotten, Jesus preached that if persons go to the altar and remember there is a sister or brother with whom they have a broken relationship, they must leave their gift at the altar and first be reconciled *to that person*. Jesus seems to go against the psalmist's declaration that "against you [God] only have I sinned" (Ps 51:4). Through an understanding of the reality of han, theology breaks through the individualistic tendencies associated with salvation. Han gives additional aid that points to the true intent of confession—not reprieve, but reconciliation. Therefore, confession and repentance that are not directed toward the victim of our sin are not far-reaching enough. Park

---

14. Park, *Wounded Heart*, 11.
15. Park, *Wounded Heart*, 102.
16. Park, "Bible and Han," 47.
17. Considine, "Han and Salvation," 88.

states, "The idea that sinners can achieve salvation by confessing their own sin regardless of the welfare of their victims is a narcissistic illusion."[18]

This is clearly seen in the story of David. What transpired when David was home instead of in battle wreaked extensive havoc upon his family, let alone Bathsheba and Uriah, who were brought into the chaos. This point again must be stated with clarity and precision. God forgave, even healed David after he is confronted with the gravity of his sin and confesses. But such repentance and forgiveness is not the end of the suffering David inflicted, and therefore is not truly complete. "David's repentance was insufficient to resolve han and the han took its course, demanding its price" says Park.[19] From David's child with Bathsheba, to Tamar and Absalom, and so on, the consequences of han become a tidal wave. This is often the case when persons are victimized. Furthermore, Park strongly adds, "By excluding the healing of the injury of the victims, the salvation of sinners loses its intrinsic meaning."[20] Creating space for the victims of sin to find healing, even in "public" venues such as worship, gives balm to those suffering. Ideally, offering this space can and should be a means of conviction and grace to those who have hurt others as well, as they see tangibly the pain they inflict. Park's point needs to be stated again. Paying attention and providing liturgical space for the healing of the victims of sin is not for the benefit only of the sinned-against. The sinner—David—who desires healing and forgiveness, cannot experience full healing while the sinned-against are left in the shadows of their despair.

This was seen powerfully in the Truth and Reconciliation Commission in South Africa. Putting it simply and briefly, it was decided by the TRC that persons who publicly confessed to their crimes (often evil acts done in the shadow and darkness of night) would not be further punished by the legal system. It is important to note that not all were pleased by this process, including many victims who felt like a public confession was not enough. Watching the commission proceedings, however, was powerful for most of the victims and their families as they heard the truth of what had happened to them. The TRC believed that restorative justice through public confession and hopefully reconciliation was a better way forward out of Apartheid; they believed that typical retributive justice that focuses largely on punishing the perpetrator offers little and often ignores the victims and families. Similar stories come out of other contexts, such as the efforts toward reconciliation and forgiveness in Rwanda after its genocide. These

---

18. Park, *Wounded Heart*, 103.
19. Park, "Bible and Han," 49.
20. Park, *Wounded Heart*, 103.

African examples were culture changing, and often very public. It raises an appropriate question about the culture of the Christian church that has so often hidden its abusers and abused alike.

Unhealed Han Causes Further Han

According to Kevin Considine, Jae-Hoon Lee and Kim Chi-Ha offer further assistance in explaining han. "Lee brings the psychology of Carl Jung and Melanie Klein into dialogue with Korean culture and arrives at three interconnected variations: won-han, jeong-han, and hu-han. To simplify, these variations are based in aggression, resignation, and nihilism, respectively. They are all of a piece, yet one variation tends to manifest and dominate the life of a [particular] victim."[21] Kim Chi-Ha emphasizes the intense negativity of han. For Kim, han is a "ghostly creature" that "appears as a concrete substance with enormous ugly and evil energy . . ."[22] Ethical conundrums arise when we recognize that the experience of han, the ugly "ghostly creature," can certainly lead sufferers to damage others. "For some, damage may become the core problem, and, unhealed, it can fester into more damage: a cycle of violence and evil."[23] Put otherwise, hurt people hurt people.

The movie *Monster*[24] poignantly exposes an ethical dilemma. It portrays the true story of serial killer Aileen Wuernos, who was convicted of luring men to their death, and who was eventually executed in 2002. The main character, Aileen (played by Charlize Theron) was abused and neglected from the beginning of her life. These life circumstances banish her to a life of prostitution. At one point, determined to straighten out her life, she tries to find legitimate work, but with little education and limited social skills, she fails at every turn. She returns to working as a hooker, hitching rides along the local interstate highway, and has an encounter with a vicious client whom she kills in self-defense. After this, however, she snaps, and begins to kill her johns, often brutally. When she is caught she claims self-defense, but is convicted for six murders. Interestingly, the movie does not portray Aileen as displaying characteristics for an insanity defense. She is sent to prison, and eventually executed. We could say that her han led her to her action. After seeing the scene of the first murder and the horror of the rape and violence Aileen endured, the movie leaves the thinking viewer

21. Considine, *Han and Salvation*, 88.
22. Considine, *Han and Salvation*, 88–89. Kim Chi-Ha, quoted in Nam-Dong, "Towards a Theology of Han," 64.
23. Park and Nelson, "Why Do We Need?," 5.
24. Jenkins, dir., *Monster*.

with the question, in what sense and to what degree is Aileen responsible for her choices?

Han that is not dealt with will work itself out in some way. For some (if it does not find a means of healing) han can inflict more han on others and themselves. Park describes han as a "black hole" and a festering wound whose energy must be channeled and resolved either to give life or to give death to one's self and others.[25] Considine writes, "The negative unraveling and continued festering of han can lead to mental illness, physical and spiritual sickness, suicide, interpersonal violence, [or] a nihilistic attachment to a great political cause that can lead to little more than greater pain, suffering, and oppression for the most vulnerable of society."[26] For Park, han will be resolved either destructively (revenge as violence) or constructively (transforming han into a graceful life). Destruction is seen in the classic and tragic pattern of adults who were abused as children becoming child abusers themselves. Tragically, this is also seen in places where marginalized groups can marginalize others. For example, the feminist movement had to eventually recognize that white women, usually of a higher class, did not speak for all women. Womanist and Mujerista movements demonstrate how "even victims can victimize the weaker and that no one is free from the potential of oppressing others."[27] This was also embodied in the Los Angeles riots of 1992, sparked by the Rodney King verdict. A great deal of violence was committed between the African American and Asian American populations.

The traditional category of sin by itself is insufficient to tackle the wounds and alienation caused by unresolved han. That is, wounds and alienation that are not healed can lead to communal, or "systemic" evil.[28] Thus the cycle of han must be broken through its healing. What Park helps to illumine plainly is that while it is true all persons have committed sins that need forgiveness, even sins that emerge from han, when persons who have been victimized are not given a place, particularly in the church, for their han to find healing, the whole body suffers (see 1 Cor 12:26).

While it is true that hurt people can hurt people, just as likely is the proclivity for victims to blame themselves. Because the doctrines of sin and salvation have been limited in scope in the narratives of the church, often brutalized victims will blame themselves. The marginalized have been taught to "look to [their] own behavior for a theological understanding of [their] suffering. Since [their] conduct is the only thing over which [they]

---

25. Park, *Wounded Heart*, 15–20.
26. Considine, *Han and Salvation*, 88.
27. Park and Nelson, "Why Do We Need?," 12.
28. Park and Nelson, "Why Do We Need?," 13.

have any notion of control, [they] long to find the key to [their] suffering within the scope of [their] own agency."[29] Park asserts that our theology has led victims to the conclusion that they should repent of their own wounds, which only conflates the problem, exacerbates the pain, and prevents healing.[30] Self-blame for another's guilt increases han, for it betrays the truth. And so, beside the common practice of perpetrators manipulating their victims into taking full responsibility for their abuse, the theology of the church can and has reinforced notions that blame the victim. And victims can ingest such false blame readily. Their disempowerment can be met with disempowering theology. Their self-hate is reinforced. And they can indeed be doubly traumatized—by their abusers and by atonement theology that hardly acknowledges their existence.

Victims, before entering any journey toward healing, often bear their suffering alone and, thus, in silence. Who can be trusted to listen without rebuttal, understand without verdict, receive without judgment? The church has often failed in offering what victims need. But beyond the question of whom to trust, silence also represents the consequences of experiencing the truly unspeakable, and of being misunderstood. For example, Terrance Des Pres has offered a study of the literature of the survivors of the Holocaust. He suggests that "silence, in its primal aspect, is a consequence of terror, of a dissolution of the self and world that, once known, can never be fully dispelled . . . Silence constitutes the realm of the dead."[31] He goes on to examine in detail the writings of the survivors of death camps, who write either during or after the experience, and strongly suggests that there is a connection between their desperate need to remember, to "witness," to objectively record what happened, and their endurance of the circumstances that killed millions. The sense of responsibility they had to not let the dead be forgotten compelled them to live long enough to be heard. From another context, "Scrawled on the latrine wall in a Soviet camp was this inscription: 'May he be damned who, after regaining freedom, remains silent.'"[32]

> The Holocaust produced an endless scream which, given time, has transmuted itself into the voice of many witnesses. This would seem, in fact, to be one of the primary aspects of the survival experience: the will to bear witness issues as a typical and in some sense necessary response to extremity. Confronting radical evil, men and women instinctively feel the desire to call,

29. Fortune, "Conundrum of Sin, Sex, Violence, and Theodicy," 125.
30. Park, "Bible and Han," 51.
31. Des Pres, *Survivor*, 36.
32. Des Pres, *Survivor*, 38.

to warn, to communicate their shock. Terror dissolves the self into silence, but its aftermath, the spectacle of human mutilation, gives birth to a different reaction. Horror arises and in its presence men and women are seized by an involuntary outburst of feeling which is very much like a scream—sometimes, as we have seen, literally a scream. And in this crude cry the will to bear witness is born.[33]

Or in the words of an actual survivor:

> This pitiful sound, which sometimes, goodness knows how, reaches into the remotest prison cell, is a concentrated expression of the last vestige of human dignity. It is a man's [sic] way of leaving a trace, of telling people how he lived and died. By his screams he asserts his right to live, sends a message to the outside world demanding help and calling for resistance. If nothing else is left, one must scream. Silence is the real crime against humanity.[34]

We know that in different instances of suffering, the ability to find one's voice is often intricately involved in one's healing. Victims of violence and abuse need to tell their stories. And they need a different story, or at least a different telling of the Christian narrative, to connect to in order to find the empathy they need. It is crucial, therefore, that we examine traditional theories of the atonement in light of the existence and experiences of the sinned-against.

---

33. Des Pres, *Survivor*, 33.
34. Des Pres, *Survivor*, 33.

CHAPTER 3

Toward Saving the Conventional Cross

Consider who Jesus is. We know that He is fully God. We know that He is rightly called prophet, priest, and king. We know that He not only represents, but in a certain sense is the true and holy God of Israel. It should not be lost on us that God's people are now called "the body of Christ." This Man who is God walks up to the River Jordan [in order to be baptized by John the Baptist]. And what happens? What should we expect to happen? Well, a person who is versed in the Old Testament and who also knows who this Jesus is might have a very reasonable expectation. In the Old Testament when the people of God come up to the waters while running from Pharaoh, the waters part. In the OT when the ark of the covenant, which was God present to His people, came to the River Jordan, the waters part. This person, well versed in the OT, when seeing Jesus come to the waters should have every expectation that they too will part. Jesus is the fullness of the presence of God, He is the fulfillment of all prophecy, He is the true Son of God, all people of God are in Him. When He comes to the Jordan, the river should break open before and

> beneath him. And yet, the waters do not part. Instead, God enters into the chaos and death of the water, and He is covered ... The mystery takes us further. That day not only does Jesus come up to the water and the water's will to swallow him up, but it is this very day that for the first time God reveals Himself in His fullness: Father, Son, and Holy Spirit to humankind. The threefold nature of the Godhead is revealed to us at the moment in which God reveals Himself as the God for whom the waters do not part ... We learn that God reveals Himself formally and most clearly in the very midst of human suffering ... this mystery of the suffering of the impassible God.
>
> —Fr. Jonathan[1]

God reveals Godself to us as the God for whom the waters do not part. God reveals Godself formally and most clearly in the very midst of human suffering. This is the mystery. Christ is born in vulnerability. The baptism of Jesus begins his ministry of suffering. It is the cross that concludes it. In roll the high and mighty waters as never before. If we do not truly understand the nature of God's heart, we should fear in that moment—not that Jesus will die, but that he won't. The cross is the highest pinnacle of God's self-revelation. To be true to himself and true to his God, Jesus must declare again that he is the one for whom the waters do not part. And so, he enters fully into the suffering of us all, beckons the waters to wash over his head, and allows himself to die.

We needed Jesus to not be saved. But does the cross need saving? The title of this chapter certainly suggests that it does. This is perhaps evidenced by the plethora of books written on the atonement in recent years. Critiques about how it has been understood traditionally have come from different directions. Such critiques are not challenging traditionalism for its own sake, but instead have strong cohesive arguments and fresh theological insight stretching from feminist/womanist concerns to pacifist concerns to exegetical concerns and beyond. There are an array of recent studies that interpret atonement passages with greater nuance and with an eye toward more

---

1. Fr. Jonathan, homily.

contemporary themes. But most remain "traditional" in the sense that the issues raised are still directed at God's forgiveness of sinful humanity. Only a handful have suggested that a second locus of atonement theology should be focused on the victims of sin. Perhaps to overgeneralize, most churches do not know how muting their narratives can be, and how inhospitable their practices.

The Atonement

Unfortunately, some of the muting of victims of all kinds has been done in the name of theology, even theologies of atonement—various analogies of a spiritual reality that intend for us to understand how humanity is reconciled to God. The silencing of victims comes from our inability to adequately deal with issues relevant to the *sinned-against*. We do not do a very good job of talking to, or listening to those at the back side of the cross. We understand that the atonement is crucial for our salvation. But we do not easily connect the cross to victims of violence, abandonment, and abuse. When people are hurt, rejected, enslaved, abandoned, whatever the case may be, does Christian faith have anything to say? We return to our book's central question: Does the atonement have anything to say to those who are sinned against, to those we have pitched out to Gehenna while others soothe their consciences? Is the meaning of the cross vast enough to speak into such darkness of those who have been victimized?

All traditional theories spell out exactly how forgiveness of sin comes from the atoning work of Christ, but do so in different ways. Interestingly, there is no one theory that is considered the "orthodox" position. No one theory dominates the biblical witness. Unlike Christology, which was more or less settled in the early church period through various ecumenical councils that produced creeds, atonement theology has never been settled in the same way. The continuing development of various theories throughout the history of the church bears out that there is no *one* correct interpretation of relevant biblical passages. However, most Christians hold to a one-correct-interpretation model and clearly believe they know what the Bible says about the atonement. The fact is that they are depending on extra-biblical sources from the early church, the medieval period, the Reformation, or beyond. Most Christians are not aware that there are so many options, but are aware only of what is most emphasized in their own tradition.

Despite some wishful thinking on the part of many, it is not a viable option to suggest that the spiritual truth of the atonement, as a reconciling act, is some mysterious combination of the dozen or so theories offered throughout the theological history of the church. In some respects, they radically oppose each other. They also represent very different views of the nature of God—some, we might suggest, quite detrimentally. It has been a common strategy in scholarship of late to indict some theories as theologically abusive themselves. The question is whether these valid and necessary critiques are reaching beyond the realm of academic endeavors to laity who can somewhat superstitiously hold to what they have been taught to be the truth about the cross. And so, a theology of atonement that focuses on the justification of the sinner in typical fashion is fraught with problems on its own, even before the introduction of the question, "what about the sinned-against" who cower at the back side of the cross? It could be said that atonement theology in general is in turmoil.

As suggested in chapter 2, the traditional emphasis seems clear enough: God forgives sinners. Unfortunately, this simple truth can lead us to rather crass conclusions. If not careful, we could imply that it does not matter what we have done and *whom we have hurt*, God will wipe our slate clean as God throws our transgressions into the "sea of forgetfulness." Often a focus on our psychological anxiety because we have not forgiven ourselves arises here. With a radical individualism at its base, we hear sermons or read books where we are reminded that God forgets, and that we should stop reminding God that we have sinned. We fail to remember, however, that it still exists for those who suffer from the wounds and pain we caused and the sometimes debilitating consequences of sinful actions. They remember all too well while we use pseudo-spiritual tactics to forget; in doing so, we forget our responsibility in reconciliation and healing.

Some atonement theories focus on God's wrath; some focus on God's love. All introduce the cross of Jesus Christ as pivotal in God's saving act for the sinner. And in this, the theology of the atonement has been "limited" in a different way.[2] Some shame that silences victims comes when their experiences are lumped into a theology that speaks only of and to sinners. Worse yet, atonement theology can go where it should never go—sucked into the black hole of implying that we suffer because we sin, or similarly, that we are sure to be healed when we confess. Blame boomerangs back on the innocent, not just from perpetrators who spit blame and who use this strategy to control their victims (sometimes even long after the acts of victimization), but by a theology that imagines justice only as God gladly sweeping away the culpability of the guilty because "Jesus paid it all." Certainly, it has often been implied, if not explicitly stated, that if victims do not forgive those who have transgressed against them as quickly and easily as God, they are

---

2. Beyond the use of the word *limited* associated with "five-point" Calvinism.

at fault—threatened by the parable of the unmerciful servant and the reimprisonment they deserve. They are threatened that if they do not forgive, the forgiveness they have received from God will be rescinded, like a cross necklace yanked from their necks due to their unworthiness to wear it.[3]

Within this constructive work, we are convinced some theological deconstruction of Christ's death on the cross needs to take place to more fully emphasize the nature and the depth of the healing God offers to all. The means by which we seek to offer help in this chapter is to employ the concept of mimesis in order to mine different ore from traditional atonement theoretical rocks. The concept of mimesis has ancient roots in the work of Plato and Aristotle. It has been appropriated by a wide variety of disciplines, including modern philosophy, art, literary criticism, and psychoanalysis, to name a few. While respecting the depth and breadth of its function in these areas, we intend to use the mimesis theory here in a similar fashion to Luce Irigaray, who advocates that one use oppressive models—in her case, misogynistic views of women—and embrace them for the very purpose of undermining them, indeed *transfiguring* them into new, liberated sets of meaning.[4] (Later in the book, we will use a different tack of mimesis, that of René Girard).

And so this chapter is based on the belief that even traditional theories of the atonement, that have been solely directed toward sinners who need forgiveness, can be transfigured into new sets of meaning for the sinned-against. Even a theory, for example, that attempts to appease the wrath of God has potential for comfort if turned on its ugly head. The format for the following pages will be to present a traditional theory, and then immediately offer its reinterpretation. The aim is to indeed "save the cross" by opening up new possibilities for perception, and thus new hope for healing. After this chapter, chapters are offered that continue to transfigure the meaning of the cross as it relates to violence, abandonment, and sexual abuse.

Atonement Theories

The types of atonement theories generally fall into two categories: objective and subjective. *Objective* theories emphasize the primary need in salvation as appeasing God, which have been called "satisfaction" theories of the atonement. Satisfaction theories (including substitutionary theories) put it this way: Jesus took our place by being punished on our behalf. Once so

---

3. This image is based on an actual account.

4. See Irigaray, "Any Theory of the 'Subject,'" 133. This is one example of the theme found throughout her work.

punished, he can take a "satisfactory" sacrifice before God as a form of payment (to God or to Satan). In response, God's wrath or God's honor is satisfied or appeased, and humans can be forgiven. The connected theological anthropology is very dark. Humans are utterly sinful, totally depraved, and completely removed from any goodness. Grace comes only because God is "paid off" by a Son who suffers the punishment we so obviously deserve.

In the more subjective theories of the atonement, the "audience," if you will, shifts. The cross becomes the greatest expression of God's love for us, *to* us. Subjective atonement theories express that God seeks to communicate, through the life and crucifixion of the Son, the lengths to which God will go to offer us reconciliation. God does not have to be satisfied or appeased in order to be merciful. The word *appease* shifts to the word *appeal*. The cross is God's making an appeal to humanity. Appeal is not to be understood in some juridical sense, as an appeal in a courtroom, but as an appeal to the heart of a beloved. God appeals to humans through the divine mediator, Jesus, that love can conquer sin. In the subjective theories there is often more optimism about humanity's condition. The image of God has not been completely obliterated by the fall, and prevenient grace can actualize potential goodness, even before our conscious reception of Christ's redemption.

It becomes clear why certain traditions focus on certain theories: what one believes about the nature of God determines what one believes about the efficacy of the cross. Is God essentially sovereign? Is God essentially love? The objective and subjective theories line up under what we believe most about God, and subsequently, what we believe about humanity. Of course, convictions about the essential nature of God spill into every systematic category, but perhaps none so essential as soteriology. The traditional emphasis seems clear enough no matter the "objectivity" or "subjectivity" of the theory: God forgives sinners. But "mimicking" these various theories opens the door to God's healing act for victims.

Substitutionary Atonement Theories

The substitutionary theories of the atonement in their traditional form (also known as satisfaction theories) focus on the idea that "the wages of sin is death" and that sin must be punished. Our salvation comes from the fact that Jesus Christ takes on that punishment by dying in our place. Jesus is the substitute. Jesus suffers, not necessarily with us but very much for us. We could go so far as to say that the consequences for our sins are taken away. We are kept "sterilized," far away from his bloody and gruesome death, because he is handling it in our place. God needs sin to be punished in order to maintain properly God's honor and/or justice. Its objective nature comes from the fact that Jesus takes on the sin of the whole world (or the elect), bears the punishment, and thus *enables* (quite literally) God to forgive those who accept Jesus' substitution (or at least those elected to be saved). Or to put it more bluntly, God *cannot* forgive sins without Jesus dying on the cross. Issac Wiegman states, "In many strands of the Christian faith, this is the context in which the good news arrives: that someone else, a perfect substitute, has absorbed God's wrath or the punishment that humankind rightfully deserves, or the death that is the proper repayment for sin."[5] The other curious issue is that this system is either established by God or one that is forced upon God by some universal justice code. Wiegman further explains:

> This cluster of views requires that God's wrath is *moral* wrath: wrath that is ignited by sin and that aims to consume impurities and satisfy the demands of justice. What kind of justice? . . . God's wrath appears to be aimed at *retributive* justice, as opposed to *restorative* justice or *distributive* justice. God's wrath is primarily aimed at giving sinners what they *deserve* irrespective of the overall *consequences* of inflicting that wrath (restoration, rehabilitation, deterrence, etc.). In other words, God's wrath is primarily a mechanism of debt collection rather than a mechanism for generating future returns. On this model, it is unavoidable that God's wrath is understood from within an economy of exchange within which each transgression is a debt that demands proportional repayment.[6]

It is quite legitimate to ask the following questions. Why would God choose to save us through this mechanism? Why would Jesus volitionally bear our sin and punishment? "By what moral alchemy does the suffering of the wronged, coupled with the punishment of the wrongdoer transmute into a morally good occurrence? Why would God operate within such a system? Why would God be bound by the requirements of retributive justice?"[7] In the substitutionary theory there is at least an implicit *why*. God's primary *modus operandi* is justice or fairness. In Calvin's penal satisfaction theory, God's justice is center stage. To forgive without punishment would be unimaginable. In fact, forgiveness is not the point, but a consequential option opened because retributive justice is satisfied. For Calvin, God then applies

---

5. Wiegman, "Divine Forgiveness," 83.
6. Wiegman, "Divine Forgiveness," 183–84.
7. Wiegman, "Divine Forgiveness," 184.

forgiveness to the elect only, showing that the response of the forgiven is unnecessary, and even arbitrary.

Here enters the governmental theory for those with more Arminian tastes. The question why, and how Arminians answer it, pushes substitutionary theory toward a more subjective answer. Why would God choose to save us from the deserved punishment of our sin? Because God is Love. But the governmental theory remains objective in that it is still addressed to God, who still needs appeasement and satisfaction through punishment. While Arminians, like John Wesley, clearly reject any notion of predestination by emphasizing that repentance (as life change) is paramount, it is still Jesus' death *in our place* that precipitates God's "ability" to forgive sin in the "governmental" form of the satisfaction theory. "Regardless of how substitution is understood (e.g., penal or otherwise), the underlying similarity is that Jesus takes responsibility for our sins and his suffering and death thereby absolve us from what we deserve or what we owe. On this cluster of views, Jesus' death is supposed to be a justifiable moral transaction,"[8] says Wiegman. But what if we question the morality of this claim? Is it possible for us to step outside the system of retributive justice? If so, "the good news should not be understood as a moral transaction within it. Rather, our bondage to the system itself is the bad news, and the good news is that God has created an ingenious way out."[9] The Old Testament assumes that God will punish the wicked for their wrongdoing, and reward those who act righteously. The Old Testament seems bound to this premise. But what if we break free from it, and see the cross as something radically new, rather than following Old Testament paradigms? Might we have something to say to victims?

Substitutionary Atonement Theories Transfigured

It seems appropriate to first challenge the idea of retributive justice, despite how "biblical" it might seem. Although entire chapters follow that deal with forgiveness, it is appropriate to introduce the topic here. It is possible to imagine forgiveness quite outside the laws of justice. In human relationships, for example, we forgive without any proportional repayment. When a person wrongs another person, it is possible for the one who has been hurt to "wipe the slate clean" of the wrongdoer. In fact, our intuitions might suggest that forgiveness is a free gift. Is it really forgiveness if we require some restitution beyond their sincere repentance? In fact, a system where punishment is required might very well create situations for abuse itself. A wife is

---

8. Wiegman, "Divine Forgiveness," 186–87.
9. Wiegman, "Divine Forgiveness," 185.

"disobedient" and thus "rightly" deserves to be beaten as payment. To fully engage in substitutionary theories forces us to see God as unable to forgive outright. The transaction between God and the cross is one that maintains God as punisher, not as *essentially* forgiving or merciful. God purposely misdirects wrath, but wrath is still expressed onto the substitute Jesus. This almost (if not altogether) requires a split in the Godhead. Jesus becomes the one willing to die for us; God remains wrathful and needs to be satisfied.

But if we remain stuck in this system, we have to accept the foundations on which it is built.

> There appears to be little more to say than that it seems . . . fitting that virtuous people should get good things and that vicious people should get bad things. However, if we ask why this seems fitting, we might simply say that it is good to love the good and to hate the bad, and that hating the bad (for instance) entails apportioning bad outcomes to people who are disposed to do bad things, namely the vicious. But we can ask a still further question of why hating the bad requires giving them bad things. Why isn't it enough to simply prevent vicious people from doing bad things in the future? . . . It is easy to see that this line of questioning has gotten us no further in justifying the requirement that bad deeds or vicious people be repaid in suffering or hard treatment.[10]

This necessitates a god who doles out punishments and rewards, which is exactly how some read the Law and wisdom literature in the Old Testament. The method of "an eye for an eye" (see Lev 24:17–21) keeps violence and retribution proportional, and keeps situations from intensifying, knowing that human nature often seeks to take more than an eye when enraged. The Law then, keeps things fair. But the entirety of the Sermon on the Mount challenges the Law, not by nullifying it, but by extending it beyond external behavior to the very heart itself. Jesus says, in fact, "For I tell you that unless your righteousness surpasses that of the Pharisees and the teachers of the law, you will certainly not enter the kingdom of heaven" (Matt 5:20). How are we to have such a righteousness? And what does this righteousness look like?

Jesus continues: "You have heard that it was said, 'Eye for eye, and tooth for tooth.' But I tell you, do not resist an evil person. If anyone slaps you on the right cheek, turn to them the other cheek also. And if anyone wants to sue you and take your shirt, hand over your coat as well. If anyone forces you to go one mile, go with them two miles. Give to the one who

---

10. Wiegman, "Divine Forgiveness," 191–92.

asks you, and do not turn away from the one who wants to borrow from you" (Matt 5:38–42). The Jewish law spoke of a kind of justice that kept the people from escalating the degree of harm to someone who had wronged them. We are prone to anger, to righteous indignation, and to a desire for revenge when we are hurt or offended. If we are living out of a sense of duty to the Law, we will be stingy with grace, love, and compassion, and retributive justice seems to make sense. Remember, the Law allows for some measure of such revenge: an eye for an eye. But Jesus stands the Law on its head. Not only should we not seek revenge, we are to treat others better than we have been treated by them. When we are slapped, our inclination is to slap back. If someone takes our shirt, we react by snatching it back and possibly taking something of theirs in return. When we are obligated to do something for another person, we will do what we have to, but not go an inch more. If someone borrows something from us, we meticulously keep score. The kingdom of God offers a different way of being in the world. It requires a very different kind of inner character to give willingly and generously, particularly when we have been offended.

Jesus raises the standard even above the Law. He puts a new law of love in place, far, far away from retributive justice. He demands that we live differently. He requires this of us as it offers us a path to deeper humanity. How, then, can we force God to stay in a retributive system? Does God require something of us that God is unwilling to do? According to Wiegman, "The crucifixion actually reveals that substitution is not a morally required transaction, and that the system of retributive punishment for transgressions is itself morally bankrupt."[11] This makes satisfaction and substitutionary atonement theory at the very least misguided, if not altogether "unchristian," particularly in what it communicates about the nature of God—who seemingly requires a type of selfless love from us that God is unwilling to express.

But before we leave such theories in our dust, the question remains on the table as to whether it can be helpfully *mimicked*. What if we could *transfigure* substitutionary theory as applicable to the sinned-against? What if Jesus could stand in for the sinner (not the victim, here) in another sense?[12] What if the crucified Jesus, who in a sense has experienced the sin of the abuser by taking it in, could offer a substitutionary apology to the victim? As substitute Jesus can lament for the victim, if not actually repent in place of the abuser who may never repent or confess to the actual victim

---

11. Wiegman, "Divine Forgiveness," 202n2. Also see Wiegman, "Evolution of Retribution."

12. For a novel take on Jesus as substitute for the victim see Alison, "God's Self-Substitution and Sacrificial Inversion."

of the abuse. Rather than satisfying God, it is the victim who needs to be satisfied, who needs justice, who needs their woundedness at the hand of the abuser exposed in the light. This is why it is so important in the healing process for the victims to tell their stories, over and over again. The truth sets us free. "As an example, consider that victims of abusive relationships will sometimes regulate their attitudes toward abusers by diminishing the abuser's responsibility for abusive actions ('she has been under a lot of stress lately') or accepting the abusive action ('I deserved that') or denying that the abuser's actions are abusive ('it didn't even leave a mark'). In none of these cases is the victim forgiving the abuser."[13] The truth of who is really guilty and blameworthy releases the abused from darkness and silence. Again, abusers must be exposed as such; too often they remain hidden from view through means and mechanisms of placing blame on their victims, which such victims wrongfully absorb into themselves. What remains "right" about substitutionary/satisfaction theories is that justice should not be set aside. What must be transfigured is that God is not the one who needs justice; victims do.

What the Arminian version of the satisfaction theory offers victims is that sinners must repent in order to be forgiven. What some forms of Christianity miss is that repentance is broader than confession to God of wrongs done. It is more correct to firmly affirm that repentance and confession must involve the person wronged. Again, from the Sermon on the Mount, "If you are offering your gift at the altar and there remember that your brother or sister has something against you, leave your gift there in front of the altar. First go and be reconciled to them; then come and offer your gift" (Matt 5:23–24). Too often the verse "against you, and you only have I sinned" (Ps 51:4) is mangled and misappropriated. It is wrongly interpreted to give credence to a "privatized religion" that neglects the responsibility of confession to persons.

How does the cross of Jesus help? Jesus himself was victimized, and thus enters empathetically with those who suffer innocently at the hands of others. Jesus can say "I am sorry that this has happened to you." Beyond just solidarity with the sufferer, the cross can represent a taking *on* and taking *in,* by the divine-human himself, of the suffocating shame and oppressing blame which victims tend to take into themselves. Christ wants the victim to expel these toxins onto him. But is it helpful in any way for Jesus to represent the abuser, take the place of the sinner (since he in fact has absorbed these precise sins and become "sin for us" [2 Cor 5:21]), and act as a substitute admitter of harm? This substitutionary apology will not completely

---

13. Wiegman, "Divine Forgiveness," 187–88.

satisfy a victim's need for justice, however. The actual abuser can still get away with it. Is it any help to the victim to believe that the abuser will not get away with it eternally? "It would be better for them to be thrown into the sea with a millstone tied around their neck than to cause one of these little ones to stumble" (Luke 17:2). Or, for victims to know that they have some say in their abuser's inclusion in the Christian community? "Truly I tell you, whatever you bind on earth will be bound in heaven, and whatever you loose on earth will be loosed in heaven" (Matt 16:19; 18:18).[14] At the very least, in a substitutionary apology, God in Christ invites the sinned-against to find their innocence, and shed misplaced guilt and shame, for the true perpetrators and their offenses are named by an Innocent Confessor.

The Moral Influence Theory

Subjective theories of the atonement attempt to communicate to humanity that God is love; emphasis is placed on the lengths to which God will go—the giving of the Son—to beckon relationship with us. There has been much criticism of such theories because they can come across as "light" on sin, as the question of *how sin is atoned for* can slip from view. But the emphasis of the moral influence theory stands as a counterbalance to images of a wrathful, angry God. It consistently addresses the human need for holistic salvation through the loving gift of the Savior, *not* God's need for justice, and can point to the need of a transformed life. The love of God influences the morality of the one who responds to it.

The obvious strength of this theory is that it radically shifts the essential character of God from justice to love, even kenotic—self-emptying—love. Justification is imagined as relational renewal rather than just juridical or forensic salvation. God's aim is an ongoing relationship with humanity. Certainly this is not absent from objective atonement theories, but there is present a primacy of new birth over justification and an expected renewal and restoration of the image of God. In other words, indicative of what it means to be human is that God created persons to be loved and to love: God, others, ourselves. Indicative of what it means to be saved is to be set again on

---

14. Although there is some disagreement on small nuances by commentators about what these verses mean, there is a common interpretation that the context is the exclusion of any who sin and resist church discipline. The images of binding and loosing also connect to Jesus' work with those who have lost control of their lives through oppression by an external force. It could, therefore, be helpful to victims who feel bound or imprisoned by their circumstances to know that loosing is very much within the parameters of Jesus' healing ministry, and the loosing of abusers is somewhat in their control.

the path of human potential, that love might flourish. Thus the moral influence theory, as well as other subjective theories, is very optimistic about the subject's ability to change. The "moral example" theory emphasizes this change; Christ gives us the example of how to live fully devoted to God, and to love as God has loved us.

Where the moral influence theory fails is twofold: although optimistic, its mechanism for change is didactic in nature and it diminishes its focus on concerns of justice. First, close examination of the theory reveals that the cross is intended to elicit an emotional-spiritual response from the sinners. If they can perceive the love of God in the volitional self-sacrifice of Jesus, they will be moved to repentance. The understanding that Jesus died "for me" as an expression of love, will influence me to "do better." But this understanding, even though based on spiritual emotion, i.e., conviction, is really a didactic device. In other words, Jesus' expression of love becomes a model for our behavior. It is not, in this sense, a means of grace. Forgiveness comes from the heart of God and is not dependent, in any transactional way, on Christ's death. Christ dies as a symbol only of the love of God. The impetus to change (repent) is a decision on the part of the sinner, who accepts love. But the love itself is not the means of any transformation. While it might first appear as if this theory meshes with Wesleyan–Arminian theology (where grace is free to all who accept it), the moral influence theory moves in a different direction by taking God's (prevenient and sanctifying) grace out of the equation. Salvation, then, moves even beyond the synergism of grace and faith, and is completely and solely dependent on the sinner's acceptance of what God freely gives. The cross is not the source of grace, but only a means of communication intended to sway us. We learn to be better by looking at Jesus. But the content of Jesus' life—the nature of his holiness—can be neglected, which brings us to our second point regarding the theory's inadequacy.

A second weakness of the moral influence theory is that it can push justice out of the picture. This needs explanation. One might argue that the moral influence theory of Peter Abelard later influences theologians of modern liberal Protestantism, which is the birthplace of the social gospel movement. What might not be as readily seen is that liberal Protestantism, like the moral influence theory itself, can be accused of being "light on sin." At its beginning, "progress" of humanity was interpreted through an extremely positive theological anthropology, where the consequences of the fall were minimized. What humanity needs, in this movement, is education. To act justly is within our ability. God is a wholly benevolent God, and serves almost as a benefactor of our own enterprise. In light of the strong-armed interpretation of God's punitive sense of justice in the retributive system, this might be a good thing. But does an overemphasis on humanity's potential leave God completely void of a capacity to see "man's inhumanity to man"?[15] This is exactly the response of neo-orthodoxy to Protestant liberalism, which reintroduced sin as a primary category of theological reflection. For all the good of a social gospel movement, appropriate social "justice" must face the true capacity of evil expressed by all human beings. Of course, neo-orthodoxy arises from the flames of two world wars, and the real possibility of a Hitler.

Clearly the Bible, Old and New Testaments alike, repeats over and over again God's intolerance of injustices, particularly enacted upon the weak and the vulnerable, the poor and the stranger, the oppressed and the victimized. This is where God's anger is directed. For example, the lectionary text (Revised Common) for Ash Wednesday reads:

> "Why have we fasted," they say,
> > "and you have not seen it?
> Why have we humbled ourselves,
> > and you have not noticed?"
> "Yet on the day of your fasting, you do as you please
> > and exploit all your workers.
> Your fasting ends in quarreling and strife,
> > and in striking each other with wicked fists.
> You cannot fast as you do today
> > and expect your voice to be heard on high.
> Is this the kind of fast I have chosen,
> > only a day for people to humble themselves?
> Is it only for bowing one's head like a reed
> > and for lying in sackcloth and ashes?
> Is that what you call a fast,
> > a day acceptable to the Lord?
> Is not this the kind of fasting I have chosen:
> to loose the chains of injustice
> > and untie the cords of the yoke,
> to set the oppressed free
> > and break every yoke?
> Is it not to share your food with the hungry
> > and to provide the poor wanderer with shelter—
> when you see the naked, to clothe them,
> > and not to turn away from your own flesh and blood?"
> (Isa 58:3-7)

---

15. Niebuhr, *Man's Nature and His Communities*, 84.

Then of course, at the initiation of Christ's ministry, he claims another passage in Isaiah for himself:

> He stood up to read, and the scroll of the prophet Isaiah was handed to him. Unrolling it, he found the place where it is written:
>
> > "The Spirit of the Lord is on me,
> >   because he has anointed me
> >   to proclaim good news to the poor.
> > He has sent me to proclaim freedom for the prisoners
> >   and recovery of sight for the blind,
> >   to set the oppressed free,
> >   to proclaim the year of the Lord's favor."
>
> Then he rolled up the scroll, gave it back to the attendant and sat down. The eyes of everyone in the synagogue were fastened on him. He began by saying to them, "Today this scripture is fulfilled in your hearing." (Luke 4:16–21)

James describes authentic religion, that which pleases God: "to look after orphans and widows in their distress" (Jas 1:27). First John goes right to the point: "Anyone who claims to be in the light but hates a brother or sister is still in the darkness. Anyone who loves their brother and sister lives in the light, and there is nothing in them to make them stumble. But anyone who hates a brother or sister is in the darkness and walks around in the darkness. They do not know where they are going, because the darkness has blinded them" (1 John 2:9–11). The writer continues: "If anyone has material possessions and sees a brother or sister in need but has no pity on them, how can the love of God be in that person? Dear children, let us not love with words or speech but with actions and in truth" (1 John 3:17–18).

Where liberation theology—theology from the "underside"—excels is in its refusal to overlook injustice, and in its declaration that God's anger is most potently directed toward oppressors. God is on the side of the oppressed. This reveals that the moral influence theory is lacking. To explain, in its extreme focus on God's love as exemplified in the incarnation and on the cross of the crucified one, it loses its ability to take injustices as seriously as they need to be, as well as a root of evil that cannot be overcome by the human will. Again, the hope of the moral influence theory is that those who sin against others (regardless of the degree) will be moved to act differently by the example of Christ, but there is no insistence on a level of transformation where sinners are converted and living justly is imperative. It implies a type of Platonic logic: "To know the good is to do the good." It implies that if oppressors understand their error in contrast to Jesus' sacrifice, they can (with their own willpower) change their ways through insight. They are "free" to do so, rather apart from grace. What the moral influence theory fails to show is that oppressors, in the light of Jesus' full expression of love, can feel themselves *condoned*, rather than condemned, and as such do not experience a type of repentance that demands change. It indeed makes "grace" (understood as willpower) "cheap" (understood as easily given). Victims need more than this type of "slate cleaning" that costs oppressors nothing.

The Moral Influence Theory Transfigured

How does a transfigured moral influence theory help the sinned-against? Put simply, it is one of the theories that illuminates the love of God most poignantly and profoundly. God is a God of love and compassion, and if anyone needs such compassionate love, it is the sinned-against. The Greek word for compassion speaks of deep feeling that arises from the very "bowels" of one's being. It is more than feelings of pity or sympathy. It is a word that implies profound motivation toward action, almost as if one is compelled toward offering care to the one in need. The word *compassion* is a compound word that means "to suffer with." Compassion entails entering into the suffering of the other. Love never waits by the sidelines. Love is moved (both affectually and behaviorally) toward action. Love cares for the needs of the other, even, as Christ's parable of the Good Samaritan shows, towards the needs of the stranger. Truly, Christ is the Good Samaritan toward all who have been wounded. Love serves the other, and takes on the attitude of volitional servanthood.

The God of love is for all who have been abused or suffered violence, for those who have been abandoned and are covered in a shame not their own. God is for the wounded of every kind. This is one of the most foundational messages of the Bible and one the moral influence theory highlights. God is *for* us. God is not our enemy; even when we are lost and estranged, God is for us, especially the oppressed. Despite the way many have been trained to think, sometimes from an early age, we are not vulnerable before God, for God is *for* us. Vulnerability has to do with the possibility of harm. Vulnerability has to do with fear. But God's love is completely trustworthy. God's love is entirely dependable. God's love is absolutely reliable. We may feel vulnerable before God, but John steps in and reassures us, "If anyone acknowledges that Jesus is the Son of God, God lives in him and he in God. And so we know and rely on the love God has for us . . . There is no fear in love. But perfect love drives out fear, because fear has to do with punishment" (1 John 4:15–16; 18). And Paul reassures us: "If God is for us, who can be against us? . . . Who shall separate us from the love of Christ? Should trouble, hardship, or persecution or famine or nakedness or danger or sword? I am convinced that neither death, nor life, neither angels nor demons, neither the present nor the future, nor any powers, neither height nor depth, nor anything else in all of creation, will be able to separate us from the love of God that is in Christ Jesus, our Lord" (Rom 8:31; 35–39). Because of love, God's power willingly concedes to God's compassion; God's wrath willingly surrenders to God's mercy; God's majesty willingly submits to God's grace, as God gives Jesus Christ up for all—especially the most vulnerable and the most damaged. At this point it is important to celebrate that the compassion as seen in the person of Jesus is true for the entire Trinity. It is not just Christ who is kenotic and compassionate love; this kenotic and compassionate love is the very center of the Divine nature, even in the Trinity's relationship with each other.

Not only is God's love for us; God as love is also with us. From the symbols of God's presence in the Old Testament to the outpouring of the Holy Spirit in Acts, God has been a God with us. Christ as Emmanuel in the person of Jesus on earth was the immanent presence to whom all of salvation history pointed. God became human in order to truly be with us, in order to fully communicate with us, and to fully understand us from a position of actual empathy. From this perspective, the incarnation is as important as the atonement. In fact, they are inseparably linked as both the person and work of the triune God in Christ. The Word dwelt among us. It is only through this immanent and embodied presence of God on earth that Jesus Christ can serve as our high priest—representing us to God through a true identification with us as human and representing God to us through true identity in nature with God. It is this "scandal" of God's "particularity" in Jesus that changed and continues to change everything.

God was potently with us in the incarnation of Jesus Christ. And God is perpetually with us through the Holy Spirit. And the Holy Spirit, of course, represents and transmits God's love for us. Pentecost is rightly seen as the birth of the faith of the church, as the Holy Spirit was manifested in particular ways. The Holy Spirit remains with us. The Holy Spirit is truly the one "called alongside" us as comforter. The Holy Spirit abides with us. God is with us. It is also the Holy Spirit that breathes life *into* us, and transforms our perception from God as *with us* to God as truly *in us*. God's love through Christ and the Holy Spirit is a love that is for us, with us, and also *in* us. This is one of the most unique aspects of Christian faith. And one that offers hope and healing to the wounded. The Holy Spirit is *in* us—the deepest of expressions of God's intimacy.

An outrageous hope for this project moves us toward the hope of the healing of woundedness and the consequential han that can keep the sinned-against in bondage. The first steps toward that healing is to experience God's love for us, with us, and in us. But whether we are persons who have been sinned-against, or are persons "on their side," a renewed ability in us to love others is also the goal. God loves the broken world *through* us. Love is Christlikeness at its core. First John, the epistle of love, says this: "We know that we have come to know him if we keep his commands. Those who say 'I know him' but do not do what he commands are liars, and the truth is not in them. But if anyone obeys his word, love for God is truly made complete in them. This is how we know we are in him: Whoever claims to live in him must live as Jesus did" (I John 2:3–6, TNIV). God heals us in order to make us authentic messengers of the gospel. God heals us in order to "purify" and make effectual the love we offer to others. God heals us in order to love through us, especially to love others who have been sinned against. In sum, a transfigured moral influence theology, transfigured through a powerful injection of love and especially grace, reminds the wounded that they are not alone with a command to "heal thyself." The very meaning of grace is that God helps those who cannot help themselves, and is precisely not a self-willed change based on a didactic influence.

The Ransom and *Christus Victor* Theory

Although the ransom theory and the *Christus Victor* theory can be seen as distinct from each other, we will deal with them together because they both deal with "the powers of darkness" that need to be defeated. The ransom theory goes back to the earliest church's understanding of the meaning of the cross. Context is important. Greg Boyd assists us:

> Owing to a number of historical factors, the understanding that the earth is a war zone between good and evil cosmic forces intensified significantly among Jews in the two centuries leading up to Christ, commonly referred to as the apocalyptic period. All indications are that Jesus and his earliest followers shared, and in some respects even intensified, this worldview . . . These depictions are obviously heavily influenced by standard Ancient Near Eastern mythological imagery, but they nevertheless powerfully communicate the understanding that the earth and its inhabitants exist in a cosmic war zone. Order in the cosmos and the preservation of Israel depend on God continually fighting against these evil cosmic forces. It's clear, biblical [Old

Testament] authors understood Yahweh's victory over these forces to be praiseworthy precisely because they believed these opposing cosmic forces were formidable and that the battles in the spiritual realm were real.[16]

Paul says that Christians' struggles are against "the rulers, against the authorities, against the cosmic powers of this present darkness, against the spiritual forces of evil in the heavenly places" (Eph 6:12; also see 2 Cor 10:35). This cosmology would have remained in the ethos of the early church, especially in the growing enmity between Christianity and Rome.

Early church writers developed the ransom theory of the atonement in this context. Essentially, the ransom theory believed that the fall of Adam and Eve effectively placed them and future humanity in the hands of Satan. Satan has held humanity captive ever since. He also demanded a ransom be paid by God if he was ever to release them. The cross and the death of the Son is this ransom. Satan frees humanity while Jesus is dead because the ransom has been paid. However, God tricked Satan. Satan did not know that Christ could never be held by the bonds of death, and did not anticipate the resurrection. But Jesus rises, and both he and humanity are free from Satan's clutches.

The ransom theory was utilized heavily for the first one thousand years of Christianity, until it was replaced in the West with Anselm's satisfaction theory.[17] (The Orthodox church never embraced Anselm's theory.) In 1931 a Swedish Lutheran theologian, Gustaf Aulén, published a book entitled *Christus Victor*.[18] Aulén challenged the idea that the patristic writers (particularly Irenaeus in the second century) understood the atonement only in terms of a ransom paid to Satan. Aulén argues that they did not see the death of Jesus as a payment, but rather that the crucifixion primarily represented the liberation of humanity from the bondage of sin and death. He goes on to say that Anselm critiqued the theory that came before as some sort of business transaction. Aulén denies that the early theologians implied such. But rather, according to Aulén, as the term *Christus Victor* (Christ the Victor) indicates, the theory should be understood as a victory of God over all the powers of darkness, over sin, and over death itself. Christ's death and resurrection are the means by which humanity is liberated from slavery to sin, and freed to live a new life in pursuit of true righteousness and holiness (best articulated as the recapitulation theory, also by Irenaeus, discussed below).

16. Boyd, "'Christus Victor' View of the Atonement."
17. Oxenham, *Catholic Doctrine of the Atonement*, xliv, 114.
18. Aulén, *Christus Victor*.

In contrast to Anselm's theory, which is fully based on the "law" of reward and punishment that says *God* must be satisfied, the *Christus Victor* motif says, God (the First Person) and God the Son are not against each other in the cross—with the first in the role of judge and the second in the role of sinner—but are united in the purpose of the destruction of the powers of sin and darkness. God is set on destroying what destroys humanity. This view, Aulén maintains, reveals the unity within the Trinity to redeem all held captive to sin. According to Boyd, "The New Testament concept of salvation does not first and foremost mean 'salvation from God's wrath' and/or 'salvation from hell' as many western Christians take it to mean—often with negative consequences for their mental picture of God and/or antinomian consequences for their life. Rather, it is a holistic concept that addresses Christ's cosmic victory and our participation in it."[19] To quote Charles Wesley, God "breaks the power of cancelled sin and sets the prisoner free."[20] It is an easy jump from this freedom to include all who are held captive to other humans.

Theologian J. Denny Weaver traces the development of the *Christus Victor* theory (or as he calls it "narrative *Christus Victor*") since Aulén and claims that many of its themes find their way into the liberation theologies of the second half of the twentieth century.[21] The *Christus Victor* motif moves us far beyond individual salvation and shows us Christ's victory over the very structures that perpetuate evil. This gives us direction as to how to transfigure the ransom and *Christus Victor* theories for the redemption of the sinned-against.

The Ransom and Christus Victor Theories Transfigured

The theology surrounding the *Christus Victor* theory of the atonement implies that God breaks us free from the darkness of sin and death. We most often interpret this to mean that we are freed from our own sin that brings spiritual death. But God's redemption is broader. According to James Kallas, "since the cosmos itself is in bondage, depressed under evil forces, the essential content of the word 'salvation' is that the world itself will be rescued, or renewed, or set free. Salvation is a cosmic event affecting the whole of creation . . . Salvation is not simply the overcoming of my rebellion and the forgiveness of my guilt, but salvation is the liberation of the whole

---

19. Boyd, "'Christus Victor' View of the Atonement."
20. Charles Wesley, "O For a Thousand Tongues to Sing."
21. Weaver, *Nonviolent Atonement*.

world process of which I am only a small part."²² Many theologians of late have emphasized Romans 8:20–22 and its ecological significance. All of creation groans for redemption. This is certainly a step forward in widening the breadth of atonement theology. But there is even more territory to explore.

Darby Kathleen Ray has written an important book entitled *Deceiving the Devil: Atonement, Abuse, and Ransom*. In it she intricately traces the connection between the ransom/*Christus Victor* theory and liberation theology. She insightfully distinguishes between earlier and later liberation theologies on an important point. At first, according to Ray's interpretation, liberation theology saw Christ's death on the cross as a profound declaration of God's solidarity with the oppressed. God is a God of suffering who empathizes with the plight of those who live under the consequences of the powerful and evil structures that keep them disempowered. So far so good. But to become too comfortable with suffering could have the effect of dulling our memory of all the ways Jesus' life reveals his resistance against the causes of suffering. Ray's critique of this idea continues: "A related problem plaguing many liberation interpretations has to do with the claim that God's suffering and pain is salvific, that God redeems evil by embracing it, by bringing it into God's own being. The danger of this position is that it tends to eternalize suffering, to offer it a theological back door to acceptability, and that, therefore, it may undermine human resistance to unjust suffering."²³ She agrees that God can accompany suffering humanity with deep empathy. But she asks, "Is accompaniment in suffering redemption? . . . Redemption from evil must mean more than suffering through it together, as vital as that may be. Salvation . . . must include resistance to evil, struggling against its causes, concrete efforts to undo it."²⁴ She affirms later liberation theologies that have "a dual emphasis on solidarity in suffering [and] *in the struggle to end suffering*."²⁵

Our back-side theology, following the sensibilities of liberation theologies, wants to proclaim loudly that breaking the powers of darkness and setting captives free involves resistance against structures that perpetuate evil and abuse. These are extremely important metaphors for the sinned-against, who struggle not with their own sins, but with the sins of others. Where back-side theology differs from other liberation theologies is in its strong emphasis that victimization is horribly *isolating*. It is not that battling racism, for example, is in any way easy! But there is a potential of solidarity

22. Kallas, *Satanward View*, 74.
23. Ray, *Deceiving the Devil*, 88.
24. Ray, *Deceiving the Devil*, 89.
25. Ray, *Deceiving the Devil*, 89.

with others of one's race in efforts at resistance. Such solidarity is often difficult to find for victims of violence and abuse; every instance is unique, and the element of shame often keeps victims from sharing their stories with others.

We now raise the question, can the ransom/*Christus Victor* theories be transfigured for the sinned-against? Put most directly, physical abuse, sexual abuse, spiritual abuse, neglect, abandonment, and other atrocities cause trauma of varying degrees, most severe. In the last few decades the effects on victims of such abuse have been studied extensively from a scientific perspective. The more we know about the brain through specialties within the field of neuroscience, the more tragic it becomes. Such studies have revealed the devastating consequences of various traumatic experiences, from delayed child development, to post-traumatic stress syndrome, to disassociation from the body, to the inability to maintain a sense of self-consciousness. We are coming to understand that even one traumatic encounter damages those abused, let alone years of repetitive harm or neglect. Psychiatrists and therapists have struggled to keep up with the discoveries found, and to find effective treatments for the traumatized.

Even though most trauma comes from the hands of an individual, there is certainly a *gravitas* that goes beyond a sinning person's sin. Such devastating consequences, where the brain itself is changed, gives rise to our intuitive sense that truly "dark powers" are at work in the world, and in each and every instance of victimization. It gives rise to our understanding that the very cosmos is disordered. There is a rip in the fabric of God's creation. Everything in us cries in protest. We understand the appropriateness of Jesus' threat of a millstone:

> He called a little child to him, and placed the child among them. And he said: "Truly I tell you, unless you change and become like little children, you will never enter the kingdom of heaven. Therefore, whoever takes the lowly position of this child is the greatest in the kingdom of heaven. And whoever welcomes one such child in my name welcomes me. If anyone causes one of these little ones—those who believe in me—to stumble, it would be better for them to have a large millstone hung around their neck and to be drowned in the depths of the sea. Woe to the world because of the things that cause people to stumble! Such things must come, but woe to the person through whom they come!" (Matt 18:27).

We can also perceive that the battle is not against flesh and blood only, but again "against the cosmic powers of this present darkness, against the spiritual forces of evil in the heavenly places" (Eph 6:12). In light of this, the world stands in need of a true conqueror, of a radical liberator, a thorough vanquisher, of a mighty God who will overcome it all. What the *Christus Victor* theory offers to the sinned-against is a promise of a justice that reaches cosmic proportions. Through Christ's victory, the potential of healing is opened as a realistic possibility, for the individual and for the whole order of things. Through the death and resurrection of Jesus, everything will be redeemed from its groaning. In turn, we can be made "more than conquerors through him who loved us" (Rom 8:37).

The Recapitulation Theory

Jesus Christ, the perfect image of God, is the "divine-human." If one seeks to hold to the traditional view that Jesus is uniquely God incarnate, this creedal truth must deal effectively with the humanity of Jesus and the hypostatic union. One early church figure, Irenaeus of Lyon, makes the humanity of Jesus central to his understanding of God's holistic salvation offered to other humans.

Irenaeus of Lyon suffered from severe persecution and was eventually martyred. While the context of martyrdom is no less important for Irenaeus than for other ante-Nicene writers, Irenaeus shaped his theology in conflict, not with the empire, but with those he deemed heretical, those who would consider themselves to be within the Christian circle. He is more known for his delineation between orthodoxy and heresy than his martyrdom; he is known for his clear demarcation of boundaries, as one of the first Christian thinkers to formalize the concepts of "orthodoxy" and "heresy."

Irenaeus furthered the early church's orthodox understanding of Christology and soteriology. Besides his endorsement of the *Christus Victor* motif, he is most known for his "recapitulation" theology and his elaboration of Jesus Christ as the new Adam (based on Romans 5). His atonement theory here strongly asserts that Jesus Christ obeyed where Adam disobeyed, and through this obedience, Jesus opens the door for us also to be fully obedient to God, and to return to Adam's original state *in this life*. It is in this context that Irenaeus's theological anthropology is born. His debate with Gnosticism, particularly its interpretation of the fall, forms his understanding of human nature. Irenaeus is extremely interested in defending the goodness of creation over against Gnosticism's tendency to call all materiality evil. The fleshly incarnation of Jesus is thus crucial. The focus of the recapitulation theory is on his humanity. And, therefore, unlike other theories of the atonement, Irenaeus's theology is not constrained to the crucifixion as the only saving event. All of Jesus' life is salvific, as he shows humanity as God originally designed it, and the humanity to which we can be renewed. While going to the cross is the ultimate act of obedience, his incarnation, baptism, temptations, and itinerant ministry all reveal his desire to do God's will. Because he is the second Adam, he empowers our obedience as we are continually transformed into our original design, precisely as humans.

In a highly original move, he perceives Adam and Eve to be "like children," implying innocence *and* immaturity. This leads us to consider Irenaeus's teaching on sin to be "the antithesis, or rather the corrective, of that of St. Augustine."[26] Irenaeus holds Adam and Eve responsible for their disobedience, but it is hardly the great disruptive event that changes the very structure of the universe, as Augustine seems to imply centuries later. Rather, sin is a result of immaturity and an opportunity for illuminating the mercy of God that will ultimately be expressed by a recapitulating Christ. It is also important to clearly differentiate between human nature and sinful nature, something, it could be argued, Augustine fails to do with precision. We do not sin because we are human. We sin, in a sense, because we are less than what humans were created to be. Whereas Augustine sees the fall as a cataclysmic event that causes a radical break with God, and total depravity within, Irenaeus's emphasis on immaturity and on the possibility of renewal preserves an optimism about human nature, the remaining *imago Dei*, and full restoration. Thus, the recapitulation theory of Irenaeus focuses just as much on sanctification as it does on justification. It also opens the door for understanding salvation as healing.

The Recapitulation Theory Transfigured

In an attempt to transfigure Irenaeus's ideas for the purposes of the sinned-against, remarkably, we do not need to leave Irenaeus's own paradigm. This comes when we consider not only his views of humanity, but also, in particular, his views of women. The gnostic myth clearly blames femaleness for the creation of an evil material world.[27] Women are the first "other" in a negative sense. If Irenaeus wanted to affirm the material world and yet condemn women, he could have easily transferred blame from the female deity in Gnosticism to Eve, as many in Christianity have done with

---

26. Rondet, *Original Sin*. Of course Irenaeus predates Augustine.

27. One form of Gnosticism believed that God's "wife" Sophia sinned against God by creating her own offspring, called the demiurge. It was the demiurge who created the material world.

devastating effects. But according to Rebecca Lyman, this is exactly what Irenaeus does not do.

> In contrast to later tradition, Eve has no special blame for the sin in relation to Adam . . . Irenaeus emphasized the unity and equality of Adam and Eve before and after the Fall . . . Any hierarchy between them is a result of the Fall itself, not Eve's particular part in it and is mentioned only in conjunction with Adam's own limitations.[28]

Key for our purposes here is that Lyman goes so far as to describe Irenaeus's understanding of the fall in terms of the *victimization* of Adam and Eve. Recall Irenaeus's view of the fall. Culpability is minimized. And for any remaining culpability, Jesus' recapitulation that transfigures Adam's disobedience into the potential for human obedience is where Irenaeus is strongest. What is stunningly intriguing, however, is his view of Eve. Indeed, "Eve is pictured as forthright and honest in her replies to the serpent and to God."[29] It is Irenaeus's high estimation of Eve that allows for his even higher estimation of Mary.

Several passages from Irenaeus may be cited that probe the relationship of Eve to Mary. It is worth quoting one at length:

> For just as the former [Eve] was led astray by the word of an angel, so that she fled from God when she had transgressed His word; so did the latter [Mary], by an angelic communication, receive the glad tidings that she should sustain God, being obedient to his word. And if the former did disobey God, yet the latter was persuaded to be obedient to God, in order that Virgin Mary might become the patroness of the virgin Eve. And thus, as the human race fell into bondage to death by means of a virgin, so is it rescued by a virgin; virginal disobedience having been balanced in the opposite scale by virginal obedience. For in the same way the sin of the first created man receives amendment by the correction of the First-begotten [Son].[30]

Just as Christ recapitulates Adam, so Mary recapitulates Eve. While this parallelism throws Irenaeus's Christology into a bit of confusion for those who want to see Irenaeus as a precursor of christological orthodoxy, it is notable that he is apparently wrestling to give particularly *victimized women* a patroness if not even a savior figure. "Mary . . . by yielding obedience,

---

28. Lyman, "Reflections on Early Christology," 3.
29. Lyman, "Reflections on Early Christology," 5.
30. Irenaeus, *Against Heresies*, V.xix.1.

becomes the cause of salvation, both to herself and the whole human race."[31] What did Irenaeus really mean by this statement? The possible implications are far-reaching and certainly captivating.

At the very least, Mary becomes a model of true discipleship in Irenaeus's estimation. Rebecca Lyman writes:

> Later categories of Mariology which focus on maternity distract us from the positive images of female discipleship pictured in Mary . . . The Christological model I am suggesting which may lie behind Irenaeus' few references is one which affirms the unity of male and female discipleship in Christ, and struggles to place feminine images of redemption into the theological model. On the level of human freedom and obedience, a parallel between Mary and Christ is hardly inappropriate.[32]

We might suggest that in light of how Irenaeus uses Mary as a pure type (to the degree of paralleling even Christ), Mary can be seen as a teleological model of female salvation and sanctification. There is also an element of "healing" in the image. Rather than needing to "become male" in order to become like God,[33] Lyman argues that "women may be in the image of Christ as women: like Mary they are second Eves."[34] Since Christ recapitulates Adam, and Mary Eve, as men and women imitate the recapitulating Jesus and Mary, they recover the image of God and progress in the process of sanctification, or healing. Lyman has more than adequately shown that Irenaeus does not resemble the later tradition that so closely ties the image of Mary to a passive, acquiescing, and simply maternal figure—a woman defined by her circumstances. In striking contrast, Irenaeus's Mary is independent, intentional, and active in her obedience and discipleship. She is more than a vessel to hold the Christ. She is like the Christ in her independent and willful obedience, and in her empowerment through the same Spirit that is in Christ. "Mary is not portrayed as 'submissive.' Her obedience parallels Christ's which is the model for the voluntary acceptance of God's will and word," Lyman writes.[35]

Thus it is key to see Mary, and especially Jesus, not as victims in light of their willful obedience, even though they were victimized. We can see them in the same way we see victims who become "survivors"—terminology

31. Irenaeus, *Against Heresies*, III.xxii.4.
32. Lyman, "Reflections on Early Christology," 7–8.
33. Corrington, *Her Image of Salvation*, 23. Corrington analyzes asceticism and martyrdom of the first centuries as attempts to "become male."
34. Lyman, "Reflections on Early Christology," 7.
35. Lyman, "Reflections on Early Christology," 5.

meant to convey that victimization (no longer) defines a person, but rather, healing and restoration is definitive of her or his essence. Mary's empowerment by the Spirit shows her as more than a passive vessel or womb. Jesus' empowerment by the Spirit propels him to be obedient, even to death on the cross, which importantly, Mary witnesses. They model *active* obedience to God and open the door to a theology that makes humanity (including victims) co-creators with God (i.e., active participants with God in the betterment, or redemption of all of creation). In Irenaeus's paradigm, they are mature and complete. As we move forward, Jesus as victim will be an important image in the following chapters. But this is not the end of his story, nor is it ours. The recapitulation theory pushes us from the cross and toward the resurrection. Even though we have much ground to cover before then, perhaps it is important here to pause and also say, there can be genuine resurrection for the sinned-against—this will be taken up in chapter 9.

The traditional atonement theories are fraught with problems. However, it is not necessary to completely discard them. In each there are remnants of value. This chapter has attempted to draw out such value through the process of "transfiguration"—a type of mimicry that subverts the traditional or obvious meaning by calling out to something deeper and more relevant for the sinned-against. In the next chapter we further explore potentially novel nuances of the atonement by transfiguring the symbolism of the cross.

CHAPTER 4

The Cross as Converted Symbol

It happened one day as his popularity grew. Early in his ministry, he had already healed many—a man with leprosy, a paralytic, a blind son, for example. The crowds were especially fascinated by his ability to drive out evil spirits, which he had also done on several occasions. He understood in his heart that they were more interested in what he could do than in who he was. But he helped them anyway. He was like that. It had gotten to the point where they followed him everywhere; so much so that he had to search for ways to be alone. Jesus crosses the lake by boat to get away, only to again be confronted by a crowd on the other side.

A rather important man approaches Jesus. The common crowds are one thing—but a synagogue ruler is something else. His twelve-year-old daughter is dying. In fact, she is dead near the end of the story, until Jesus performs an incredible miracle and brings her back to life. But there is another character in this story. A woman who reaches out of the crowd that is pressing in on Jesus—and touches just a bit of his garment—is changed forever. On the surface, we see another person who is sick, another person whom Jesus heals. But there is so, so much beneath the surface.

For what has felt like an eternity, this woman has suffered, but not just physically. We know that she has been bleeding for twelve years! In case we forget how long that is, she's been sick as long as the little girl has been alive. What we don't immediately realize is that in Jewish law, once a month, when a woman bleeds, she is considered untouchable. This woman had been untouchable for twelve years. This woman is in a sense a social leper, but one without a colony with which to commiserate. She is ignored and isolated, yes. She is socially "untouchable," but she is also, literally, not to be touched at all. Absolutely no physical contact . . . for twelve years. She could not have been married. It would have been impossible. She was probably divorced. There was a loophole in the law. One could have only twelve wives in any given year, and they could be dismissed for any reason. Many a woman who had been rejected by her husband, for various, often trivial reasons, turned to prostitution to stay alive. Not an option for the bleeding woman in our story. No one would have touched her. Even lowlifes who used prostitutes. No one. How did she exist? Rejected even by the very lowest of society?

She must have been a beggar. But if anyone knew her problem, they would stay clear of her too. Perhaps she moved around a lot. She would have been shamed and blamed for her infirmity, clearly a sinner in the imaginations of all she encountered. Unknown. Alone. Outcast. Unclean. Unclean. Unclean. Physically sick? Yes. But also psychically tortured. She represents, symbolizes, embodies an utterly broken woman. So desperate, she reaches out voicelessly, anonymously she hopes, and touches the hem of his garment. He, her only chance. She, healed and restored to life, whom he now calls "daughter." If there has ever been a healing by Jesus that rippled across to all aspects of a person's life, this was it. Truly redeemed; fully healed.[1]

---

1. Based on Mark 5:24–34.

The last chapter offered the reader reinterpretations of the more classical theories of the atonement. By "transfiguring" them into messages relevant for a wider audience than just sinners, the atonement is opened to wider meanings. It is crucial here to realize that to address the needs of victims, we do not have to find another salvation method. The cross retains dynamic capacity as a strong metaphor for the sinned-against, but the narrative of the cross needs to be told differently. The symbolism is there; it needs to be "brought to bear" (up under) the victimized.

The Cross as Symbol

Paul Tillich represents one theologian who reflected on the theological meaning of religious symbolism; many have followed in his footsteps through examinations of analogy and metaphor as aids in the theological task. Tillich's discussion is older and more concise, as represented in his classic *Dynamics of Faith*. He offers six characteristics of a symbol, using it broadly, referring to its various secular and religious applications. But his main point is to show the nature and power of Christian symbolism. First, symbols, like signs, quite simply point to something else. A symbol stands in as a type of shorthand for more elaborate sets of meaning. Second, unlike signs, symbols not only point to something, they also *participate* in that to which they point. It is here that Tillich indicates that it is extremely difficult to purposely extinguish a symbol; a symbol can change meaning (for example, the swastika from a symbol of triumph to a symbol of hate), but very seldom do symbols become void of meaning. The third characteristic of a symbol is that it opens "levels of reality" that are otherwise closed, a reality that cannot be reached in any other way. "In the creative work of art we encounter reality in dimension which is closed for us without such works," according to Tillich.[2] Fourth, symbols "unlock dimensions and elements of our soul . . . and open up hidden depths of our own being."[3] The fifth characteristic is that symbols cannot be created intentionally. Certainly signs can. We can create signs that we hope become symbolic. But a true symbol is accepted widely primarily through the collective unconscious of a group. And finally, symbols grow and die independent of our manipulation. As said above, it is nearly impossible to purposely kill symbols. If they die, it is because the cultural situation or context changes. "They die because they

---

2. Tillich, *Dynamics of Faith*, 42.
3. Tillich, *Dynamics of Faith*, 42–43.

can no longer produce responses in a group where they originally found expression."[4]

It is rather obvious to say that the cross is symbolic since it has been used symbolically for two thousand years. But what has it symbolized? For the Christian, it symbolizes the means of "salvation." It is an ironic symbol, in that it points to life out of death, healing out of suffering, victory out of defeat, to name a few. But also in a sense, the answer to the question of what the cross symbolizes depends precisely on what atonement theory one embraces. For some, it is the greatest symbol of God's love. For others, it symbolizes the appeasement of God's wrath. For still others, it is a symbol of paying a ransom to Satan for the captive souls of persons. But whether it is portrayed as "morally influencing," "satisfying," "paying," or "conquering sin," its symbolism has been limited to dealing with the guilt and salvation of the sinner. And yet, it is pregnant with possibilities for symbolizing help for the sinned-against. If we look at the cross from its back side, themes do emerge. Namely, the cross of Jesus Christ is symbolic of 1) death; 2) violence and scapegoating; 3) abuse and abandonment; and 4) nakedness and shame. Discussions of each follow here, with full-length chapters after this chapter's introduction of their meaning. The goal is to open up new dimensions of reality, and open up the hidden depths of our own being. Again, we are not creating the symbol, but bringing what has been in the shadows into the light.

Death

The cross is first a symbol of death. And the symbolism is compelling. All theories of the atonement agree that it is the *death* of Jesus that is salvific (although certainly not divorced from his previous life and his imminent resurrection). There is some sense in all of the theories that Jesus died for humanity. One biblical reason comes from the oft-quoted verse, "The wages of sin is death" (Rom 6:23). What Paul announces here would not have shocked his readers, and it should not shock us. He is not, in this first part of the verse, offering some revelatory truth that is novel or surprising. He is stating what should be obvious to all. Sin kills. He is also not speaking only of some eschatological and spiritual consequence of sin, as if announcing that sin will bring ultimate and permanent condemnation. His words are existentially apparent, and experientially known. In other words, someone's sin can ultimately lead to the literal death of another, as the story of Cain and Abel so poignantly demonstrates. (Not poignant in that Abel died per

---

4. Tillich, *Dynamics of Faith*, 43.

se, for many have died at the hands even of brothers since, but deeply disturbing because one of the first "recorded" sins was so extreme.)

Christians in Rome were all too familiar with conflict and conquest, with armies that killed and maimed, and even with rulers who sometimes arbitrarily inflicted pain, suffering, and death on those who seemed to oppose them. Certainly Roman Christians had experienced oppression and violence themselves. The sin of persecution led to their martyrdom. And ultimately Paul himself met his end at Rome's hands. Sin can lead to death, quite literally. In light of holocausts, genocides, homicides, and infanticides, we should not move too quickly to a metaphorical meaning.

But Paul does imply more in this verse, of course. There is spiritual death that comes when human beings sin. In Romans 7, Paul wrestles with the consequences of sin apart from Christ. After describing sin, almost in anthropomorphizing terms as his master and he the slave, he finally desperately cries out: "Who will rescue me from this body of death?" (Rom 7:24). Who will free him from the corpse he carries around that is rotting his flesh and eating him alive? Sin destroys. A common interpretation of Paul's words here echo a major theme in the entire biblical witness—sin brings spiritual death to those who do not participate in God's mercy and grace. As God said in the garden, "You must not [sin], or you will die" (Gen 3:3). Another biblical message is that all have sinned. In light of this reality, atonement rises as our only hope. "The wages of sin is death, but the gift of God is eternal life in Christ Jesus our Lord" (Rom 6:23).

In the New Testament, and in the Pauline writings in particular, Christ's work on the cross is the means of finding forgiveness and justification, redemption and regeneration, adoption and reconciliation with God. Sin brings death, Christ brings life. Sinners are "saved" through faith in what Christ has done on their behalf. "The old is gone, the new has come" (2 Cor 5:17). Salvation through *faith alone* becomes the Protestant mantra. Truly, what a relief!

What has not been as apparent in Christian theology, especially in our theology of the cross, is that the *sinned-against* have also died, and apparently no one has come to save *them*. Slaughter, famine, war, violence, unspeakable abuse, all create victims—victims of sin, victims who die quite literally. But for every actual death, there are countless more spiritual deaths. Experiencing sin from the back side as a victim of its effects does not lessen its death blow. It is not just the sinner who dies in his or her sin. When persons are sinned-against, humiliated, abused, shamed, and used, they are dehumanized, and experience some level of "nonbeing." How can we say that a young girl who is sold to a brothel at age three, who dies there at age fifteen, has ever really lived? When such atrocities occur, lives are altered in radical ways. Victims who live must grieve the lives they once lived or never lived, for their reality has changed, or their ability to truly live has never emerged. They are emotionally, psychically, and spiritually damaged. They are, in effect, according to Jürgen Moltmann, truly the godforsaken. And while the question of *why* such things happened may linger justifiably, the question eventually must change to *how*—how do they go on? How do they continue to live, also carrying a corpse with them: not the corpse of their sin[5] like Paul, but their own corpses that have "died" at the hands of another? Being forgiven by a gracious God seems surprisingly irrelevant.

A passage from *Night* seems appropriate here:

There was a young boy in Buna concentration camp who was in the service of a commander who had 700 prisoners under his command. Usually such a "piple," as they were called, was hated because of his relationship to the German officers, but this boy was surprisingly well-liked, and it was said that prisoners smiled just at the sight of him. Someone beautiful in such a horrific place. The block where he lived was found out to have been involved in the sabotage of the electric plant on site. And an investigation found weapons in the block. All were questioned, including the boy. He refused to name names, even though he was tortured. He was then sentenced to death. He was executed with two others in the gallows. The rest of the prisoners looked on.

> The two men were no longer alive. Their tongues were hanging out, swollen and bluish. But the third rope was still moving: the child, too light, was still breathing...
>
> And so he remained for more than half an hour, lingering between life and death, writhing before our eyes. And we were forced to look at him at close range. He was still alive when I passed him. His tongue was still red, his eyes not yet extinguished.
>
> Behind me, I heard the same man asking:
>
> "For God's sake, where is God?"
>
> And from within me, I heard a voice answer:
>
> "Where is He? This is where—hanging here from this gallows." That night, the soup tasted of corpses.[6]

For many victims of violence and abuse, they are like the boy lingering between life and death—literally perhaps; surely psychically, emotionally, spiritually. For many, their most existential question: "For God's sake, where is God?" The more common biblical question "what must I do to be saved?"

---

5. See Rom 7:24.
6. Wiesel, *Night*, 65.

cannot afford to linger in the realm of the eternal that concerns itself only with the propitiation of the sinner's sin and the offer of future "reward": it is a question that must be answered in the literal, where literal "salvation" is often its chief command, and its initiating gruesome circumstance is painfully real and present. In other words, the meaning of the words "what must I do to be saved?" is radically different when they come from different mouths. From the sinner: how can I escape the eternal consequences of my sin? From the sinned-against: how will I survive this present[7] existential horror? How can we speak words of resurrection to victims, if we have utterly failed to see that they have died?

Violence and Scapegoating

The cross is a symbol of violence. Jesus endured unspeakable violence which started with his scourging. The flagellation of Christ is seen more in liturgy and art than in the Gospels themselves. The words "Pilate had him flogged" appear in Matthew and John; in Mark and Luke it simply says that Jesus was beaten. The scene has been depicted in art through the centuries. Most paintings depict a violent, angry, and obviously painful scene, some wrought with blood and wounds. Films, such as *The Passion of the Christ*, burn horrific images into the minds of the viewer, as Jesus' back becomes a gaping mass of bloody flesh and exposed muscles and sinews. In Jewish law, flogging is limited to a maximum of forty lashes. The Romans had no such limitation. The Roman soldiers would have first stripped the victim and tied his hands to a post or column above his head. The whip was made of several pieces of leather embedded with pieces of bone and lead. Two soldiers, one on each side of the victim, usually did the flogging. It is very probable that Jesus would have succumbed to shock from a copious amount of blood loss. Liturgically, the flogging of Christ is one of the Stations of the Cross, memorialized on Good Friday.

The horrific nature of the crucifixion itself is often hidden by our too romanticized vision that in essence blocks our understanding of its full effects. After the scourging—which could be seen as Pilate's intent at full punishment before being pushed toward crucifixion and the Barabbas debacle—Jesus begins to journey toward the cross.[8]

He walks, attempting to carry the load of stocky wood on his de-fleshed back, until he collapses in the street. Once at Golgotha, one account says

---

7. Literally present, or "present" in the sense that post-traumatic stress syndrome can take a person back to a memory that feels present tense.

8. Perhaps 650 yards.

that Jesus is offered wine mixed with myrrh, a mild analgesic mixture. He refused to drink it. The soldier then drove a metal nail through the wrist and into the wood. He moved to the other side and repeated the action, being careful not to pull the arms too tightly, but to allow some movement. Then, Jesus would have been lifted as the cross beam is affixed to the wooden pillar. With his knees bent, his feet, one behind the other, the nails would be driven in. The weight would have caused excruciating pain in his wrists, his nerves. In order to breathe, he would have had to lift himself up, putting weight on his feet. Eventually, lifting himself would become more and more difficult. Hanging by his arms, the pectoral muscles would become paralyzed and the intercostal muscles would become unable to act. His joints and muscles were stretched and dislocated. Finally, carbon dioxide would have built up in the lungs and in the bloodstream. Deep pain would increase as the pericardium slowly filled with serum and would begin to compress the heart. There are several possible explanations for how he died. He could have died through a heart attack, blood clots to his lungs, suffocation, or shock.[9]

This truly violent event is interpreted as the means of salvation for the whole world, and has most traditionally been associated with justification. But a crucial concern arises with an overemphasis on a juridical justification—which accentuates a legal salvation for the guilty, even the

9. See Davis, "Physician's View of the Crucifixion of Jesus Christ."
"People often ask, 'What was the cause of Jesus' death on the cross?' We really don't know for certain; many theories have been offered. Although we believe that Christ was in good health, His extreme suffering and severe pain could have brought about a sudden, catastrophic heart attack. He could have suffered from a cardiac arrhythmia or arrest. He may have developed blood clots in the calves of His legs early on. If these clots migrate to the lungs, they cause a pulmonary embolus, which would shut off the respirations. This is one of the common causes of death in older people in the hospital. There is another interesting theory. If Christ had suffered a heart attack early on, blood supply to a portion of the heart would have been blocked. As a result, a portion of the heart muscle would die and the area would become soft or mushy. With continued torture, it is possible that the heart muscle could have been torn open. Christ would have experienced bleeding into the sac that surrounds the heart, the pericardium. He would have died from internal hemorrhage. There is no question that Jesus experienced shock. Shock represents inadequate blood flow, depriving vital tissues of oxygen and nutrients. When this develops, a patient becomes weakened and nauseated. He vomits. He lapses into unconsciousness or coma and slowly dies. There are three principal forms of shock. Traumatic shock results from tissue injury and pain. Hypovolemic shock results from diminished circulating fluid volume, due to bleeding and dehydration. Cardiogenic shock develops when the heart is no longer strong enough to pump blood under sufficient pressure to vital organs. Breathing would become more labored as the lungs fill with fluid (congestive heart failure). In my opinion as a surgeon, shock was the ultimate cause of Christ's death on the cross." Green, "Crucifixion of our Lord Through the Eyes of a Surgeon."

perpetrator—is that it seems to assert not only God's forgetting sins done against others, but also God's apparent (and deeply ironic) blessing of violence.

Besides the temptation to be Marcionistic in our view of God as a result, the multiplicity of biblical views of violence has led some atonement theories to suggest that God ordains some levels of violence, and even *needed* violence toward Jesus in order to accomplish forgiveness. In strong reaction, some contemporary renderings completely deny that God could have any hand in Jesus' death at all, as if God is caught by surprise that Jesus suffered.[10] Negotiating these extremes leads to a legitimate question in atonement theology: how do we interpret God's relationship to violence, particularly in this book where we will bring victimization, pain, and suffering from the shadows into a prominent hermeneutical space? Did God *need* to use the violence against Jesus—his scourging, his beatings, his torture, his crucifixion—in order to save us? Did God *will* the cross? Does God ever will violence for some greater end? When this is simply assumed, and when a Christian blessing or romanticizing of violence occurs, it can lead some to believe that God may be inviting "faithful Christians" still today to engage in personal violence as doing God's will. Worse yet, it can imply that God uses (even wills) violence against a person for that person's ultimate good. And theodicy again raises its uglier head as we misquote Romans 8:28. The assumptions that reach such conclusions about God's condoning and using violence must be carefully explored. (Such will be offered in the next chapter.)

What is clear is that Jesus suffered violence. In the background, in the shadows, we "see" hidden people look on with keen perception of the pain,

---

10. Alan Lewis writes, "Theologians today sometimes suggest that the death of Jesus was merely an accident which overtook him: not the conclusion which issued from the logic of his preceding life but an illogical and disconnected catastrophe which befell him. (See Pannenberg's discussion in *Jesus, God and Man*.) The principal target of that interpretation is the idea that the events of Jesus' life and death were not genuinely open history but the predetermined outworkings of a divine plan for 'salvation history.' The corollary of that, also subject to attack, is that Jesus was clearly conscious of this plan and went through life, or at least his years of ministry, willing and securing his own demise and liquidation. In fact, a much more subtle and imaginative analysis will discover no contradiction between Jesus' deliberate choice of firm obedience to his Father's will, which had death as its inescapable conclusion, and his involvement in freely developing historical events which were beyond his control even though they meshed with his own intentionality. In other words, the fate of Jesus was neither an accident nor suicide, but the result of actions against him by others, who had been provoked by actions of his own. In order to obey the God he believed in, he had entered into conflict; and he died both as victim to those who contradicted him, and in consequence of his own opposition to them." Lewis, *Between Cross and Resurrection*, 45–46.

for they are familiar with its visceral reality. They truly understand. Who are they? They are the children huddling in their closets praying that their father will not come tonight and do unspeakable, truly violent and violating things to them. We see the woman in the mirror trying to cover the bruises with makeup, to no avail. We see a young Asian woman running naked down a back road in Vietnam. We see a man, instantly consumed by nuclear fire in Hiroshima. We see skeleton people waiting their turns for the "showers" at Auschwitz. We see beaten children, rape victims, the dismembered and neglected bodies of veterans, the elderly who die alone, slaves of all kinds, the diseased, the desperate, and the despised. We see people—intermingled yet solitary—who tentatively and slowly move toward the foot of the cross, and quietly beckon: "Speak to *me*!"

Jesus was violently killed. He understands violence that affects body and soul; bone-chilling, bone-cracking, flesh-tearing, heartbreaking violence. He indeed has something to say to these sinned-against victims, those who are godforsaken. His response is not limited by the isolating and confining helplessness of pain, though he experienced it to the core of his being. He comes with priestly care and whispers, "By my stripes you are healed" (see Isa 53:5).

In the Old Testament, the blame for persons' sins was symbolically placed on a goat, who was then sent out away from the people. The word *scapegoat* has made its way into cultural as well as religious imagery. A scapegoat is a person who is unfairly blamed for something that others have done. Thus scapegoats are innocent, and do not deserve the punishment that should be assigned to the guilty. Thus Jesus is a symbolic scapegoat who vicariously steps in and bears the guilt of the world by enduring and absorbing the violence of the cross. As such, he is fully able to empathize with victims who are so often scapegoated, also innocent of any guilt for the crimes against them. In chapter 5, violence and scapegoating will be explored in detail.

Abuse and Abandonment

The cross is a symbol of abuse and abandonment. Jesus suffered at the hands of the soldiers, who followed the orders of the powerful of Rome and the synagogue. To state the obvious, he was clearly abused physically. He was victimized, suffering violence at the hands of others. But, this must be said "delicately" because theologically, it is crucial to also say that Jesus embraced the cross voluntarily. In the garden of Gethsemane, Jesus could have said no to God. We have to maintain this, or else risk falling into the dangers of Monophysitism, where Christ's temptations are no longer real as they are subsumed under a strictly divine nature. It is essential to maintain his freewill choice to allow himself to die. And yet, it is also vital to say that the cross was not merely suicide, without perpetrators. Christ actively allowed himself to be victimized and abused, unlike all other victims. But he did so to enter into full solidarity with them.

There were persons involved in the whole passion narrative who stand guilty—directly or indirectly—of Jesus' death. A traitor killed him as Judas gave him up for a bag of silver. A group of self-righteous religious men killed him as the synagogue rulers found him guilty of blasphemy. A crowd killed him, as they preferred Barabbas over Jesus. A Roman governor killed him as Pilate washed his hands of the whole matter. A few soldiers killed him, pounded the nails and threw lots for his clothes. And his own disciples either fled or passively watched him die. Peter denied him outright. This is where we speculate: Jesus was clearly physically abused, but what about emotional or psychological abuse? In what sense can we say that Jesus was traumatized? Clearly the anguish and frustration toward his disciples in the garden—"Could you not keep watch with me?"—illustrate this emotional and psychological pain, enfleshed in drops of blood. Although finally victorious as he cried out, "It is finished," there were other moments on the way to the cross and on the cross where we see the emotional as well as physical strain.

This is most acutely seen in his cry *"eloi eloi lama sabachthani,"* "My God, my God, why have you forsaken me?" Not only have human beings denied, whipped, tortured, deserted, and killed him, God as Godself has abandoned the Son. It has been a theological conundrum to try to decipher what occurs in the trinitarian Godhead in the death of Jesus Christ. Some have suggested it crucial to affirm that the whole Trinity died and that there was no essential separation, on the one hand; to others it has been imperative to say that the First Person turned away from the Son, truly abandoning him to die and thus fracturing the essential Trinity, on the other. For our purposes here, what matters is Jesus' existential experience of God's abandonment. This experience is crucial to our assertion that Jesus, the abandoned one, empathetically suffers with all those who have experienced godforsakenness. Jesus was, therefore, not only a victim of human abuse and neglect. Jesus was a victim of God. At the very least God's failure to intervene in this despicable evil drama must be reckoned with. Jesus' victimization is thus crucial to our overall thesis. This theme will be thoroughly expounded in chapter 6.

Nakedness and Shame

The cross is a symbol of nakedness and shame. The full weight of this can be difficult for modern (Western) readers to access. More recent scholarship (biblical as well as patristic studies), has shown how deeply embedded an honor-shame system was in early Christian culture. What is missing now is the sense that Jesus Christ fully empathizes with those covered in shame, particularly with those whose shame has been imposed upon them by guilty others. If we make the cross only a symbol of triumph, we leave the shamed hovering at the back side of the cross. It is theologizing that (appropriately) transfigures the cross from death to life, from sin to holiness, from hate to love, from weakness to power, and from shame to honor. However, at face value, in its historical context, the cross was a symbol of all that was repulsive. It is only in a post-crucifixion culture—where the symbol of shame eventually lost its power—that we can romanticize, even glamorize a cross. Yet victims often view themselves as repulsive, unacceptable, even ugly. The message that Jesus bore the shame of the cross, experienced its utter humiliation, and died naked can communicate to victims that they are not alone. Chapter 7 will elaborate on this powerful imagery.

The cross is a powerful symbol. The cross is a symbol of violence, abandonment, and shame; we should be cautious about a type of romanticism about the cross that drains it of these realities. We will now enter chapter-long treatments of each of these subjects, and explore more deeply the travail that each of these tragic circumstances inflicts on victims. In each instance, Christ's empathy and solidarity are crucial in the binding up of real wounds. While purposely avoiding cheap answers to extremely difficult questions, the sum of these next chapters is intended to move toward the claim that the cross is also a symbol of healing. As much as we might like in this book, and in real life, to jump quickly to therapeutic ends, we must first walk the "*Via Dolorosa*" in order to get there. Thus, we venture into difficult territory, fraught with the danger of both despair and oversimplification.

CHAPTER 5

Violence and Scapegoating

After she awoke and finished her morning chores, her "uncle" found her and said her next appointment was ready. However, he was not really her uncle, but simply a friend of her father. Her mother died in childbirth and her father had been killed in a senseless brawl. She was only twelve when he died. She was an only child and now she was truly all alone. A friend of her father told her that she could live with his family as long as she "earned her keep." What began as household work escalated to "entertaining" her uncle's business associates. Her uncle told her this was necessary in order for him to be able to put a roof over her head and food in her stomach. She had no choice.

She would never forget the first time she was asked to be with one of her uncle's friends. He was older, with deep wrinkles on his face. He reeked of alcohol and had not showered in weeks. He was rough with her, hit her, debased her, humiliated her. She had never felt such excruciating pain. She was wracked with shame. She tried to learn how to feel nothing at all.

Eventually when she turned twenty, she had enough and ran away to a village that was a three-days' journey from her hometown. She tried to find work in order to support herself, but in the end she was forced to turn to the only marketable skill she thought she had. She had no other choice. It was this or death. Perhaps death would have been the better option in light of what she endured. But at least now she would be in charge of whom she would "work with," and she could keep one step ahead of homelessness. Her client base grew consistent enough she could buy new clothes and eat meals that did not leave her hungry afterward.

She was meeting with a regular client, a husband and father of three. Their appointment was almost over when she heard men shouting. Suddenly the door to her apartment burst open and men were screaming and yelling insults at her. Several of these men were religious leaders she recognized from town. Others were men who were her regular clients. They were hurling insults at her, "slut," "prostitute," "whore." All of these labels were true, she knew, but she questioned them in her heart. She was trying to survive. They grabbed her by the hair, ignored the man she was with, and began dragging her down the street. Fear gripped her body. The penalty for her behavior and lifestyle was death.

They threw her in the middle of town where a crowd had gathered around another man. A cloud of dust billowed after they tossed her soiled body to the ground. Some men who had been shouting at her were now shouting at this other man. She did not hear all they were saying initially but soon she heard the law referenced and that the penalty for adultery was stoning. Fear seized her. Certainly, this other man was a religious leader also, who could also condemn her to death. Her poor and sad life flashed before her eyes as she sobbed in fear. Her accusers had stones in their hands and were ready to be given the permission to execute the righteous judgment.

While waiting to hear her death sentence, her body was strewn on the ground, her eyes closed with tears flowing down. Yet the shouting stopped and there was silence. The silence was deafening, her life was in the balance. Though her eyes were closed, she could hear what sounded like someone writing in the dirt. Then he spoke.

With a gentleness of fierce intensity, he said plainly, "Let anyone who has not sinned throw a stone." Again, silence. The silence was only broken by the sound of rocks hitting the ground as her accusers, religious leaders, and her clients (some were both), walked away.

Then he bent down and looked at her. Many men before had looked at her, often as an object who could bring them pleasure. While she had been looked at often, she had never really been seen. Yet, he looked at her and his eyes pierced right through all the fear, shame, and pain.

He asked her, "Woman, where are those that have accused you?" She looked around in disbelief, not sure if this was a trick, but said, "No one is still here."

Then, he gently picked her up from the ground. He looked at her again with a countenance that pierced her soul with a love and hope she had not experienced.

He said, "I don't condemn you either; go and leave this life behind." Her life would never be the same.[1]

While this is a story based on the eighth chapter of the Gospel of John, it could be the story of countless women and men (even boys and girls) who are trafficked, enslaved, and abused today. Too many people, though, have no one to save or free them so directly. It has become clear that sexual acts such as rape should be seen primarily as acts of violence, where lust and rage are indistinguishable. What the Gospel account shows us is that such violence is as old as time. What we can hardly face is that little has changed despite all claims that we live in a much more "civilized" society.

This story has most often been used in the church to paint a negative picture of those religious leaders who were simply trying to trap Jesus in his view of the Law. The focus has been on their hypocrisy, and the story

1. Based on John 8.

has been a vehicle to illuminate the growing tension between Jesus and the Pharisees. Yet too often, the church ignores this woman, or perhaps more precisely, uses her for other purposes, and thus objectifies her. If she is given any attention, it is to speak of God's grace that can offer forgiveness to someone as despicable as she.

So why would men drag this woman to Jesus? Was it really about their desire to uphold the Law? We rarely inquire about the man who was with her who should also be involved in this scene, and what punishment *he* deserved. Perhaps their frustration with Jesus was an expected expression of the anxiety of religious leaders who were living in an occupied land, where Rome could easily wipe them and their temple off the map. Holding to the Torah while also trying not to incite Rome was a delicate balance. Jesus upset the balance, suggesting common sinners could believe and be made righteous because God loved them. The mob forms with its own angst, wanting to see Jesus toe the line and have this woman killed as a sign of his loyalty to the Law. In many ways, this woman is the perfect scapegoat. If Jesus would have followed the Law and given permission to kill her, perhaps he would have eased the tension between him and the Jewish religious leaders. Perhaps with the Law executed correctly, they could forget the ominous shadow of the Roman spear.

It is curious that church tradition has assumed the guilt of this woman without any knowledge of her context. It is not often preached that women who were prostitutes were so out of a desperation to survive, not out of lust for a life of sexual pleasure. Prostitutes were abused, and blamed for it. Of course this is also true today. Sex workers (as only one example of those on the *back side of the cross* who have experienced violence) have been told by the powerful (and culpable) that such violence against them is needed and justified, that they deserve no better. When the violence done against a person is thus rationalized, labels of *innocent victim* are exchanged with labels of *guilty criminal*. It is clear the accusers in John 8 felt completely justified in stoning this woman. The tragedy is that women like her have not been saved from violence, guilt, and shame to this day.

Does God Need and Bless Violence?

In John 8, the woman was spared from the violence of execution, and from the life that perpetuated her abuse. Jesus often gave the people he encountered alternatives leading to new life. Yet violence was not spared to Jesus himself, the innocent Son of God. Within the complexity of the atonement, the question concerning God's relationship to violence needs attention.

Does the First Person need an innocent victim to die in order for forgiveness and restoration to come to those who need it? For many Christians the answer is simple and easy. Yes, Christ had to die in order for God to be able to love and forgive us. This is the *theological* foundation for most discourse of the atonement. For those on the front side of the cross (powerful sinners) rarely see this as a problem. Yet from the *back side of the cross*, the idea that the First Person needs an innocent One to take punishment and be a scapegoat is deeply problematic. For many, the First Person's blessing and need for such a violent transaction seems to reinforce the message that their own innocent victimization and violence should be endured as blessed, endorsed, and needed by God. How is one to discern when the First Person might desire or need violence against the innocent to help the powerful and guilty, especially when far too many victims are told by their perpetrators, or even by abusive spiritual leaders, that they deserve such treatment? So does the First Person need physical violence in order for the forgiveness offered in the atonement to "work"?

Specifically to those who grew up in an evangelical denomination, it is commonly ingrained from an early age that Jesus' death was necessary and willed by the First Person. When asked why Jesus had to die, most evangelical Christians will offer some variation of "Jesus died to pay the price/penalty of sin," affirming some variation of the penal substitution/satisfaction theories (discussed in chapter 3). While many Christians are quick to offer this interpretation of the cross, the theology of such a statement needs to be considered in light of concerns around the subject of violence. Some questions that arise from such a statement are these: Did the First Person will and cause Jesus to die on the cross? Is the cross more for us or for the First Person? Is the cross good or evil? Did Jesus have to die on the cross? Is the cross necessary for our salvation, and did the First Person need the cross in order to forgive us?

The biblical witness is clear about what happened; Jesus was born, lived, died, and on the third day, the First Person raised him from the dead by the power of the Spirit. But it is not clear about the meaning of these events; they must be interpreted theologically. Most Christians focus on the death of Jesus Christ as central to the Christian story, but to such a degree that Jesus' life and teachings are often marginalized and seen as peripheral to Christ's salvific work. This centrality and fixation on the death has largely resulted in the assumption that everything that occurred in Jesus' passion was necessary to the salvation of humanity. Within those Christian traditions that affirm God's total sovereignty of power to the point of determinism, such assumptions are easy to make. For some Christians all that occurs in life, and specifically in the life of Jesus, occurs at the will and desire of

God. Yet even those who affirm other atonement theories can still need the violence and death of Jesus to occur, necessarily.

Did God Will the Cross?

The will of God should be nuanced to distinguish between God's *causal* and *permissive* will.[2] Simply put, God's causal will is that which God *brings about* and hence *desires*. God's permissive will is what God *allows*. Within both of these spectrum positions, there is an underlying belief that nothing occurs that God does not *cause* or *allow*. Yet, to the point of this chapter, did the First Person *cause and desire* the killing of Jesus or did the First Person simply *allow* it? Exploring these questions is essential, especially for those who stand at the *back side of the cross*.

Some Christian traditions affirm and emphasize the sovereignty of God's power as determining everything. All things that happen God not only *allows*, but also *causally wills*. Since God controls all things, nothing can happen that God does not desire. Most who claim such control also affirm that God is loving and good. Yet such a theology, where God controls and causes all events, makes God responsible for all the suffering, all the atrocities, all the rapes, and all the murders of the world. God is, in essence, the author of evil, no matter how we might try to wiggle out of this reality. Furthermore, if God controls humans they are then not responsible for actions such as these, and the category of evil as willful sin and love as purposeful choice evaporate. Worse, it forces us to redefine what is good, by insisting that whatever God does, it must be good. Logically, in a world where God is claimed to be good and the power behind every action, all things that occur in life must be interpreted as good, or for good, somehow.[3] However, eventually for many it becomes impossible to hold both of these claims that God is good and controls all events. When pushed by the logical dilemma known as theodicy, many Christians simply back away from God's sovereignty of power (controlling and causing all things) and want to hold onto God as loving. Yet for both of these options, evil done to the sinned-against is lost in the complexity of theological noise.

---

2. Aquinas, *Summa Theologiae* Prima Pars, Q. 14 and 19 and *Summa contra Gentiles*, bk. I, chs. 72–88 and *Quaestiones disputatae* De malo, q. 3, a. 1.

3. "Beth," a sexual assault survivor, says this: "I don't think that the rape of a child, the rape of me, is good—in any sense of the word; and I resent like hell the people who imply that, in some way, it will be good. People at church have said, 'Well, at least it will make her stronger.' That infuriates me. Suffering was not good." Blumenthal, *Facing the Abusing God*, 231–32.

Those who hold to the side of God being loving suggest that God allows (permissive) evil. This only pushes God's responsibility back one notch. Why does God permit the evil of innocent suffering? This does not offer a theodicy or answer the problem of evil, because while God does not will or cause all events, no event happens that God does not allow. God is just as responsible for letting evil happen when God could stop it, as God is by God causing all evil and/or suffering. The benefit of a theology where God allows evil is that humans are (also) responsible for causing evil. This brings us to the question, was everything that happened to Jesus, especially at the passion, caused by the First Person? And even if the First Person only allowed it, in what sense did the First Person will it?

One of the most powerful christological narratives recorded in Scripture is the account of the garden of Gethsemane. Jesus and the disciples just celebrated the Passover, yet Jesus transformed this Passover meal with the assertion that the bread and wine of which they were partaking were symbols of his body and blood. After they sang a hymn, they went outside the city to the Mount of Olives. This evening was as confusing as it was weighty for the disciples. Beginning with foot washing, charges of betrayal, pledges of ultimate allegiance, awkward events regarding Judas, and Jesus' proclamation that Peter and all the disciples would not be faithful made it an evening of promise, peril, and pain.

Once Jesus and the disciples arrived at the garden of Gethsemane, Jesus asked Peter, James, and John to come with him and pray. The Gospel writers describe in visceral detail the amount of excruciating despair, pain, and grief Jesus was experiencing, so much so that he was sweating drops of blood in anguish.[4] Meanwhile, the disciples are comfortable enough to drift to sleep, exacerbating and foreshadowing Jesus' isolation. Within the Gospels' retelling of the garden narrative, Jesus' petitions and desires that the coming events and cup might pass and be removed from him, since all things are possible with God. This is Jesus' will and desire. Even more than a fear of the pain and torture, he is facing the blackness of death. But in a powerful statement of obedience and worship of the First Person, Jesus announces, "Not my will, but your will be done."[5]

In light of Jesus' prayer of devotion, trust, and love to the First Person, much of Christian theological history has assumed that everything that happened following Christ's garden prayer must have been the First Person's

4. Luke 22:44; Matt 26:36–46.

5. See Matt 26:36–46; Mark 14:32–42; and Luke 22:39–46. It is also noteworthy that in both Matthew and Mark Jesus prays in three different movements, back and forth from the sleeping disciples. Three different prayers are intentional for these Gospels to connect to the length of Jesus' death.

will. This speaks directly into the problem of evil. Theological traditions emphasizing divine determinacy can answer this question with ease; God willed it all. Other traditions, that affirm the gift of free will among humans, see in Jesus' prayer an invitation for the First Person to do with Jesus what the First Person wills. Since Jesus is tortured, beaten, and crucified, one can assume that this was all part of the First Person's causal or permissive will. Moreover, if the First Person (who is good) willed the killing of Jesus, then this event must not be evil but also good. The First Person cannot will evil, so it is not evil. Moreover, it follows that if the First Person causally or permissively wills the killing of Jesus, the First Person must *need* the killing of Jesus for the salvation of humanity.

Therefore, in traditional atonement theories, the killing of Jesus is argued as necessary for the redemption of the world. In fact, many find affirmation in Hebrews 9:22 on the necessity of blood being shed. "In fact, the law requires that nearly everything be cleansed with blood, and without the shedding of blood there is no forgiveness" (NIV). According to many, if the triune God desires and seeks the redemption of the entire world, then the First Person needs the killing of Jesus for creation's redemption. The First Person needs the violent killing of the innocent one to aid and benefit the guilty. Of course, other verses and narratives challenge simplistic interpretations of this bloody passage,[6] but most still point to the needs of sinners. For those *on the back side of the cross* to affirm that the First Person willed/desired/needed this act of violence upon the innocent Christ for redemption becomes dangerous in the least. What if God still wills violence against the innocent themselves?

If asked, many Christians would have no problem in affirming Roman and Jewish powers were evil and guilty in their killing of Jesus. However, it is often spun that "what humans meant for evil God used for good." This creates problems. If the First Person willed the Son to be killed, then the Romans and Jews were actually doing the will of God, which is always good; the killing of Jesus was a good thing and is emptied of its evil. The killers are not sinning and are not guilty if this is followed. In a similar vein, it is often told to victims, even of violence, that God has a plan for all that has happened to them; this is intended to convince them that it is not really evil they have experienced but something good, buttressed by the underlying

---

6. For example, Jesus refers back to the prophets who note God's disdain for the sacrificial system. Jesus quotes Hosea 6:6 in Matthew 9:13, and also similar verses of Isaiah 1:11 and Amos 5:22. Some are quick to suggest with other verses that while the blood of bulls and goats was not sufficient, Christ's blood was sufficient. However, part of the prophetic critique and plea was that what God desired was not their sacrifices, but God wanted each person as a sacrifice; this is equally problematic for the sinned-against.

subtext that God has brought about this event. The idea of God needing evil in order for good to come moves toward an extremely problematic dualism, and back to the notion of a sadistic God.

The issue is raised with greater intensity by asking the question: Would it have been better for Pilate, Herod, Caiaphas, and/or Caesar to have confessed their sins and become disciples of Jesus, or was it better that they killed Jesus? Which is more consistent with God's purposes? If the cross is willed by the First Person as absolutely necessary, Jesus' opponents and executioners should be praised for bringing about this plan.

> [T]hose who killed Jesus must also have been acting in a sense as agents of God. In this case, Jesus' actions ceased being the revealer of God, and his opponents are entrusted with the divine mission of killing Jesus as punishment on humankind, which stands in direct contradiction to the claim that in his mission Jesus' human will cooperated in complete obedience with the divine will that sent him.[7]

J. Denny Weaver's claim here is that either God is being revealed through the actions of the innocent Lamb of God willingly laying down his life, or through the actions of those who killed Jesus. While some may postulate that God is being revealed through both, Weaver finds such a claim wanting. How can the words of Jesus to love one's enemies, act nonviolently, and not enact lethal punishment on other humans (via the Sermon on the Mount), be consistent with the First Person *needing* quite opposite actions by those who killed Jesus? Raymund Schwager asserts, "If the New Testament conviction of God's revelation is not to be destroyed, the action of God in Jesus must be clearly separated from possible 'divine' actions of his opponents."[8] Schwager suggests that many other Old and New Testament texts must be interpreted through such a lens. Christ becoming a curse for us (Gal 3:13), and, the First Person made Christ to be sin (2 Cor 5:21) should not be read with the First Person as the agent of the killing of Jesus. Thinking specifically about 2 Corinthians 5:21, Schwager concludes, "God was not the direct actor, but he sent his Son into the world ruled by sin, and thus, through the excess of sin making use of the law, he became sin and a curse."[9]

Therefore, one of the important theological claims from the back side of the cross is that God did *not* causally will, desire, or need Jesus to be killed to forgive and redeem creatures. The will of the First Person into which

---

7. Weaver, *Nonviolent Atonement*, 58.
8. Schwager, *Jesus in the Drama of Salvation*, 163.
9. Schwager, *Jesus in the Drama of Salvation*, 167.

Christ submitted in prayer from Gethsemane to Golgotha (really from the baptism forward) is not that Christ be killed, but that he be willing to suffer the ultimate consequence of evil. He would refuse fear in the face of violence, refuse counter-violence, and willingly take the stance of a lamb, silent before the shearer.[10] This, the First Person wills and allows. As subtle as the difference is, it is key.

This whole discussion highlights a not-often-heard claim that God is, by nature, nonviolent. We understand the intense complexity of this statement in light of primarily Old Testament passages that seem to suggest the opposite.[11] There we find texts that ascribe to God commands that the Israelites inflict violence upon others. The Christian canon offers multiple narratives of God's supposed blessing of genocides and infanticides; difficult passages to say the least. Other narratives, specifically those in the New Testament placed in the mouth of Jesus Christ, condemn violence towards enemies. This has been a perpetual hermeneutical question long before the writing of this chapter. How do we rectify the God of the Old Testament and Christ of the New? The early church heretic Marcion concludes that they cannot represent the same God. His heresy at least tries to answer the question of such an apparently strict contrast between them. We will stay in the muddle of such a dilemma unless we use the often utilized hermeneutic that presses the point that the Old Testament must be interpreted in light of the full revelation of God in the person of Jesus. Again, Jesus is the fullest revelation of God. It is impossible to continue imagining God as violent if interpreted through the lens of a nonviolent Christ. Either God is schizophrenic, or God-in-Christ's nature is the hermeneutical key.

But this leaves another question on the table. Denying that the First Person causally willed the cross, as the above discussion does, the question remains as to whether the First Person permissively willed the violence of the cross. Certainly the First Person allowed it. This is where the claim that God is by nature nonviolent must be said with one caveat. God can (permissively) will violence *against God's own self*. Not randomly, not masochistically, but for the purposes of the self-emptying characteristic of agape love specifically. In this way Jesus can legitimately say that he lays down his life for his friends. The love expressed in the death and the laying down of his life, and not the death alone, is what is truly redemptive.

What is *crucial* in the celebration of Christ's death, then, is *not* to make a universal ethic that glorifies violence; it cannot be explicitly or implicitly suggested that innocent victims must silently endure the abuse of evil

---

10. Isa 53:7, Acts 8:32.

11. The story of Ananias and Sephira in Acts is just as problematic.

victimizers as if following Christ's example. Christ, and therefore the triune Godhead, viscerally entered/enters into the suffering of the innocent to be present to them and thus, in love, to redeem them. In an ironic twist, through his death Jesus illuminates, chastens, and undoes violence itself. The Son became flesh in Jesus Christ to confront the pervasive disease and power of sin and death. Thus, the mission of God through the incarnate Christ is to confront the evil powers of sin through the inauguration and unleashing of the reign of God, a reign that radically differs from reigns of power where violence is liberally used and abused. Weaver notes, "Jesus' mission was not to die; his dying was the direct result of posing an ultimate threat to the powers of evil."[12] This threat to those powers led to the response of the powerful to eliminate Jesus. "Thus his death seems inevitable although not willed by God to satisfy a divine need or as Jesus' specifically chosen goal. Nonetheless, he was willing to die in pursuit of his mission, and it was the will of God that Jesus carry out his life-bringing mission faithfully, even unto death."[13] Thus the death of Christ is not needed by the First Person for payment or penalty, according to this interpretation; but it is how God destroys and undoes sin, evil, and violence itself, by refusing to participate in it. David Brondos suggests:

> Paul understood Jesus' death primarily as the consequence of his dedication and faithfulness to his mission of serving as God's instrument to bring the awaited redemption of Israel, which would also include Gentiles throughout the world . . . [Jesus' death] is salvific because God responded to Jesus' faithfulness unto death in seeking the redemption of others by raising him so that all the divine promises of salvation might now be fulfilled through him.[14]

The triune God's willingness to face and undo the reign of sin, evil, and violence are then defeated themselves in both the kenotic divine passion of Jesus laying down his life, and in his subsequent resurrection, where the eschaton of God's reign breaks into history.

From the shadows of the *back side of the cross*, then, care must be taken when speaking of the atonement. Does God bless, use, and condone abuse upon the innocent for other "good" ends? Extreme care must be taken when affirming a God who uses Christ's death for our good. Without care, even affirming the revelation of God's love expressed in Christ's willingness to die could reinforce the sentiment that God wants us always to endure the abuse

---

12. Weaver, *Nonviolent Atonement*, 162.
13. Weaver, *Nonviolent Atonement*, 162.
14. Brondos, *Paul on the Cross*, xi.

of evildoers, and never resist. From the *back side of the cross* the emphasis must be on the notion, not that the First Person willed or desired Jesus to be killed, but that God ultimately exposes violence for what it is, evil.[15] The First Person's desire for Jesus Christ not to fight or flee evil, and to endure the suffering of the cross, must never lead to the idea that God desires or needs the innocent and vulnerable to similarly suffer against their will.

Here, it would do us well to pause and ask, so what do we do with metaphors such as turning the other cheek? Jesus' words, we believe, presuppose an inner power of the one struck. Today we often call persons to self-denial before they have experienced a self to deny. Whether it be political oppression, social structures, cultural norms, family dysfunction, and certainly abuse, or innumerable other reasons, there are countless human beings who have been severely disempowered, even split off from any sense of personhood or selfhood. In more psychological terms, self-loathing, self-criticism, and a complete lack of a healthy view of self is rampant today. And yet, we can find the church preaching unhealthy forms of self-abuse, even using the metaphor of "self-execution." Such preaching misses the mark for innumerable people. There are those who even say that self-esteem is not a biblical concept and take a pejorative view of loving one's self *as* loving neighbors. But is it true—is it true that the Scriptures teach this self-annihilationism? No. Too many persons have been oppressed in the name of Christianity on this point. By way of analogy, to tell a slave—who has no freedom—to choose to live as a slave is nonsensical. Indeed, this supposedly biblical injunction was used in the rhetoric in the South to condone slavery before the American Civil War. Or similarly, to tell the poor to give up their overabundance of wealth also makes no sense. In the same way, to tell persons who have no sense of selfhood to deny themselves is as existentially mystifying as it is implicitly cruel. But do Christians have an alternative? Yes. The biblical messages of resurrection (as we will see in a future chapter), restoration in the image of God, empowerment for life and service, new birth, and new creation, all point to the power of God released into the life of those who follow Jesus, through the indwelling power of the Holy Spirit. In all its applications this life in the Spirit never washes away our personhood. In fact, the opposite occurs. Life in God enlivens us, brings us to real life through the liberating grace of God. We find our*selves* in God! It is only as we find this Godly sense of self that we can *then* in turn give ourselves away in love, or here, turn the other cheek. It has also been suggested that

---

15. Christianity has, of course, in its history used violence for its own gain. Miroslav Volf makes an important claim in light of this. "[T]he cure against religiously induced or legitimized violence is not less religion, but, in a carefully qualified sense, more religion." Volf, "Forgiveness, Reconciliation, and Justice," 269.

turning the other cheek in that historical context would have had a shaming effect on the aggressor and can be interpreted as nonviolent resistance toward the aggression and aggressor.[16] To put it most simply, God does call us to a costly discipleship. But the difference between this and those who suffer at the hands of others is that the disciple has a choice; sufferers of violence and abuse have no choice in their victimization.

Violence and the Mimetic Theory

We now turn our attention to the specific violent practice of scapegoating, as it relates to Jesus Christ's sacrifice of his life, to humanity's tendency to scapegoat others, and to victims who bear undeserved shame. René Girard, philosopher of social science and philosophical anthropology, observes how *sacrifice* plays a powerful role in the history of humanity, and even in human cultures today. While some anthropologists have been hesitant to see violent sacrifice serving any common narrative across cultures, Girard hypothesizes that most cultures use sacrificial rites "hoping in this way to protect themselves from their own violence by diverting it onto expendable victims, human or animal, whose deaths will not cause violence to rebound because no one will bother to avenge them."[17] Girard named his hypothesis the mimetic theory. Put simply, this theory asserts that whenever an innocent person becomes the locus of violence unjustifiably, by being forced to take on a blame that is not theirs, they become "mimics"—or what has come to be known as "scapegoats." Mimesis, then, is the common cultural practice of scapegoating.[18]

Girard examines many cultures and religions, including non-Western ones, and finds many similarities in their cultic practices. He also considers how the Christian narrative of sacrifice, specifically in the sacrifice of Jesus, both participates in the sacrificial practice of scapegoating, while at the same time completely subverting, undoing, and ultimately exposing it. In this, Jesus uncovers transactions between victims and victimizers, often based directly on the practice of scapegoating, as truly "savage."

Girard's main premise is that as persons engage others, they come to desire what others have (e.g., Cain's longing for God's pleasure over his sacrifice that was given to Abel instead). A rivalry can develop over "objects" that only one person can possess and that are impossible to divide. Girard notes, "The more intense the desire, the more [the object of desire] seems to

16. See Hays, *Moral Vision of the New Testament*, 319–29.
17. Girard, *Sacrifice*, x.
18. This use of the word needs to be distinguished from its use in chapter 3.

be ours and ours alone." We claim it. "But this experience is deceptive. It is not by chance that the most intense desire is always the most frustrated."[19] It is intriguing that while often the rivalry grows in significance over the desired object, the object itself becomes of less and less consequence. The rivalry itself becomes the focus and the object, as object, is lost. Girard notes this occurs when a feud crosses a "threshold of intensity; the rivals forget, misplace, or destroy the disputed objects and lay hold of one another directly. Hatred of the rival then prevails over the desire for the object."[20] This is reminiscent of family conflicts when a feud goes on so long that persons on both sides forget what the actual issue was; all they know is that enmity exists.[21]

In such a rivalry, one option is to try to kill whoever possesses the object that one desires; many have taken that option. Yet this bloodshed comes at great risk to oneself and to the community. For example, the other persons could defend themselves and cause harm in return. The conflict itself becomes threatening to the community. If the loss of either person is seen as a "great" loss to the community, an alternative must be found. Rather than kill the one who possesses what the other desires, the community finds a third party to blame for the conflict (what Girard labels, then, as a scapegoat).[22] This third party chosen by the community becomes a common enemy of the two rivals. It is the practice of mimeticism (unconscious, of course) that helps find this often arbitrary scapegoat who can help reconcile the two rivals. As more and more of the community join in the need for this common enemy, the system moves to "unanimity against a single adversary, a scapegoat chosen by mimeticism itself."[23]

Girard further suggests that often these communities become united because of the loss of a differentiation of sides, such that it "polarizes an

19. Girard, *Sacrifice*, 19.

20. Girard, *Sacrifice*, 25.

21. One of the most notorious fabled family rivalries from the United States involves the Hatfields and McCoys.

22. It is perhaps important here to point out that Girard is in fact using the word *scapegoat* wrongly. In the Old Testament (see Lev 16), there were two goats involved in purification. One goat's blood was spilled and sprinkled on various objects as a symbol of cleansing. The second goat, however, is kept alive. The people's sins are symbolically put on it, and then it is cast out of the community. It is not killed. It takes their sins and impurities away, as in spatially. Thus, when Girard considers Jesus as the "scapegoat" he has mis-associated them, and mistaken the first sacrificed goat used for its blood with the living goat that leaves the community. Girard is not unique in this misunderstanding. Popular culture also associates the word "scapegoat" with those killed in place of another.

23. Girard, *Sacrifice*, 26.

entire community against a single individual, a supreme enemy who all at once appears solely responsible for the catastrophe and is promptly lynched."[24] However, Girard notes that out of the frustration and confusion over this jointly held desire causing such chaos, the move to blame the scapegoat comes about through a dulling of the community's sense of how it all started. It is almost in the frenetic need to find resolution that the community loses its ability to be aware of the actual situation. This dulling of the senses helps to make it easier to deduce how this scapegoat is the real culprit and to move blame from the guilty and powerful onto the fragile and innocent—though labeled guilty—victim. "Anything that diminishes the acuity of perception favors the success of the sacrifice."[25]

It is intriguing to consider how the mimetic theory of scapegoating illuminates some of the most evil and heinous activities in the history of the United States. The lynchings of African Americans is an indelible stain and scar upon the soul of America to this day. While the majority of these acts of violence were done in the South, the entire country was culpable, both those who committed the acts and those who chose not to stop them. Many, if not most, happened after the Emancipation Proclamation. The animosity of the Civil War was certainly not eased by its ending. Tensions between the North and Sound remained, but violence toward each other now had to be submerged and suppressed. Ex-slaves became scapegoats. Specifically, one can imagine how the lynchings of African Americans enacted the mechanism of scapegoating as an outlet for the angst of whites who had other areas of trouble that diminished their sense of power. It seems easy to see that most whites in the South hated African Americans in light of the conflict of the Civil War. They lost the power to enslave them legally.

While it seems true that persons must be taught to hate, clearly the condoning of slavery of African Americans in the United States from the start told the story that persons' value and worth was based on the level of pigment in their skin. Yet not only were African Americans hated and treated as animals, as nonpersons, because of their "darkness," in many cases, they were also feared. What if they banded together against their common enemy, the slaveholder? Some of the most horrific abuse occurred from the mingling of hate and fear.

Abraham Lincoln, of course, freed all slaves in the 1865 Emancipation Proclamation, but for a long time the treatment of African Americans in the South worsened. Moreover, with all the great hardships the South immediately faced in Reconstruction, the African American was the ideal scapegoat,

---

24. Girard, *Sacrifice*, 26.
25. Girard, *Sacrifice*, 55.

deemed guilty for all the hardship experienced. Hence, the lynching of African Americans was *just* and *right* in the eyes of whites whose very way of life was quickly disintegrating. Again, according to Girard's paradigm, those doing the killing direct their angst "to a second-rate victim, a stranger, a vagabond. They propose to the god, in short, a false culprit, an insignificant scapegoat in place of those responsible, the actual sacrificers."[26] Certainly, many who lynched African Americans had a deep-seated racism, bigotry, and hatred for African Americans themselves. All the excuses often given about how African Americans were the cause of problems in the South were real fabrications. They, in fact, had little power to cause anything. But the mechanism of mimesis was also surely at play. They were blamed, literally, branded, even though they had been the innocent victims.[27] After the war, then, tensions between Southerners themselves were very real as they tried to reconstruct their lives in a chaotic aftermath. The scapegoating—in the form of lynching—of those who had been enslaved united whites against a common enemy, and obscured the complexity of new desires and new rivalries inherent in knitting a nation back together.

This is but one example. There are countless others. We might well consider the anxiety in Europe after World War I, which gives rise to a leader such as Hitler, who scapegoats six million Jews. That level of hate, based on fear and terror of the other, needed to commit such an atrocity is staggering. The Jews were sacrificed like sheep for slaughter, while millions of non-Jewish Germans watched, indeed sacrificed, rather than see Hitler as an enemy of their community. It is interesting to interpret this part of history in light of Girard's theory.

Girard summarizes the purpose of sacrifice:

> Sacrifice is a strategy for preventing violence from spreading throughout the community, for diverting toward an expendable victim the dangerous disorder that the murder of a personal enemy would precipitate, were it allowed. Sacrifice is an attempt to outwit the desire for violence by pretending, as far as possible, that the more dangerous and therefore more fascinating victim is the one being sacrificed rather than the enemy with whom we are obsessed in everyday life.[28]

But scapegoating, to the degree of the Holocaust, or to the degree of sacrificing only one victim, is "bad therapy" that solves nothing by simply

---

26. Girard, *Sacrifice*, 55, 58.

27. It is intriguing to notice the evidence that a lynching could cool things, but only for awhile; the rage would always return, paving the way for the next murder to occur.

28. Girard, *Sacrifice*, 57.

pushing relational angst down the road while killing innocents in its wake. Girard notes that this scapegoat mechanism as a mechanism of substitution was "utterly convincing by its unanimity so long as its mimetic nature goes unnoticed."[29] This system can sustain itself as long as the lie of its true purpose and function keeps the masses ignorant. He continues, "To have a scapegoat is not to know that one has one. As soon as the scapegoat is revealed and named as such, it loses its power."[30] Scapegoating functions through the blinding of the reality that the powerful are killing the innocent to momentarily qualm their desire to kill others. Yet to kill an innocent provides no real reconciliation, actually destroys community, and creates more han, if you will, to all involved. Perhaps the next obvious question to ask in a chapter on the violence of the cross is whether or not Jesus was a scapegoat. And if he was, how can the cross be saved from such a stigma?

Scapegoating, Mimeticism, and Jesus Christ

Mimeticism offers a unique lens with which to view the killing of Jesus. Girard speaks specifically about how mimeticism illumines parts of Jesus' passion, and affirms "that mimeticism plays a major role among the passive witnesses, as it does among those who actively participate in the essentially collective violence of the crucifixion. The mimeticism appears foremost in the mob and in the imitation of the mob to which all the spectators of the crucifixion surrender."[31] While certainly the Jews were nervous about Jesus' presence, teaching, and ministry, the Romans had largely ignored him. However, the mob[32] outside Pilate's court collectively chants—after being

29. Girard, *Sacrifice*, 57.

30. Girard, *Sacrifice*, 72.

31. Girard, *Sacrifice*, 67. (All should not refer to his followers at the foot of the cross; Mary, etc.)

32. Girard has a great deal to say about mob violence and mimesis. It is beyond our scope here to elaborate as specifically as we might like, or as may be warranted. Here is a snapshot in miniature. Girard's theory states that along with rivals joining forces against the scapegoat, often others in the community also join in the forming of a mob when existential angst arises. Mob formation elicits humans to do collectively what they would never do individually, as a part of the dulling of senses into a pack mentality. Mobs form in a variety of contexts and ways, sometimes with external causes such as epidemics, draughts, floods, or famines. Other times the cause is manifested in political strife or religious disagreements. While the causes vary, Girard notes, "The strongest impression is without question an extreme loss of social order evidenced by the disappearance of the rules and 'difference' that define cultural divisions" (Girard, *Scapegoat*, 12). During the rise of the mob, fear grips and then moves the group towards places of anarchy. "Institutional collapse obliterates or telescopes hierarchical and functional differences, so that everything has the same monotonous and monstrous aspect" (Girard,

stirred up by the chief priests (religious powerful and elites)—for Barabbas to be released and for Jesus to be crucified.[33] The crowd, who is traditionally identified as the same crowd who had celebrated the Palm Sunday entrance, is frenzied into chanting "crucify him" and calling for the release of Barabbas. Pilate, who wants little to do with Jesus, and who is even warned by his wife, submits to the fury of the crowd by having Jesus flogged and then crucified, though he claims to find no guilt in Jesus by which to do so. The Gospel of Luke also notes that after a bizarre interrogation of Jesus by Herod, Herod stands in agreement with Pilate to kill Jesus. Even more odd is Luke's narration that on this day of killing Jesus, Herod and Pilate became friends, when before they had been enemies.[34] Both Herod and Pilate have a difficult time finding anything at fault with Jesus. For Girard, a classic sign of mimeticism is that reason is absent in a mayhem that has lost touch with reality. "To reveal its purely mimetic nature, as the Gospels do, is to understand that there is nothing in the scapegoat phenomenon intellectually or spiritually deserving of faith; it is to see that the persecutors . . . hate him *without reason,* by virtue of an illusion that propagates itself irresistibly but no less unreasonably among them."[35] Here the mechanism of mimeticism moves forward through a movement of mystic ignorance and illusion. What is perhaps most surprising is the fact that the disciples, and particularly Peter, are also caught up in the frenzy. While most of the disciples scattered, Peter followed Jesus at a distance. But when asked if he even knew Jesus he rebuffed the thought with great vigor and sustained anger, unto his ultimate

---

Scapegoat, 13). While the roots of such anxiety are complex, those in power are often gripped by terror. "The terror inspired in people by the eclipse [change] of culture and the universal confusion of the popular uprisings are signs of a community that is literally undifferentiated, deprived of all that distinguishes one person from another in time and space. As a result all are equally disordered in the same place and at the same time" (Girard, *Scapegoat,* 15–16). Girard highlights how this inability to be undifferentiated (where the powerful and weak are not easily demarcated) actually leads to a culture on the verge of chaos and anarchy as no one can "rightfully" find his or her place. When all are the *same,* there are no longer any borders or boundaries. This undifferentiated crowd moves out of deeper disordered angst toward persecution; as it fails to deal with the real causes of its angst, often a change in culture and a perceived loss in power, rage moves to action. Instead of dealing with its root cause of angst, it attempts to deal with the unrest by feeding on an appetite toward violence. "Those who make up the crowd are always potential persecutors, for they dream for purging the community of the impure elements that corrupt it, the traitors who undermine it" (Girard, *Scapegoat,* 16). It is this crowd, united by a sense of societal angst they do not consider, that seeks to find a culprit to punish for their anxiety. The crowd can quickly become a mob.

33. Mark 15:11.
34. Luke 23:12.
35. Girard, *Sacrifice,* 72.

shame. Girard also notes that even the thieves on Jesus' left and right, who are also being crucified by Rome, joined with the mob in the sarcastic mocking of Jesus (Mark 15).

Clearly, the linking of the Jews and Romans against Jesus, while complex, is illumined by a mimetic interpretation. The killing of Jesus as scapegoat could at least shortly cool Jewish and Roman enmity. Girard notes how the Gospel of Luke connects the mimeticism of the mob to scenes from the Old Testament, where prophets were often falling victim as scapegoats to various powers. Even though the Jewish leaders and Roman officials were rivals, both parties were united by seeing the killing of Jesus as the way of dealing with the momentary threat to peace.

This entire mechanism is a classic triangulation, where a third (innocent) party cools the vicious anger of often powerful enemies. While the Jews were not in power overall, but rather subjugated to Rome, the religious leaders used their power in the community as a means of control. Jesus threatened that control, and so they subversively maneuver those over them to accomplish their purposes. It is also striking that for Girard, this killing of an innocent victim to keep enemies at bay is not about any real healing or reconciliation, but postponing eruption until the next conflict arises. In striking contrast, the kingdom of God as embodied by Jesus invites true reconciliation among enemies, that acknowledges and deals with their true anxiety and inner chaos, and subsequently removes the need for scapegoating victimization.

Christianity's Unmasking of the Scapegoat Myth

Girard notes that the Christian story participates, just like other cultic myths, in the killing of the scapegoat. Yet the Christian story, while narrating the sacrifice of the scapegoat on some level, also unmasks the myth held in the "archaic" sense by proclaiming the innocence of the scapegoat Jesus and exposing, not the victim, but the victimizers as the evil and guilty party of this scene. Girard notes that if the death of Jesus is a *sacrifice* in any sense, it is found in Jesus' consent to die in order to reveal the lie that innocent blood sacrifices elevate the true sources of conflict and violence.[36] The killing of the scapegoat by the powerful is seen as justifiable and righteous in light of the scapegoat's guilt. However, the life, death, and resurrection of Jesus as the sacrificial scapegoat illumines that the *Lamb of God* is innocent, and that the killers are guilty. For Girard "the sacrificial process appears and

---

36. Girard, *Sacrifice*, xi.

loses its efficacy"[37] and is as fraudulent and illegitimate as killing God. In other words, there is no redemption when guilty persons blame, shame, and kill innocent victims. Through Jesus' innocence, the guilty parties are seen as truly evil; the killing of the innocent scapegoat exposes who the guilty really are. Put directly, this sacrificial killing of the scapegoat has only made the evil perpetrators, even though united in transferring their competitive desire for power, more evil.

The passion of Jesus "makes visible the mimetic contagion and the inanity of the accusation."[38] The Gospel accounts expose the guilt of the executioners. While Peter was caught up with the mob on the night of the arrest, on the day of Pentecost Peter speaks the truth by exposing the evil. Empowered by the Holy Spirit (and precisely not by the "will to power"), Peter now speaks the truth that sinfully wicked people killed the Son of God by nailing him to the cross. Yet God raised him from the dead, exposing the futility of earthly power, and conquering the spiritual power of sin and death.[39] Peter's proclamation was about both the power of God and the evil killing of Jesus as the innocent Lamb of God. It should be clear, then, that the killing of Jesus is not (a) good! And the victimization of any scapegoat is inherently evil.

The mimetic theory helpfully exposes the passion of Jesus as evil. For Girard, Jesus is a scapegoat in a precise way.[40] "The extreme solitude of Jesus is the other face of the anthropology of the scapegoat. It is so absolute that the victim has the impression of being rejected by God himself: 'My God, my God, why hast thou forsaken me?'"[41] It is this point in Girard's analysis that is also so central for those on the back side of the cross. Often scapegoats feel completely isolated, shamed, and even guilty, even though they are innocent victims. Thus Girard notes that in the killing of Jesus, there is the potential of illuminating the actual effects of violence, rather than validating and endorsing the scapegoating sacrifice of the innocent.

While the Gospels give us everything we need to expose the insensibility and foolishness of the culture of violent scapegoating and subvert it, Christian theology unfortunately went where it should not have gone. It allowed an interpretation of Christ's death that condones the killing itself, and as a result, can condone other killings of other innocents. This must be resisted. But to say that the killing of Jesus is evil, and that evil cannot be

37. Girard, *Sacrifice*, xi.
38. Girard, *Sacrifice*, 74.
39. Acts 2:22–24.
40. Girard, *Sacrifice*, 69.
41. Girard, *Sacrifice*, 69.

causally willed by the First Person, does not prevent God from transfiguring this specific killing into a redemptive act.

Innocence of Victims at the Hands of the Powerful and Culpable

Truly Christian theology would never speak about the sinfulness of Christ. Hebrews 4:15 affirms indeed that Jesus was tempted in every way we are yet was without sin. No Christian theology should ever speak about the guilt of Jesus. Christians celebrate that he is the spotless Lamb of God who takes away the sins of the world. No Christian theology should ever say in any form that Christ deserved what he received on the cross. Christ was innocent. This is central to atonement theology, regardless of which theory is propagated.

Girard's mimetic theory reminds us how central to the human condition it is for the sinful and powerful to blame the innocent and marginalized for their own state of despair and misery. Repeatedly, the powerful seek to shift the blame onto another and really enforce that this scapegoat is guilty, thus forgetting and even denying their own culpability.

There is a different way to imagine the life, death, and resurrection of Jesus both for those on the *front* and *back side* of the cross. Christ's death was for the redemption of the world, not for a deficit in God. Jesus came to redeem the woman caught in adultery, a victim and oppressed scapegoat. Jesus came to redeem all scapegoats, all victims, all who suffer at the hands of others. Let's return to our primary example given earlier: the lynching of former slaves. How does Christ's death redeem them, and those who stand in their wake?

James Cone, in his viscerally painful and prophetic book *The Cross and the Lynching Tree*, names how many African Americans find salvation in Jesus as a fellow sufferer, as one who was also lynched. The primary lens of atonement for Cone is that of liberation. But his hope is not simply the liberation of isolated persons, as important as that is; he hopes for a cosmic liberation that also undoes structures of oppression and the mechanism of scapegoating. Not only are individual humans transformed and redeemed, there is a potential for the reconciliation of all creation in the cross of Jesus. "Fellowship with God is now possible, because Christ through his death and resurrection has liberated us from the principalities and powers and rulers of this present world."[42] Cone notes the paradoxical event of the cross. "The Cross is a paradoxical religious symbol because it *inverts* the world's value

---

42. Cone, *God of the Oppressed*, 209.

system with the news that hope comes by way of defeat, that suffering and death do not have the last word, that the last shall be first and the first last."[43] Again, the danger is to see the First Person as the one bringing the violence rather than absorbing it in order to defeat it. We see power, not in a God who wills the cross upon the Son, but in a triune God who endures the cross in order to expose violence and defeat death. In this way, Cone notes that the cross is "God's critique of power—white power—with powerless love, snatching victory out of defeat."[44] For African Americans during the lynching era (1880 to 1940),

> [T]he lynching tree joined the cross as the most emotionally charged symbols in the African American community—symbols that represented both death and the promise of redemption, judgment and the offer of mercy, suffering and the power of hope. Both the cross and the lynching tree represented the worst in human beings and at the same time "an unquenchable ontological thirst" for life that refuses to let the worst determine our final meaning.[45]

As Christ actively allowed himself to be a victim, Christ is the redeemer who enters into the pain of the sinned-against. For many African Americans the "cross was the foundation on which their faith was built."[46] Moreover, "the final word about black life is not death on a lynching tree but redemption in the cross—a miraculously transformed life found in the god of the gallows."[47]

Cone notes that those who have experienced brutal torture and humiliation can see in Jesus one who has also experienced humiliation and despair. Victims of evil are not alone, for Jesus is a fellow sufferer. Jesus hangs from a tree. However, persons and cultures who have experienced similar brutality and victimization should not find Jesus' torture as torture, or death as death, redemptive. That would make the whip and hammer the instrument of salvation; rather, it is in Jesus' overthrow of violence by exposing it where atonement and redemption are best imagined.

Jesus experienced what it means to be blamed and punished though innocent. For those on the back side, God in Christ enters into their shame, pain, alienation, and godforsakenness and communes with them. As has been said throughout this conversation, while all other victims do not

---

43. Cone, *Cross and the Lynching Tree*, 2.
44. Cone, *Cross and the Lynching Tree*, 2.
45. Cone, *Cross and the Lynching Tree*, 3.
46. Cone, *Cross and the Lynching Tree*, 21.
47. Cone, *Cross and the Lynching Tree*, 23.

choose their oppression, Jesus kenotically chose to lay down his life, in order to bring healing and redemption to those who suffer at the hands of others. Put most simply, God in Christ experienced violence as a victim. Christ came to redeem all, not only the sinful, but those who have been sinned against. Indeed, as Jesus exposes the sins of the powerful—*those on the front side of the cross*—inviting them to see their guilt and repent, Christ, who desires to liberate all, also provides healing for the sinned-against in the communion with his wounds. This healing and redemption of the sinned-against, the scapegoats, the vulnerable, the wounded, is not pretending no injury or godforsakenness occurred. Rather, this healing is a statement of God's lament on their behalf, and of God's desire that they know themselves innocent and infinitely loved.

CHAPTER 6

Child Abandonment

It was a clear day filled with promise. I was all alone, yet I felt the strong and powerful presence of God undergirding my breath and giving my feet strength. I was alone, but I was not alone. I was still chanting the praises from a powerful worship service. While my life had its share of challenges and difficulties, as I took stock of all the blessings of God, my heart was bursting forth with praise. The Lord had blessed me with a wife and children all of whom were the delight of my eye. My household was full of faithful servants who helped me tend to our growing family business of crops and animals. There had been hard years of low yields and disease, threats from neighboring clans, yet through it all God had been faithful. I have lived long enough to realize that God indeed blesses those who are faithful followers. I knew that all of the blessings of life are gifts from God and I knew the Lord was pleased with my desire to live righteously in God's sight. As I was contemplating the blessings of the Lord, I almost lost track of where I was until a servant rushed to my side and startled me from my daze of thankfulness and joy. Like someone startled awake from a deep and peaceful sleep, this messenger not only tore me from my meditation of praise, but offered news that began to tear away all that I knew.

I could barely understand him as he had run a great distance. Clearly, he came with a report that was important, but I could tell from his countenance that it was terrible news. As I encouraged him to catch his breath, he informed me of how one of the neighboring clans had come and taken all our oxen and donkeys. Worse yet, all of the servants caring for the animals had been killed, and he was the only one who survived. Many emotions began to stir within me: anger, confusion, sadness. Yet as I was trying to make sense of this awful act, another one of my servants came with the same look of desperation and pain. I initially assumed he had another account of this same occurrence. Yet as he began to speak, I could tell his news was different. He recounted how a mighty fire from the heavens had burned up all the sheep and the servants charged to care for them; similarly, only this servant had escaped. I began to go numb. This new information had hardly sunk in when a third servant approached with a similar look of pain and horror. This servant recounted the tale of a different neighboring clan who had come and taken all of our camels and again killed all the servants except her. Certainly all of these accounts could not be true. Had these neighboring clans conspired against me? My mind was spinning and I could sense a paralyzing shock come over my body. This was too much to handle. Unthinkably, another servant came with another terrifying look. I thought there is nothing left, all my animals had been stolen or destroyed—there was nothing left to take. Yet the pain in his eyes moved me to a place of grief I did not know existed. He told me of a party that my oldest son had hosted for my other children. He spoke of a great wind that had come almost from nowhere and caused the house to collapse with all my children inside. And then, he uttered the words no parent can bear to hear: "They are all dead." This servant alone had survived. Something within me went cold. While the pain of the loss of servants and animals was a bitter pill, the loss of my children tore open a wound in my soul that has never found balm.

My wife came to hear all these servants and as she heard each account, distress, disbelief, panic, and pain caused her to collapse. Yet when I looked at her in our moment of deepest grief, it was not one of shared sorrow and dismay she offered, but a look of anger as if I had done something wrong. She refused my consolation and she ran off. I was alone.

I was all alone. Even though the sun continued to shine, all I could feel was cold. No longer did I sense the presence of God in my breath and under my feet. I had no strength to stand. I was all alone. I tore my robe, shaved my head, then collapsed to the ground. Yet in my despair and pain I did the only thing I knew to do when hardship came. I attempted to worship the Lord. Yet I still felt all alone. Where was God?

The next month was a blur of overwhelming emotion. My wife and I did not find a way to share our grief together. We barely spoke. She also found it too difficult to worship with me. As often happens in tragedy, I was worried these unspeakable disasters were driving a wedge between us. I was struggling, wondering why all these things had happened. I knew in my heart that God's righteousness was at work in me. I always feared the Lord. But my loneliness consumed me. My wife felt distant, as did God. I wanted to feel their presence again.

The next morning I awoke and noticed sores over my body, while they were simply annoying at first they became more and more painful as the day progressed. I noticed these sores not only hurt, but they caused such irritation to my skin, and they began to itch tremendously. At first, I resisted, but soon the prickling was overwhelming. I broke a piece of pottery, and took a shard and started to relieve the itching by scraping it over my body. The momentary relief was worth more than the blood that oozed from these boils from scratching.

Was this how it would end? I was all alone. Alone in my grief, pain, and now my outside body matched the sores within my soul? Yet in my heart I still longed for God. I still found the strength to trust in him, but I felt like God left me, perhaps forever.

Two days later my wife came close, and I thought she had come finally to mourn together. But like that shard of pottery, her words tore open the wounds of my soul. Her venomous disgust for me oozed from her countenance as her words dripped with resentment. "Do you still think you are so righteous and holy now? Clearly all our livestock, all our servants, all of our sons and daughters are dead because of your sin! This is all your fault. Your sin has caused this! Why do you keep on with this holy charade? Simply curse God and die! We would all be better off." She was not angry at God, she was angry at me. She believed God honors and blesses the righteous while God curses and brings destruction to the wicked. Several friends stopped by and at first sat with me. But soon they made the same indictment: I must be to blame for God to punish me so severely. I was confused about these understandings about God's justice. I knew what we were supposed to believe, but I also knew deep in my heart that I was not the cause of this destruction. I was not among the wicked. But where was God? Why would God abandon me in my point of greatest pain? Why would God not speak to these others in my defense, to let them know that this destruction to my family and estate was not a result of my sin? After my wife made her disdain and revulsion clear, she wanted me gone. No longer would she see my faith in God as genuine because she felt God had judged me and condemned me by bringing such destruction that saturated every area of my life. I felt alone and abandoned by everyone. Would God ever show up again, I asked myself? I felt lost in the shadows of my despair. There was no one to console me, only to accuse me. I cried within, "Lord, why have you forsaken me too?"[1]

---

1. A rendition of the early chapters of the book of Job.

The book of Job provides a narrative that is hard and painful, yet necessary. It challenges simple theological clichés, but ones that are not completely false when we look at other Scriptures. The books of Psalms and Proverbs celebrate how those who live a righteous life will receive blessings and protections from God. They are clear that evil will be punished. "No harm overtakes the righteous, but the wicked have their fill of trouble" (Prov 12:21, NIV). "Surely, Lord, you bless the righteous; you surround them with your favor as with a shield" (Ps 5:12, NIV). "Be sure of this: The wicked will not go unpunished, but those who are righteous will go free" (Prov 11:21, NIV). With this wisdom, it is so easy to assume that if our life is healthy and blessed, God is pleased with us, and if our life is filled with destruction, disease, and despair, it is a result of our own sin.

Still today the idea that one's hardship and pain is punishment for sin, persists. For many on the *back side of the cross,* not only is their life one of immense heartache, there is the added burden of being accused, that they are experiencing God's justice, meted out upon them for their own sin or that of their family. In many ways, they can feel completely desperate and abandoned, especially by God. Grasping for any sense of power, some who have been hurt, abused, and marginalized find temporary relief in blaming themselves for their pain and destruction. We see this even in some abused and neglected children. They are psychically incapable of placing blame on perpetrators, particularly when the children need them in order to survive. Psychiatrist Leonard Shengold writes these intensely difficult words:

> Some of the stories that patients tell about their parents and childhood could make the psychiatrist weep: my father beat us so badly he broke bones; my mother put lye in my brother's oatmeal; my mother kept the bedroom door open when she brought men home for sex; my stepfather took baths with me and taught me [sexual acts], and when I told my mother she slapped me and called me a liar. Sometimes the accusations do not primarily concern beatings and sexual abuse but hatred and mental torture; or they are about complete indifference, neglect, and desertion. They present parents who are psychotic, or psychopathic or alcoholic. Love and empathy are described as never or only intermittently present—cold indifference or destructive hatred reigns. Often one hears of a kind of brainwashing, a cultivation of denial by the parents that makes the child doubt the evidence of his or her own senses and memory.[2]

---

2. Shengold, *Soul Murder*, 24–25.

Later, abused adults can continue to carry the shame for what happened to them because at the time they were dependent on their abuser, falsely thinking they could choose not to be dependent. They blame themselves because to do otherwise would mean facing the unfaceable—their absolute helplessness in the midst of the original abuse. It is more emotionally tolerable to bear guilt, which maintains some semblance of power, than to see their complete and explicit powerlessness clearly.

At the same time, the victimized must face the more "spiritual" reality of the abandonment of God. Simon Wiesenthal, who survived the concentration camps of Hitler, wrote of his experiences there. One night two friends were discussing some news they had heard from the outside, while Simon was desperately trying to sleep.

> Suddenly Arthur gripped my shoulder and shook me.
> "Simon, do you hear?" he cried.
> "Yes," I murmured, "I hear."
> ". . . You really must hear what the old woman said."
> "Which old woman?" I asked "I thought you were talking about what you had heard from the BBC? . . . What could she have said? Does she know when we will get out of here? Or when they are going to slaughter us?"
> "Nobody knows the answers to those questions. But she said something else, something that we should perhaps think about in times like these. She thought God was on leave." Arthur paused for a moment in order to let the words sink in. "What do you think of that, Simon?" he asked. "God is on leave."
> Let me sleep, I replied. "Tell me when He gets back."
> [The next day] I had time to ask Arthur how much of what I recalled was a dream and how much real.
> "Arthur," I asked, "what were we talking about last night? About God? About 'God on leave'?"
> "Josek was in the Ghetto yesterday. He asked an old woman for news, but she only looked up to heaven and said seriously: "Oh God Almighty, come back from your leave and look at Thy earth again."
> "So, that's the news; we live in a world that God has abandoned?"[3]

Wiesenthal carefully depicts the strong faith of his friend Josek throughout his book, yet he also presents the reality that many Jews lost

---

3. Wiesenthal, *Sunflower*, 10–11. The purpose of Wiesenthal's book is to probe the question of forgiveness of the Nazis. See chapter 10 for a more detailed discussion of forgiveness and justice.

their faith as a result of the Holocaust. One author has juxtaposed survivors of the Holocaust with survivors of abuse on this point.[4] One thing they have in common is that experientially, God is nowhere to be found. God seems to have abandoned them, like the refuse tossed to the margins of our culture. Like Job, the pain of unjust suffering and victimization is not the pain of the abuse alone, but also of God's abandonment, and of God letting it happen. At best God apathetically does nothing to stop innocent suffering; at worst, God is seen as the cause of it.

This is where we must move from our rejection of evil being causally willed by God in the previous chapter, to the acknowledgment that God's permissive will is also very problematic, not only theologically, but existentially. Regardless of the root of suffering, for many on the back side of the cross one of the most devastating effects is feeling all alone. Job's most desperate cry was for God to show up and be present. It is very difficult to have the tenacity of Job, who resolutely believed that, despite what his friends and wife said, his devastation was not a result of his sin. For most, an overwhelming sense of abandonment is the primary response to the unexplainable pain of abuse. How do they find salvation from God, who, as the same God, did not prevent the abuser from wreaking unspeakable havoc on their bodies, souls, and spirits? Why didn't God intervene? Why God allows suffering moves quickly to the cry of where was God? And where is God now? Unfortunately, too many Christians today, like Job's wife and friends, have little to offer to those who feel abandoned. With good intentions, we attempt to make sensible the senseless. But such explanations perpetuate the cycle of shame. Worse, Christians imply that it is not right to ask the hard questions such as these in the first place.

Some take the course to deny there is a God. Atheism is not a lament (for even laments are grounded in trust); atheism is a relinquishment of the question altogether, and a protest against a theological game that is stacked against them. It is absolutely true that the problem of evil can make persons of faith into atheists. But it should not be because Christianity has absolutely nothing to say. While God does not always stop unjust evil from happening, and while God does not logically answer the "why" questions Job and other victims are asking, God does act in both the incarnation and crucifixion of Jesus Christ. It might not offer a nice clean answer to theodicy. But in all its putrid messiness, God-in-Christ enters into the pit with the abandoned, and becomes one who is also abandoned by the First Person. For those on the *back side of the cross,* a powerful source of hope is not only seeing that Jesus died at the hands of his accusers, but that he was also someone

---

4. See Blumenthal, *Facing the Abusing God.*

abandoned by the First Person. As important as it was to establish that the First Person did not kill Jesus, it is just as important, perhaps paradoxically, to look directly into the face of a Jesus who also cries out "Why have you forsaken me?"

The Crucified God

Jürgen Moltmann, in his *The Crucified God*, powerfully invites the reader into the sorrow of Jesus Christ, specifically in his cry of pain and despair on the cross, "My God, my God. Why have you forsaken me?" Moltmann is convinced that the church—largely those in power on the front side of the cross—has failed to soak in the depth of despair of the Son of God, Jesus Christ, on the cross. It is important to provide some context for Moltmann's work before moving on to application.

Moltmann grew up in Germany and, at the tender age of late adolescence, found himself in Hitler's German army. Later, he came to learn the depths of evil that occurred within Germany and neighboring countries as the evil of the concentration camps came to light. Moltmann became profoundly shaped by the narratives of the survivors. He began to resist those in power who had helped put them there, people who looked very much like himself. He then became interested in the stories of victims of all kinds, and began to write to find theological and practical ways to help them.

Moltmann's first major work speaks directly into the fear, oppression, and despair of the Cold War. In 1967, as unrest and anxiety were building all over the globe, he wrote *A Theology of Hope*. While many had abandoned hope for fear, moved from comfort to consternation, and replaced prayer with a nuclear arsenal, Moltmann declares with a prophetic boldness that in the resurrection of Jesus Christ, God is making all things new. Yet while this book was received well by those who had been held captive by the imagination of fear, Moltmann noticed that many in power and of means, who were accepting his message of Christian hope, were not motivated to enter into the margins with compassion to help those who had been cast out and rejected. Instead of this recovery of hope from the resurrection of Christ making all things new—motivating people to continue the incarnation of Christ's ministry to the lost and least—it was simply providing a consolation for those in power in this life that our next life, whenever it comes, will be good and pleasant. Moltmann became increasingly frustrated by many Christians with power and influence who were not drawing upon this hope to participate in the redemption and healing of those in the ghettos of life. In many ways, Moltmann writes his next book as a counter treatise for those who had embraced *The Theology of Hope* so easily, and to recall that this hope in the resurrection is the resurrection of *The Crucified God*. God in Christ humbles himself to lay down his life and experience total and complete abandonment by the First Person. Moltmann's primary thesis, captivating and incisive, asserts that "through [Christ's] own abandonment by God, the crucified Christ brings God to those who are abandoned by God."[5] Especially for those at the back side, Christ first helps not by virtue of his power over evil, but by the virtue of his voluntary entrance into weakness and suffering—indeed, even into the experience of rejection and abandonment.

The First Person Abandons the Son

Moltmann is convinced that too many Christians from the *front side* of the cross have failed to consider the depth of Christ's suffering and despair, narrated most powerfully with the cry of derelection on the cross. There are many hermeneutical and theological approaches that seek to undo the scandal of Jesus' cry of forsakenness. Some can easily explain it through the Pauline concept found in 2 Corinthians 5:21, that Jesus Christ was made sin for us. In some theological systems the First Person must turn away because God cannot be present to, or contaminated by sin—even the sin Jesus innocently bears on the cross.

Moreover, the popular substitution theory steps in to say that while, yes, Jesus did not sin, Jesus must die to pay the price of the sins of the world and restore the honor of God. Jesus' death is justified and warranted and so the First Person's abandonment is therefore justified and warranted. The First Person is justified in "killing the Son" because of the bad things others have done; sin that is now placed on Jesus is rightly punished. If Jesus' death is divinely required in this way, then Jesus' lamenting cry is a failure on Jesus' part to accept the necessity of the First Person turning away from "his" sin. The First Person forsaking the sin-bearing Son is mandatory in the transaction. Yet for those on the *back side of the cross* there are some toxic conclusions that could be drawn from this. For one, in some ways the abused also absorb the sin of the perpetrator into themselves. In every sense of the word, they bear it "vicariously." It is a small step to take to conclude that God cannot be present to the sin they bear (although innocently, like Jesus), and that the First Person's apparent abandonment is (pervertedly) justified.

---

5. Moltmann, *Crucified God*, 46.

It is certainly appropriate to question the traditional idea that God cannot be present to sin in the first place; this is an extremely dangerous theological move. It is also appropriate to offer a very careful alternative interpretation of Jesus' experience of abandonment. Something more profound and engaging can be imagined for those who suffer forsakenness beyond simply asserting, first, that they are receiving punishment for their own sin, or second, that they, like Jesus, are receiving retributive justice also in a substitutionary way. Could there be other ways of considering the passion of Christ that would not so taint Jesus' experience, or our experiences, of the abandonment of the First Person?

Moltmann wants to hold on to the radical horror that the First Person's abandonment of Jesus really was by denying any sense of its logical necessity. He also wants to emphasize that by it a serious rupture occurs within the Trinity. "The abandonment on the cross which separates the Son from the Father is something which takes place within God himself," that was unprecedented.[6] Further, "As there was a unique fellowship with God in [Jesus'] life and preaching, so in his death there was a unique abandonment by God."[7] But to be clear, for Moltmann a crucial part of the atonement centers around God becoming the God of those who have been abandoned by God. This is a beguiling way of posing and answering the question of the dereliction's meaning.

Moltmann offers what is a surprising conclusion drawn from the Gospel accounts, even as it stretches the mystery of the hypostatic union. Moltmann suggests that part of the cry of dereliction and abandonment is not simply about Jesus' own existential pain, but arises from the fact that the First Person has failed Christ by nonintervention. Jesus died as one rejected by a First Person who, in the end, does not save, and thus acts very ungodlike. Jesus died, according to Moltmann, with every expression of the most profound dismay. Moltmann suggests the Gospel of Mark provides the most historical account, where Jesus offers no affirmation of trust in God but simply gives a loud scream and dies.[8]

Important here is that Jesus did not know for certain that he would be resurrected. Jesus died without any such supernatural knowledge. We take the real sweat, the real blood, the real anguish, the real humanity out of the garden of Gethsemane and out of the cross itself if Jesus knew absolutely that he would be resurrected and return to God. Jesus' agony is not about the physical pain he has to endure while he waits, *certain* of his death's

---

6. Moltmann, *Crucified God*, 152.
7. Moltmann, *Crucified God*, 149.
8. Moltmann, *Crucified God*, 147; see Mark 15:37.

resolution in three days. Jesus' real agony is about the abandonment, and the threat of his own eternal death. In Jesus' cry on the cross there is real torment. He is not calling simply for the compassion of the First Person upon his own temporary personal predicament, but for the revelation of the righteousness of the First Person *who has promised* "not to forsake the work of his hands." "Abandoned by God, the righteous [Jesus] sees God's deity itself at stake, for he himself is the faithfulness and honour of God in the world . . . The prayer of Psalm 22 calls upon the faithfulness of God for God's sake."[9] In his cry, Jesus asks the First Person, why you have forsaken *yourself?*[10] But the First Person does not act. Jesus dies despairing. Following Moltmann's provocative hypothesis here, we can see in his cry of abandonment, and the First Person's failure to respond, that Jesus dies believing that this would be the end of the gospel he has proclaimed and embodied. For the Divine-Human One to be humiliated and killed was also a humiliation and the killing of the good news of the kingdom of God that Jesus believed he inaugurated. Here there is an implicit charge of God's guilt. Perhaps Jesus died believing that his death was a refutation of his divinity and message. After all, they put him on trial and succeeded in killing him for blasphemy. There was no vindication of Christ's identity. And there is no vindication of the God who supposedly saves. Only when we accept this level of despair, though, does God become the God of those abandoned by God—the God of the godforsaken.

Up to this point in the conversation on the First Person's abandonment, this chapter has been vague and messy in not conclusively interpreting what it means that the First Person abandons and forsakes the Son. Moltmann is equally vague in his text as to why there is suffering in this world, and does not answer the problem of evil. Yet as Moltmann considers the role of the First Person in the Son's abandonment, the cry of Christ becomes symbolic of all the ways and places *God fails to stop evil and unjust suffering.* In other words, the First Person's abandonment is not because God cannot stand to be in the presence of sin, nor that God is punishing sufferers by removing affection through absence. In fact, the direct opposite is affirmed: even though the First Person does not prevent Christ's suffering and death, and even though God does not prevent our sufferings and deaths, God in Christ is present with us in it because Christ's abandonment is an event in the triune God itself. The God who abandons is the same God who is abandoned, and this same God, through the Spirit, is present with those who are abandoned. Those on the *back side,* though abandoned and forsaken,

9. Moltmann, *Crucified God,* 150.
10. Moltmann, *Crucified God,* 151.

are not alone. In Jesus Christ, they find fellowship and communion in their abandonment as God becomes the God of those who have been godforsaken. This forsakenness is not a sign of God's absence from them, but actually a moment of intense communion with them, because God empathetically and emphatically understands. It is not a rational answer to theodicy, but it is more than existentially relevant to those who suffer.

Recalling the entire incarnation as an act of kenotic humility and the love of the triune God, God does not suffer passively as we suffer, "but God can actively suffer, the suffering of love, in which [he] voluntarily opens [himself] to the possibility of being affected by another."[11]

Julie Hopkins suggests that in the incarnation there is the presence and "scandal of the vulnerable God."[12] Similar to Moltmann, for Hopkins God enters into the brokenness and suffering of the oppressed. God indeed is present in the death of Jesus not because suffering was necessary for satisfaction, but because God desired to be present to, and commune with suffering humanity. Jesus' entrance into suffering was not masochism, but "his ministry was life-affirming; he sought to eradicate pain and social distress and preach Good News to the poor and heavy hearted."[13] Hence, while Christ's death was not willed by God (for Hopkins) it was a "tragedy and a prophetic exposure of the nihilistic tendencies of those who idolize power." Indeed "God was present at the crucifixion not as an impassive transcendental observer, but as actively sharing with the victim in a solidarity of suffering and grief."[14] Again the syntax of abandonment and forsakenness is not one of God's apathetic distance but of an intimate presence of communion through Jesus Christ.

For this reason, the grief of the First Person is just as important as the death of the Son. The triune God chooses to enter into communion with those who have experienced forsakenness and abandonment in newer and deeper ways. The Son suffers dying, the First Person suffers the death of the Son. It is not only the Son who suffers; the First Person suffers as well. Too often in the atonement conversation God, the parent, has been either completely ignored, or worse depicted as a passive observer or a wrathful tyrant. But we can forget what God loses in such a portrayal. Too much acceptance of a dispassionate First Person led the church to condemn Patripassianism as heretical. But the First Person and the Son are united in their willingness to suffer in order to love us lavishly. "This is how God showed his love

---

11. Moltmann, *Crucified God*, 230.
12. Hopkins, *Towards a Feministry Christology*, 55.
13. Hopkins, *Towards a Feministry Christology*, 56.
14. Hopkins, *Towards a Feministry Christology*, 56.

among us: He sent his one and only Son into the world that we might live through him. This is love: not that we loved God, but that he loved us and sent his Son as an atoning sacrifice for our sins" (1 John 4:9–10, NIV) to the point of entering into all of human experience, even the experience of abandonment itself.

Within the continuum of the passionate condescension of the entire incarnation, during the passion there is an intensification of kenotic self-giving. As the Son refused to run away from the cross and allows himself to be forsaken by the First Person, so too the First Person allows the Son to be killed and forsaken, and in so doing shows the divine capacity for grieving with us. The forsaken God and the forsaking God are most intimately united in their kenotic Trinitarian sacrificial love for us. The First Person suffers the grief of the death of the Son who is allowed to die. "The Father suffers in his love the grief of the death of the Son. In that case whatever proceeds from the event between the Father and the Son must be understood as the spirit of the surrender of the Father and the Son."[15] The First Person delivers Jesus up for the godforsaken, but the Son actively also gives himself up to godforsakenness. In this way, for the sake of the godless (those in power who choose away from God) and the godforsaken (those sinned-against for whom God does not prevent evil), the triune God was united in suffering love for a hurting creation. "Father and Son are most deeply separated in forsakenness and at the same time most inwardly one in their surrender" on behalf of us, for Moltmann.[16] And here comes the rest of the good news. Within this event between parent and child "the [same] Spirit which justifies the godless, fills the forsaken with love and even brings the dead alive ... It is the unconditioned and therefore boundless love which proceeds from the grief of the Father and the dying of the Son [that] reaches [the] forsaken in order to create in them the possibility and the force of new life."[17]

It is only appropriate to speak of resurrection after the previous points have been established. There is a danger always in Christianity to rush too quickly to the empty tomb. But now we can say the following. Moltmann notes that while Jesus' death was apparently a nullification of the gospel that Jesus espoused, the resurrection all the more verifies the validity and truthfulness of the gospel Jesus proclaimed and embodied. "Behind the preaching of the resurrection of the crucified Jesus there lies the refutation of this refutation of his death."[18] In other words, while the resurrection does not

---

15. Moltmann, *Crucified God*, 245.
16. Moltmann, *Crucified God*, 244.
17. Moltmann, *Crucified God*, 244–45.
18. Moltmann, *Crucified God*, 123.

make Jesus divine, the resurrection verifies that Jesus has always been the Messiah, the Lord, the Son of God, part of the divine Trinity, and that the kingdom which he inaugurates is present and expanding. Again, it is crucial to note that the resurrection does not erase the visceral reality that Jesus had been forsaken by the First Person for the sake of the world. The resurrection does not undo the horror, humiliation, and godforsakenness of the cross. But it does reveal with exact precision the kind of God God is. This God breaks open new hope that comes specifically for those on the back side of the Cross. (See chapter 9 for more on the significance of the resurrection for the sinned-against.)

For many the notion that Jesus dies feeling that the First Person had failed him is too much for their Christology to bear. Yet with the passion narrative as told by Moltmann, the reader is confronted with the power and depth of Jesus' despair and abandonment, with the sheer and shocking grief of a First Person who turns his face away, and with the knowledge that all was done for love's sake—a love that does not just forgive the sinner from above, but a love from below that has entered into the bodiliness and bloodiness of human suffering with everything it has.

Those, then, who are oppressed and alienated can find communion and help in the cross. Christ's sufferings are a symbol of their sufferings. Jesus identifies with those who feel enslaved, mistreated, or left behind as he took such pain upon himself. Jesus was and is with them in their suffering. Even more, as Paul says in Romans 6, for those who have died with Christ in their suffering, there is hope that they will be raised with Christ in his life. God in Christ, experiences death. God is the crucified God. To this end, death no longer alienates humanity and God. God is not contaminated by sin, but rather, sin has been contaminated by love. Moltmann notes that with the hope of the resurrection "God is my beyond."[19]

Hope and freedom for those on the *back side* comes first in their identification with Jesus on the cross, "My God my God, why have you forsaken me?" This identification moves from solidarity and communion in forsakenness, to the hope of being raised (presently!) with the Christ who loves them infinitely. Even though God is on the hook for allowing the evil to occur, God comes in gracious solidarity and meets them in their deepest pain, despair, and lament. As with Job, God never answers the "why" question, but extends the invitation to encounter the love and healing of God. Atonement occurs "whenever God is incarnate (made flesh) in any context of violence."[20] Jesus' blood being shed is not about a bloodthirsty God; it

---

19. Moltmann, *Crucified God*, 217.
20. Heyward, *Saving Jesus from Those Who Are Right*, 138.

is about entering into solidarity with those whose blood has already been or is being shed. Carter Heyward says, "We need to say no to a tradition of violent punishment and to a God who would crucify us—much less an innocent brother in our place—rather than hang with us, struggle with us, wait with us, and grieve with us."[21]

And so, for those on the *back side of the cross* the Son is not killed to punish the innocent victim; there is no salvation in that. But the triune God experiences both abandoning and being abandoned, forsaking and being forsaken, death in the death of the Son in order to bring healing to those who have been abandoned and forsaken, ironically, even by God. In the death of Christ the power of God is redefined as an unparalleled depth of love that will work to transform and redeem all creation, sinners and sinned-against alike, by showing exactly how far such love will go.

---

21. See Hopkins, *Towards a Feminist Christology*, 171–75.

CHAPTER 7

The Sexual Abuse of Jesus

The Frost and the Fire

I feel cold,
   Like when a cousin pushed my face in the snow,
     and wouldn't let me up for air.
I still feel the frozen fury
   of being completely smothered and silenced,
   of always being misunderstood.
Or like the feel of my raw fingers
   on the day I first sailed.
The weather so miserable—
   I, so miserable—
   That I forgot
To feel the wonder
   of steering myself,
   only me directing my course.
     I could only feel, or not feel,
   the numbingly cold rain on my bare face,
   and the deadening circumstances to which I had to return.
     Wonder ever since has

Played Elusive.
It was a time long ago, when I enjoyed nothing, felt nothing,
   and could voice nothing—as one choked by another's gripping
     power.
I silently shouted "bloody murder" within,
   for someone was killing me slowly;
     in the grave there, hit with shovel after shovel of cold wet shit.
Molestation—I was a blinded mole; light beyond my station.
Somehow the inescapable halted,
   arrested, at least abated;
   strangely enough. Was enough.
I started the journey toward self-reclamation,
   But it still led me through valleys of the dead.
My unrelenting sickness came also as the sensation
   of being wrongly burned;
   like I'm on fire with no relief.
   Like a poker set in the embers too long, red hot;
   it stabs into my fleshy heart, and it sizzles as it sears.
   And it moves outward from the core, and into every pore, of
     my being.
Cold death-blows come from the silence of icy sadness.
   This other kind comes as a desperate scream—
   to stop the charring pain and the relentlessly ironic agony of
     being profoundly pissed.
   And I wonder what it is like to burn to death.
But here and now, and here again—
This time 'round, I am cold once more.
My cold feet will hardly do: this narrative task.
My own cold gizzards, frozen solid,
   could easily break triple-pained stained-glass windows with
     just a toss.
Stomach and bowels; hell, my whole body now curls into a petri-
   fied ball!
Rock-solid frozen, with no motion at all.

> *The logs all jammed up in the ice, and no chance for an early spring.*
> *I wonder what it is like to freeze to death.*
> *All, all, all I want is the warmth that comes as safe, still arms.*
> *I wonder where they are, and hope, yes, hope that I perceive them.*
> *And hope that I receive them, like a healing under wings.*[1]

Sexual abuse is an experience that has occurred millions of times over, with countless fugues of variation. All putrid. All devastating. All unnecessary. All meaningless.

In a chapter entitled "The Conundrum of Sin, Sex, Violence, and Theodicy," Marie Fortune writes of our common perception of the abused: "We are looking for some meaning because we earnestly believe that the only thing worse than suffering is meaningless suffering."[2] We would be hard-pressed to find anything meaningful in sexual abuse. This is a raw suffering that is simply absurd, without an ounce of some greater purpose. In fact, to try to find purpose in sexual abuse is often to re-traumatize the victim. Further, those who try to ascribe meaning or purpose or explanation to *another's* suffering often do so from a distance and from a position of power, with possibly devastating results. Fortune continues:

> [A] healthy desire . . . to address the issue of theodicy frequently runs head-on into a dominant moral framework which, for the marginalized (those who by virtue of race, gender, class, sexual orientation, age, ability, or other factors have less access to power and resources and are therefore less able to determine our own futures), does not offer adequate answers. Marginality often means increased vulnerability to abuse or violence. So according to this dominant framework, victimization or other suffering usually derives from the sin of the victim . . . [We] often ignore the agent of harm who abused, assaulted, or violated her/him.[3]

1. Leclerc, "The Frost and the Fire," previously unpublished poem.
2. Fortune, "Conundrum of Sin, Sex, Violence, and Theodicy," 124.
3. Fortune, "Conundrum of Sin, Sex, Violence, and Theodicy," 124.

The dominant moral framework needs to ascribe blame, but has too often placed blame on the victim and not on the victimizer. This is especially true of sexual abuse. How often is a rape blamed on the one being raped, for example. The woman (in most instances) is questioned about her *own* morality. Such accusations only reinforce what the marginalized are often already asking: "What did I do to cause this?" Statistics are clear that many women would rather avoid a trial (and therefore often not prosecute a rape), than take the stand and risk an assault on their own character. This, and many other examples, can be used to show that in the absence of the victimizer accepting responsibility, and in light of the almost cosmic need for such responsibility to fall somewhere, victims will often bear that responsibility themselves, even apart from us demanding it.

As we have hinted at before, an intriguing theological question arises when we invoke the idea that Jesus was a victim. As said in previous chapters, it is very important to understand that Jesus volitionally accepted the cross. Unlike other victims, he had full agency in the matter. It is also important to reject any notion of suicide by being able to name his *perpetrators*—from Judas to Pilate to the soldiers who pounded in the actual nails, and many others who helped facilitate the crucifixion. We have proposed that being able to name the perpetrators keeps us from any notion that the First Person killed Jesus in a causal way. Yet with this said, we have also suggested that the First Person abandoned the Son in order to be the God of the godforsaken. (God is not without "fault" in Jesus' anguish on the cross.)

We have already suggested that Jesus is clearly a victim of physical abuse. Only a dualistic gnostic Christology, where Jesus does not have a real human body, could keep us from the visceral intensity of the physical torture he endured during his flagellation and crucifixion. But here we now deal with a very difficult, but very relevant question: was Jesus a victim of sexual abuse? Did he have the experiences that would enable him to fully enter and empathize with those who have suffered in this particularly horrific way?

This chapter asserts yes, in two ways. First, it is certain that Jesus was stripped naked on the cross. This introduces him as a bearer of shame. Clearly it is an innocent shame, distinct from a guilty and humiliated criminal dying on a cross. But those who saw him would not have seen an innocent man. The shame of being stripped naked was significant in that culture, and should be significant in our consideration of all Jesus experienced. Second, Jesus has also been stripped, through centuries of Christian theology, of his sexuality; this has led persons to believe that if they are to be like Christ, they too must be "asexual" and repressed, or worse, perhaps, ashamed of their sexuality. These two abuses require a treatment of Christology that has rarely found the light. They take us where we would rather not go. We begin with a naked Jesus.

The Naked Jesus

One aspect of the cross of Jesus is surely found in his willingness to absorb its shame. The cross itself was deeply connected to shame in the context of the first century. The cross was reserved for the worst of criminals, or for those who were deemed so wretched that utter humiliation was an appropriate punishment. That Jesus was innocent makes the symbol of the cross profoundly ironic. Jesus was willing to absorb a shame that was not his own. Alicia Batten provides an introduction to the discussion:

> [The] cultural values of honor and shame figure centrally in various New Testament texts' articulation of Christology. It is widely agreed that crucifixion was one, if not the most dishonorable forms of execution within the Roman Empire. It was a horrible death and perceived as such by Greco-Romans and Jews. The victim would be stripped naked and publicly put to death. This public dimension of the death was especially humiliating. Thus the New Testament authors faced the challenge of the fact of the crucifixion and its dishonorable nature. In the Gospel of Mark, for example, Jesus is abandoned by his disciples, tortured and strung up upon a cross, where he cries out to God. Mark does not belabor Jesus' suffering, but he does not hide it either. The element of dishonor that Jesus has suffered is in fact a central element of Mark's overall Christology. Here, the Christ is the suffering Son of God, degraded and bereft. In a sense, Mark grants a certain honor to something that most ancients would find repulsive. Mark redefines, in many ways, what it means to be a Messiah or Christ. The true Messiah is a humiliated, tortured figure. Such an idea must have been quite difficult for many ancient people to comprehend or even want to consider.[4]

Much of Christianity has followed Mark's lead in making the humiliation of Christ "honorable." But in doing so, it has often divorced itself from the immensity of the original shame, which Mark does not do. We have forgotten the level of dishonor and degradation of the cross. But the societal shame of crucifixion created a socially appalling savior.

The honor and shame system of both the ancient and modern worlds is important here. It is recognized as practiced in most non-Western cultures.

---

4. Batten, "Honor and Shame in the New Testament."

It is the cultural worldview of the majority of the world. Halvor Moxnes offers a helpful summary:

> What then are the main characteristics of honor and shame as a system? Honor is fundamentally the public recognition of one's social standing. It comes in one of two ways. One's basic honor level, usually termed ascribed honor, is inherited from the family at birth. Each child takes on the general honor status that the family possesses in the eyes of the larger group, and therefore ascribed honor comes directly from family membership. It is not based on something the individual has done. By contrast, honor conferred on the basis of virtuous deeds is called acquired honor. By its very nature acquired honor may be either gained or lost in the perpetual struggle for public recognition. Since the group is so important for the identity of a Mediterranean person, it is critical to recognize that honor status comes primarily from group recognition. While honor may sometimes be an inner quality, the value of a person in his or her own eyes, depends ultimately on recognition from significant others in society. It is a public matter. When someone's claim to honor is recognized by the group, honor is confirmed, and the result is a new social status. With this status follows the expectation of honorable behavior.[5]

The roots of this system have been traced back to Hellenistic times, and it was certainly used in Roman culture. As Batten has said above, the honor and shame system was in full play in the first century CE. Jesus was most assuredly stripped naked on the cross, as an attempt to manipulate him into a debased place of disempowerment and dishonor. Again, the cross was the most shameful, humiliating way to die in Jesus' lifetime. This is because it was a form of execution reserved for the most vile. But it is not as often explicitly stated that it was shameful precisely because these criminals were literally stripped. Three significant factors need to be addressed in order to understand the shame of Christ's nakedness, relevant both then and now: first, shame is evoked *in us* by a naked Jesus who reminds victims of their own intense vulnerability; second, the interpretation of Jesus' shame is aided by the ancient concept of the "gaze"; third, his observed nakedness then would have involved a subsequent "emasculation" of Jesus.

---

5. Moxnes, "Honor and Shame," 67.

Naked Shame

Most of us feel ashamed ourselves when we think of a naked Jesus. We have covered him up in our imaginations, and unquestionably in our art through the centuries. The thought of Jesus without the traditional loincloth can mortify us at a deep and disturbing level. Perhaps it forces us to truly see his vulnerability, something we most often find distasteful in our gods. But it also connects us to our own nakedness, which is hugely problematic for victims of sexual abuse.

What we don't always recognize is that there is a significant difference between shame as an emotional response to our own wrongdoing and a shame we feel even though we are innocent. The Genesis narrative speaks of the first kind. Adam and Eve sin, and they are suddenly ashamed. God seems to know of their sin by their attempts to hide and cover their nakedness, which they had not noticed before. More modern sensibilities have wanted to move us toward distinguishing between guilt and shame. If we sin, it is appropriate for us to feel conviction, or "godly sorrow" over what we have done. Shame, however, is conviction run amuck. To perhaps oversimplify it, guilt is experienced as "godly sorrow" about what I have done. Shame on the other hand, is experienced as believing and feeling that there is something inherently wrong with who I am. There is strong support for the idea that shame is always destructive. Guilt can bring repentance and forgiveness. Shame leads only to hopeless despair. As theologians, we do not believe that shame is a God-given healthy emotion, even if it comes out of legitimate wrongdoing. But innocent shame is horrific and tragic. It is taking others' guilt onto ourselves. It is being forced to swallow blame for something someone does to us, at no fault of our own.

It is psychological manipulation for an abuser to convince the abused that they are to blame for their abuse. This manipulation often involves stripping the person, figuratively—stripping them of personal freedom, personal dignity, of being able to perceive reality, of other relationships that might intervene. But the manipulation often involves stripping the person, literally. Nakedness takes us to our most vulnerable place. In a loving relationship, it moves us toward intimacy. In sexually abusive relationships it moves us to such severe humiliation that the self can evaporate. It moves victims to see themselves as ugly, grotesque, even ghostly figures, stripped of decency, security, and worth. If victims are young, they have no capacity to reject such inappropriate shame. Leonard Shengold states:

> Sexual abuse, emotional deprivation, physical and mental torture can eventuate in soul murder. Brainwashing keeps the

condition of emotional bondage going. Children are the usual victims, for the child's almost complete physical and emotional dependence on adults easily make possible tyranny and therefore child abuse; because he or she cannot escape from the tyrant-torturer, the child must submit to and identify with the abuser.[6]

Besides the physical damage of sexual abuse, abusers wreak havoc on all levels of personhood. In fact, those who have been sexually abused as children have brains that under- or over-function, and look different on scans. Further, victims are often manipulated to depend on their abuser emotionally, sometimes even for their life's sustenance. They are manipulated to believe they will always be rejected by others as damaged and disgusting. How can they possibly reject what they are told? This is a type of brainwashing that can take years and years to unpack and discard. Healing is very dependent on casting off the thick and persistent shame imposed by perpetrators.

One consequence of being inappropriately shamed and absorbing it is that it will become a lens through which victims view themselves. It deeply affects their self-esteem. Again, besides becoming convinced that they somehow deserved to be hurt, there is also the tendency to believe that they are unworthy of healthy forms of love from others. This can influence victims to continue to put themselves in abusive relationships later on. This then becomes a cycle that reinforces their sense of worthlessness. They can become "shame-based" to the point of interpreting even positive care and concern negatively. Or, absorbing shame can be accompanied by being perpetually on "high alert" in every encounter with others, as a form of grueling self-protection (often unconsciously). Post-traumatic stress disorder is just as real for a survivor of sexual abuse as it for a war veteran. Surely, such abuse has long-lasting consequences. Jesus experienced shaming nakedness.

The Gaze

Jesus would have taken on a shame at that time that we do not fully understand. A naked crucifixion is better understood when we connect it to the meaning of shame in first-century Rome through the ancient concept of the "gaze." Roman culture was concerned, first of all, with demarcating Roman from "un-Roman" space. The land occupied by the Jews had been co-opted by Rome in a sense. But even within this foreign Roman place, there were spaces undignified and thus differentiated as un-Roman. The places of

---

6. Shengold, *Soul Murder*, 2.

executions of criminals, such as Golgotha, had this type of rejection of the ground itself. A Roman soldier would have sensed the shame of the place itself. "Those dying . . . have been exiled into the non-Roman space; their sufferings are those of the uncivilized world."[7]

In addition to the shame of space is added the shame of the gaze. When we think of nakedness today, especially in Western cultures, we only apply shame to the one who is *seen* naked. But in the culture of Jesus' time, the viewer of nakedness is also a subject of shame, perhaps even more so. Since the crucifixion was a public event, it would have been a "spectacle." We use the phrase "she has made a spectacle of herself" to mean a person has embarrassed herself. It is thus embarrassing to us to watch it. A spectacle in its literal meaning in Roman culture had to do with the production of plays, where actors take on a persona. But an actor needs an audience. We also find in the definition of spectacle an understanding of an exhibition. In its place, the arena or theater where the actors are gazed upon is acceptable. Outside this accepted space, a spectacle or exhibition would have brought feelings of outrage at the misplaced spectacle. Again, it would have brought *the viewer* shame as well. In order to counteract these feelings of shame, the viewer would enact an intense "gaze" that represented great anger at the naked person for his or her horrible offense that threatened to dishonor the observers. Interestingly, we often use the word *exhibitionist* to denote a naked person. Thus Jesus dying on a cross naked, as all who were crucified, would have elicited shame and subsequent rage by those who saw him. The insults the crowd poured out upon him were socially fitting.

Gaze theory, as it is known, has been developed by more postmodern thinkers doing critical analysis, such as Michel Foucault, Jean-Paul Sartre, and Jacques Derrida. In their opinion the concept of the gaze illustrates power relations in the sociopolitical order. Foucault was interested in the gaze as a form of subjection, as a mechanism of discipline in the prison system he studied.[8] At its essence, the gaze denotes unequal power differentials. The concept has been used in film theory, the historiography of the colonial period, feminist theory and womanist theory, and psychological constructions, to name a few. Overall, the gaze is about objectifying the person seen and exalting the viewer to a position of more and more power. According to psychoanalytic theory, healthy parents of a child (usually the mother) look at her/him lovingly, and offer a type of mirror that is key to ego development. When this is absent, children develop a distorted view of themselves;

---

7. Gunderson, "Ideology of the Arena," 15, as quoted in Caldwell, "Religion and Sexual Violence," 198.

8. See Foucault, *Discipline and Punish*.

when the gaze is for the purpose of subjection or outright abuse, the child's development can be dysfunctionally arrested.

Especially important here is the theoretical concept of the "male gaze." The male gaze is also known as "scopophilia," which sexualizes the concept of the gaze; literally it means sexual pleasure through looking. The anger and outrage is still there, but the degradation of the object by the viewer becomes sexualized. Anger boomerangs back to the victim for causing sexual feelings. Since over 80 percent of perpetrators of sexual abuse and assault are male, the concept of the male gaze is extremely relevant to our discussion.[9] The *desire* to act out sexually is intricately connected to the *desire* to dominate when children, women, and men are abused, molested, or raped. The effects of such trauma on the brain, and on the whole person, can best be described religiously as being "de-souled."[10] One devastating consequence is that it often damages their sexuality. Their nakedness has covered them in shame; the gaze they have endured has controlled and humiliated them to an unspeakable degree. We now turn to another source of humiliation for the naked Jesus.

The Emasculated Christ

The third aspect of Jesus' shame on the cross is very hidden from us, but also extremely pertinent. In the humiliation associated with crucifixion, in the shame and the anger of the gazer, is its intention to rob the criminal of his maleness. A man's role was crucial in the honor-shame system. To intentionally strip a man was to shame his sexuality to the point of making him into a "dishonorable" female. This objectification and feminization of the male body was widely used during this time. It shows up not only in practice, but also in the rhetoric of the first centuries. When one wanted to discredit his ideological enemy, he would call him "womanly," or question his ability to control his women.[11] This even shows up in the Christian rhetoric between Alexander and Athanasius on one side, and the supporters of Arius on the other, prior to and during the Council of Nicaea.[12] Since there was a certain amount of shame embedded in femaleness, to call an opponent "womanly" was designed to humiliate the man and nullify his truth and honor. A naked Jesus was an emasculated and feminized Jesus. As such,

---

9 Mallett, "Women also Sexually Abuse Children." Mallet records that 20 percent of abusers are women.

10. Shengold, *Soul Murder*, 2.

11. Cameron, "Virginity as Metaphor," 191.

12. See Rusch, *Trinitarian Controversy*.

he was an appropriate bearer of shame. In retrospect, Jesus' teaching and ministry could then have been subject to criticism by his high treatment of women, a particularly strong theme of the Gospel of Luke. To empower a female was to lessen a man's masculinity.

What might this emasculation and feminization of Jesus say to victims of sexual abuse and assault? Again, since the majority of perpetrators are male, victims are open to the sexualized rage of the male gaze; victims, both female and male, can suffer from severe objectification, sexual domination, and physically forced subjection due to their female gender, or often in the case of boys and men, their genderization as female. This is not to overstate the point and forget that women also abuse. Female perpetrators also do grave damage to their victims. They also objectify and dominate their targets on many levels. But the social stigma of femaleness embedded in most cultures even today, especially in honor-shame cultures, needs to be recognized as a potential contributing factor when both genders are victimized and brutalized.

The stripped Jesus lost his male honor in the eyes of those who gazed upon him. He was emasculated in the anger of his male viewers. He was feminized by his humiliation and public shame. He died that way. But fascinatingly, when he arose, the Christian church through the centuries has taken away part of his humanness (as at least most would include sexuality as a key part of what it means to be human). But we have effectively stripped Jesus Christ of any sexuality at all. Do we, then, in any way diminish his humanity?

The Desexualized Jesus

The recorded history of Jesus, from the New Testament onward, is silent about Jesus as a sexual being. But in the wake of that silence, a dangerous interpretation arose that still has adverse effects. The desexualization of Jesus has occurred from many different perspectives. We begin by reviewing the history of asceticism in the early church.

An extremely important event in the history of Christianity was the conversion of Constantine. Prior to Constantine's reign, Christians were persecuted and martyred. While empire-wide persecution was sporadic, it was severe. Local persecution could be just as brutal. We have strong records that support the fact that innumerable named and nameless Christians were tortured and martyred. Martyrdom narratives are numerous enough to have their own genre. There is strong evidence that martyrs took on the highest place of honor and holiness in the eyes of the church. We can even speak of a "cult of martyrdom" with its own theology. But persecutions of Christians eventually ceased in the Roman Empire.

When Constantine was vying for power and a singular hold on the emperorship, he went into battle and supposedly heard a voice that said, "By this sign you will conquer." He looked into the sky and saw a sign that signified, in his interpretation, the Christian Christ. He won the battle. As a result of this experience, Constantine issued the edict of Milan in 313 and "legalized" Christianity. Constantine also promoted Christianity as the preferred Roman religion. Debate is fierce about the genuineness of Constantine's "conversion" because he continued to be very syncretistic and was not baptized until he was on his deathbed. But at the very least, Constantine used this event as a religious shift to his political advantage.

The results of such a turnaround are ambiguous. On the one hand, persecutions ceased, certainly for the betterment of the Christians themselves. On the other hand, masses of persons from the Roman populace were baptized as Christians immediately, without catechism or discipleship. Certainly this "watered down" the faith. The question quickly arose: how are we to know who is truly holy? The martyrs can no longer hold the highest place of holy honor, since martyrdom ceased. Who would take their place? It is no coincidence, it is theorized, that just after Constantine's edict of toleration, a "new martyrdom" developed, particularly in the east.[13]

This "new martyrdom" is the rise of asceticism. If one no longer had the opportunity to be literally crucified (by various means) with Christ, there was at least the option of metaphorical self-crucifixion, or self-mortification. People began to practice rigorous physical disciplines as a means of spiritual purification. Severe fasting, poverty, chastity, and even self-mutilation were commonplace among ascetics. This further developed into the practice of hermitages. Men, and a few women, headed for the Egyptian desert in particular, where they lived primarily in solitude with few interactions with each other. These, from then on, were known as the desert fathers.[14] Eventually these hermits or "eremitic monastics" formed communities that gave rise to what is known as "cenobitic monasticism," which spread throughout the empire. These would be similar to what we know today as monasteries or convents. In any case, the ascetics were identified by other Christians as the new "holy ones" who replaced the martyrs as Christian heroes.

At the very center of this new asceticism, was the call to virginity. Celibacy came to dominate the Christian narrative, beginning in the fourth century. After 325, nearly every post-Nicene father was celibate. Rhetoric

---

13. Not in any reductionistic way.
14. There were also desert mothers.

around virginity was very widespread and very forceful. In an important theological move, virginity becomes the means toward approximating the original creation. John Chrysostom, a father of the fifth century, was a very strong advocate of this position, and represents the Eastern position on virginity and marriage. In sum, "[Chrysostom] posits that virginity is the true human condition, not just the angelic one . . . By adopting virginity, we not only become more godly, we are also recalled to our true human nature."[15] While some have argued that Chrysostom's high evaluation of the potential of virginity lessened through his life,[16] it may be more correct to attribute his change of rhetoric to a change of audience. His early work, *On Virginity*, is addressed to fellow ascetics, while his later homilies were primarily addressed to married persons. In *On Virginity*, his denunciation of marriage was often brutal.

> [The married are] like fugitive slaves who have been bound by their master, first separately, then to one another, each pair fastened at their feet by a short chain: they are unable to walk independently because each must follow the other. Thus, the souls of married couples have both their own private cares and a second constraint arising from the bond between them. It strangles them more fiercely than any chain. It robs them both of freedom.[17]

Another early church father who advocated strongly for virginity was Jerome. While he mentions the renunciation of wealth and property on occasion, it is renunciation of marriage and family that most occupies his rhetoric. There are several situations where Jerome's ascetic theory goes to extremes. Many become evident in demands on ascetic women who followed his teaching. Paula and her daughters were Jerome's "most loyal champions."[18] Jerome is extreme in his advice for them to give up the roles of wives and mothers. God had not created them for marriage and sexual reproduction, for these were a direct result of the fall. Virginity is "the preferred mode of human life."[19]

In these early theories that promote virginity as the highest way to live the Christian life, it then becomes quite necessary to emphasize a celibate Jesus. He is the model of Christian perfection, which begins to become equivalent with his virginity. This is the case in both Eastern and Western

---

15. Clark, "Introduction," in *On Virginity; Against Remarriage*, xiv.
16. See Ford, "Misogynist or Advocate," 77–80.
17. Chrysostom, *On Virginity*, 41.2 (trans. Shore, 62).
18. Wiesen, *St. Jerome as Satirist*, 118
19. Clark, "Theory and Practice," 30.

ascetic understandings. Also, in order to preserve Jesus from any taint of sexuality (and original sin), the virgin birth takes on new significance and emphasis around this same time.

For our purposes here, it is important to remember that throughout the history of the Christianity it has been necessary to eradicate sexuality from Jesus. From the early monastic belief that virginity best approximates true humanity and holiness, to early feminist ideas of the need for an androgynous Jesus (which extends the conversation beyond sexuality to gender), Jesus' sexuality has been almost completely ignored. Except in an occasional nod toward the question of the nature of Jesus' relationship with Mary Magdalene in film and literature, Jesus is most often envisioned as asexual. It is shameful for most people to look at Jesus and think he had sexual temptation, or even a sexual thought (which counters the biblical statement that he was tempted in every way as we are). But in this unreflective place, we have stripped Jesus of a vital part of his humanity. We have thus abused him. And we have damaged ourselves. With Jesus as our model of holiness, we can believe that deep sexual repression is somehow Christian, that feelings of sexual urges are inherently sinful, and that sexual expression should elicit shame, no matter the context.[20] This can cause serious psychological and spiritual wreckage. We only have to look at the extreme negative effects of what has become known as "purity culture" in evangelical circles to see the damage.[21] Our point here is that such a long and pervasive message of an asexual Jesus has been destructive, i.e., abusive, to many. Being a sexual being at all is often deeply shameful in conservative Christianity, let alone having that sexuality wounded by the perversion of another through abuse, perhaps even another Christian. The Christian church must do better at offering healthy "sex education" in general, even before it begins to help those damaged by sexual abuse.

Jesus entered the realm of sexual abuse through his week of trial and most acutely in his crucifixion. It opens him to true empathetic presence to those who have been sexually abused and assaulted, just as he is present to victims of violence, and to those who have been abandoned. It is our strong conviction that such experiential empathy can have a powerful effect in the lives of the victimized. But we also believe that it is not enough to have a God who weeps with us, as poignant and even healing as that may be. It is not even enough to believe that God is presently and actively working against the injustices of the world, as crucial as such an affirmation is.

---

20. Consider Augustine's theory of sexuality particularly. See Leclerc, *Singleness of Heart*, chapter 2.

21. See, for example, Beck, *Unclean*.

And so we intentionally move next to the heart of back-side theology: to an acknowledgement of God's guilt, and our opportunity to forgive "divine neglect."

CHAPTER 8

Forgiving God

A child huddles in the dark
hiding in the back of the closet.
She rocks and cries and pleads.
 "Please God, help me."
Her father is done with her sister and they cry.
Her turn will be next.
And the pleas go on, and the years go on
and the hurt and the shame and the blame goes on.
All hidden in secret.
She rocks and cries and pleads.
 "Please God, help me."
But Father finds her in the dark nevertheless.
Decades pass. The hurt and the shame and blame remain.
She seeks God.
He finds her in the dark. And healing begins.
But one nagging question always stays:
 Does God hear the cries, the pleas, the prayers of a child?
 If he doesn't, how is this God powerful?
 If he does . . .

If he does . . .
If he does, how is this God good?

—*by* "Kerri," a survivor[1]

Kerri needed to ask these questions. They are the questions of theodicy in raw form. In working with Kerri, one author of this book came to understand that a key to resolving the inner turmoil of victims is the need to forgive. The problem is that it is very, very seldom that perpetrators confess and seek forgiveness from those they have wronged. In chapter 3, we suggested that in a type of transfiguring of the substitutionary atonement, Jesus, who became sin for us, can step in for the perpetrators and offer a substitutionary apology, thus opening the door to some level of forgiveness of the other, *not for the sake of the other*, but for the sake of the abused. And yet, we need to say more.

We here present the outrageous idea of forgiving God. Some might dismiss this idea as heresy. "You can't make God culpable!" But Kerri was helped, first of all, by being given permission to protest and lament. Her Christian father had sexually abused each one of her two older sisters when they reached adolescence. She knew what would happen to her. Do we believe that God heard her desperate cries and pleas to escape what her sisters couldn't? If we believe God did hear—could have intervened and did nothing—is it that heretical to believe God might allow Godself to be forgiven? In fact the very premise of lament calls out God's failure to prevent evil from occurring. Kerri was moved further along in her healing by not only being allowed to protest, but by being able to see the cross of the crucified God as a means not only of an empathetic identification with her pain, but also as an opportunity to forgive God for allowing her suffering. And so we begin with a crucial discussion about God's guilt.

God's Guilt

Humans have a natural proclivity to want to blame someone for pain and suffering. That is why the ancient system of retribution was deeply satisfying.

---

1. Written by a parishioner in a church pastored by Diane Leclerc; modifications by Leclerc. Used with permission.

We have talked about Job previously in this book, but it is necessary to return to him. The retributive system was the paradigm of Job's friends: pain and suffering are a direct result of persons' transgressions. This is why the figure and book of Job are so disconcerting—Job's innocence overturns the commonly held beliefs of punitive justice. The readers (hearers) of the book would not have been surprised at Job's friends' suggestion that he was suffering such calamity precisely because he had sinned and would not repent to his punishing God. Marius Timmann Mjaaland states,

> As long as they remain quiet, these old friends share a moment of unity. And when Job finally cries out, a cry of torture and despair, it could be the expression of common lament (Job 3:1–26). Yet the friends are disturbed by his words. Job accuses God of being unjust because he has caused or allowed such immense suffering, completely beyond the proportions of an economy of retribution. The friends are provoked by Job's lament. They are not prepared to accept such accusations, and so protect themselves from the disturbing thought that the guilt must be laid upon God rather than on Job. According to the principle of retribution common in the Near East, Job's suffering must have been a result of sin . . . The economy of retribution was fundamental to the entire cosmos, and if one doubted this order of being, then one called into question the bases of faith, hope, justice, and moral responsibility.[2]

But this is exactly what Job does. "It is not only [the friends'] arguments that provoke Job but also their mistrust and hostility toward their friend. They prefer to defend God against Job's accusations and, in doing so, defend themselves against the challenging tone of Job's cry."[3]

It is no wonder that much later Jesus is asked to explain what would have been quite the conundrum for those who had not been convinced by the innocence of Job to the point of overthrowing the principle of retribution. He is asked, "Who has sinned, that this man was born blind?" The innocence of a child certainly precludes blindness as a direct punishment for that child's sin. But it would seem unjust and unfair for the child to suffer the consequences of the sin of his parents (although this was also a common belief). No wonder they ask Jesus for some logical help. Jesus, of course, avoids the logical conclusions they want to push. They, like we, need someone to blame.

---

2. Mjaaland, "Fractured Unity," 101–2.
3. Mjaaland, "Fractured Unity," 102.

We do not like innocent suffering. It jars us most profoundly. For example, severely sick children disturb us deeply, and proclamations rise within us that it should not be like this.[4] The killing of innocent children is unfathomable to us; even if we have a perpetrator to blame, it does not satisfy us completely, and we search for underlying reasons why such atrocities occur.[5] This is why those who suffer, those who are "disfigured," those who disrupt the "norm" are sometimes repulsive to us. They confront us with the reality we do not want to face, because, like Job's friends, we attempt to reach circumstantial security by being pure ourselves—if we do the good we will get the good. We want the easy answer—to explain all forms of suffering as direct punishment for obvious sins. Our tendency to "blame the victim" is representative of the vestiges of this ancient system we are reluctant to release. We need someone to blame.

Traditional Christianity has looked to ancient Scripture in the search for someone to blame. Innocent suffering finds its source in the "fallenness" of the world, thus our first parents started it all. It was their sin that not only corrupted humanity and allowed for us to sin against each other; it was their "fall" that brought sickness, death, and unexplained agony into the world, according to traditional Christian theology. At their hands even creation fell, and now groans for redemption (Rom 8:22). And yet, behind the sin of Adam and Eve, we must recognize that in the choice to create the way God created, God created the *possibility* of sin and suffering; this is the "shadow side of the God who created," according to Karl Barth.[6] Typical theodicies have not shied away from this original reality. They try to answer it. Some take away God's culpability by removing choice from God's creative nature: God could not have chosen not to create, so to speak, in the way that God created. Some dismantle God's omniscience as a means of justifying God's decision—God did not know what would transpire in the future, and thus cannot be held accountable. What is known as the freewill defense attempts to explain, indeed justify, why God would create in the first place in light of the ineffable culmination of human sin and suffering that would

---

4. For an interesting theological reflection on this see Hauerwas, *Naming the Silences*.

5. This section of the chapter was originally written just days after the school shooting in Connecticut that killed twenty children (six to seven years old) and six adults. While the shooter who killed himself was obviously guilty, social media was consumed with comments about gun control and the needs for better mental health care in the United States.

6. Barth's concept of nothingness is also relevant here. See Karl Barth, *Church Dogmatics III/3*, 1–78.

contaminate all of human history. This option is challenged by a series of theodical statements, if taken to their logical end:

1. God created humanity as good, yet with the free will to choose the not-good.
2. If not by foreknowledge, then at least by God-filled wisdom, God knows/predicts that the effects of the choice against the good plays out in a devastating and lasting fallenness of the world.
3. The consequences of such fallenness include wars, holocausts, famine, oppression, slavery, abuse, and the like; it will also introduce disease and the resulting physical suffering into the world.
4. God chooses, despite the consequences, to create free will as integral to humanness.
5. Therefore, God bears some responsibility for the consequences of the fall.

Granted, there is much speculative theology in the above affirmations. Clearly various theologians have chosen to address the "problem of evil" in a variety of ways. "Solutions" are widely varied, often based not only on a theology of God, but also on an underpinning of philosophical assertions.

Most Christians, however, follow a rather traditional line of thinking that would include affirmations 1 to 4 above, but would not allow point 5 to follow. God's innocence must be strongly maintained. We might suppose that there is some comfort for our suffering in understanding its theological origins through the Genesis texts that places the blame on the first humans. Existentially, there is little, because whatever ways there are to explain God's actions "in the beginning," we must admit that even in this "best of all possible worlds" there is still an unexplainable anguish in the human story that seems quite unjustifiable. And God bears some responsibility for *continuing* to allow the consequences of the fall to impact individuals and groups who suffer "innocently" when God can stop them.

This leads us to the conclusion of God's guilt—in creating a world where suffering seems to follow, perhaps not necessarily, but at least inevitably,[7] and by a level of present and persisting inaction that leads us to conclude that God fails us. Most resist this conclusion with as much force as they can muster. But logically, we must either strip God of omnipotence in order to explain away this continuing culpability of God, or allow for a sadistic view of God who is justified in atrocities through a severe theology of sovereignty that has no problem making God the author of evil.

---

7. See Niebuhr, *Nature and Destiny of Man*, 251–60.

We must acknowledge that the sinned-against must be able to speak the fifth affirmation above out loud, and to add that God bears some responsibility for allowing abject evil to continue. In other words, in light of the magnitude of human suffering throughout human history, or in light of the suffering of even one person sinned-against, *protest* theology must remain a viable option, and protest theology is only possible when we open the door to challenge God's innocence. For some who have been sinned-against it is the *only* option that stands up to the absurdity of their suffering.

The existential need to lament—to hold God responsible—cannot be overcome through rational theodicies that get God off the hook. We need someone to blame, and often that need takes the form of crying out to God. Lament is holding God accountable, and despite our sensibilities that this is somehow wrong, the biblical witness never condemns this form of lament. If there is a perpetrator who has been violent or abusive, the question still remains, why does God allow such atrocity and cruelty to happen?[8] Why has God abandoned persons in their tragic experiences, so far ranging from holocausts to individual children crying out to God for protection and not receiving it? And in those cases of suffering where there is no perpetrator except fate, we must still ask, where is God? It is a question at the heart of all who suffer at the hands of another or suffer trouble or sickness from the fallenness of the world.

Particularly if there is no direct offender responsible for suffering, blaming Adam and Eve is not enough of an explanation. Lamenting to a God who created even the possibility of a "fallenness" that opens the door to human anguish seems wholly appropriate, and perhaps poignantly helpful. Lamenting to a God who continues to choose not to intervene against evil is just as fitting. There is the stark truth of injustice in these situations that are clearly not retributive or punitive in nature.

In this sense, we introduce here an idea that unsettles us to our core: there are victims of God—victims of God's original choice, and victims of God's abandonment and God's silence in its wake. And these victims need someone to blame. More importantly, they need someone to forgive. What we know of God's nature matters here, especially as it is revealed in Jesus Christ. The fundamental question is, is there a place infinite enough in the loving heart of God where there is a willingness to not only forgive, but to be forgiven?

---

8. Of course, one form of theodicy is to deny that God has the power to do so.

The Humility of God

Theology literally means "words about God" or the study of God. Christian theology interprets words and ideas about God through the lens of the full revelation of Jesus the Christ. Christian theology is, of course, based on Hebraic images of God, but also breaks through with new vision, and thus novel theology. Christian theology asserts that the old revelation must be interpreted in light of the new. But as soon as we invoke the idea of Christian theology, we are confronted with the reality that there is no singular interpretation of the Christ event, let alone the variation we can find in all the systematic categories beyond Christology. By some estimations, there are over 40,000 different denominations in the world, all with great or slight differences from each other. We might invoke the important creeds of the church as the essential message of the faith. Even if we could say that all denominations are centrally creedal (which we cannot), the creeds themselves leave a vast amount of theologizing left to be done. As we have tried to show, atonement theology itself represents a wide variety of positions about the meaning of the cross in the salvation of humanity. Moreover, each atonement theory is founded on different ideas about God. And so, we are confronted with the question, does back-side theology have an underlying set of beliefs about the nature of God? In one sense, no, if we want the affirmations of this book to cross denominational lines. But in another sense, yes. There are doctrines of God that can be identified as cross-purposed from this entire project. The purpose of this chapter is to propose extremely important premises about the nature of God that are necessary in order to be faithful to the sinned-against. We began with the difficult, but necessary affirmation of God's guilt. We then move to a particular aspect of God's love.

God's essential nature will always remain a mystery to some degree. As Luther described, there is an aspect of God which is described by the words, *theologia gloria* (or *Deus absonditus*). There are aspects of God that are always hidden from humanity's view. Yet, everything necessary for life and salvation has been fully revealed to us in Jesus Christ: God is also *theologia crucis*, or *Deus revelatus*. Jesus Christ (especially on the cross, for Luther) reveals the essential characteristics of what we need to know about the nature of God. While there are multiple aspects of God's nature that Jesus reveals, central to *back-side* theology is the strong belief that God is *essentially* love (1 John 4:8; *essentially* means a divine quality *necessarily* in God's nature).[9]

---

9. This could bring into play the debate over whether God is any particular characteristic by *nature* or by *choice*. (Sometimes labeled as the natural and moral attributes of God.) This was debated by scholastic theology in the medieval period under the topic of volitionalism. Pushing the argument perhaps too far is to ask the question whether

Further, love should be seen as the *primary* way of understanding God. And thus, love becomes back-side theology's primary hermeneutic for interpreting God, and for interpreting every aspect of systematic theology, including soteriology and atonement theory.

In addition to affirming a God whose essential characteristic is love, it is also important to affirm here that this God is also *essentially humble*, as revealed in the humanity of Jesus Christ. To take on flesh is an act of humility in and of itself, since the Latin for *humble* means low. God came to a lowly state in a lowly manner. But further, we affirm that God did not just act humbly; God is humble by nature. What we hope to show is that this characteristic is essential to our understanding of the nature of God, and essential to God's "posture" before us, especially before the sinned-against. Again, we know who God is because we have seen Jesus.

The Incarnation

God became human in the person of Jesus Christ. Ever since Nicaea, Christianity has declared the paradox that Jesus is fully God and fully human. The incarnation is salvific in and of itself.[10] We see a God who is, to a certain extent, divested of unlimited power through the volitional choice of embodying the Son. There is indeed a scandal of particularity here. The proclamation that God became human and entered concrete existence should shock us in its radical reshaping of what humans have perceived and believed about God, and, actually, about humanity (because Jesus reveals to us what humanity without sin is created to be; Jesus reveals the full potential of redeemed persons). We now proclaim that God is fully and finally revealed in a person. If we want to know what God is like, we look at Jesus, particularly how he lived.

Luther portrayed the incarnation as God's great *condescension* to humanity, which is certainly important. But what we find problematic in condescension language is that it can imply a change in God's *modus operandi*, as if the Wholly Other suddenly decides to become immanent through the incarnation, or as if this God puts on flesh to *disguise* God's essential sovereignty and almightiness. We would like to propose that the humility seen in God's condescension is revelatory of God's very nature.

God can choose *not* to love. If God can so choose, then God is not essentially love. But to make this move seems to limit God's freedom, logically. We would want to affirm that God is *not* limited in choice by what God essentially is.

10. This is especially true in the theology of John Wesley. See chapter 3's section on recapitulation.

The question could be stated this way: when Paul proclaims Jesus, who being in very nature God humbled himself (see Phil 2), is he saying that Jesus was being incongruous with God's nature or expressing God's nature? We think it crucial to understand Jesus and his life of sacrifice as congruent with God's nature. This then implies that humility has *always* been at the heart of God's essential characteristics; the humility expressed in the incarnation is not out of character for God, but fully expressive of it. Important for the sinned-against is that Jesus reveals God as potently with us, and as one who has always been with us. God is infinitely near, not exclusively distant as a Wholly Other beyond our comprehension, and unable to "sympathize with our weaknesses." In the incarnation of Jesus, God has experienced life as we experience it. This is not to collapse the Trinity into Christ only. But as Christ's humanity pierces into God through *perichoresis*, God can be known as innately immanent to us.

Jesus' Baptism

During Jesus' day, baptism was a liturgical method by which non-Jewish persons, or "God-fearers," became Jewish by choice. What makes John the Baptist's message so radical, and so offensive, is that he was calling Jews to be baptized. This was not without historical precedent, of course, for "washing" in the Old Testament was ritually common. In Leviticus, God instructs the people to cleanse themselves from impurities, contracted through being exposed to a leper or touching a corpse, for example. Closer to the time of John the Baptist's ministry, washing fulfilled the legal requirements of ritual purity to sacrifice at the temple. Nevertheless, these types of impurities did not imply a need for the repentance that John called for, for they were unintentional "sins." They were part of living in a "dirty" world. Thus, John's call associated baptismal washing with true repentance, which offended the Sadducees and Pharisees especially.

Jesus intentionally traveled to the Jordan where John the Baptist was preaching repentance. According to Matthew, John is immediately struck with the absurdity of Jesus' request (Matt 3:13–14). John had proclaimed Jesus as the Messiah, and as the one who would baptize them with the Holy Spirit and with fire, implying a deeper, more cleansing baptism than he himself could offer (Matt 3:11–12). The Gospel of John tells us that John the Baptist saw Jesus as the perfect Lamb of God, who would take away the sin of the world (John 1:29), not as a sinner in need of repentance. And so, he was stunned that this savior would submit himself to baptism.

What do we make of Jesus' request? We could understand that Jesus uses this act of initiation when Gentiles become Jewish, as symbolic of his initiation into his official ministry. We could see Jesus as washing himself of the impurities that surrounded him, as anyone living in the world. However, if we focus on John's shock and reluctance, we can see Jesus' request as a profound act of humility, in his association with sinfulness—he would have appeared sinful to all who saw his baptism through John's hands. This is a foreshadowing of what is to come of Jesus. In his submission to baptism, we see a heart willing to submit to a cross—the symbol of sin and shame.

This submissive humility offers particular help for the sinned-against. Traditionally when we say that Christ became sin *for us*, we are referring to the mechanism by which he has the ability to forgive sinners. But because he took on sin innocently, that absorption of sin into himself makes him empathetic to those who too are forced to absorb sins, which are not their own, into their innocence. "God made him who had no sin to be sin for us" (2 Cor 5:21). Overall, we see God in Christ willing and humble enough to absorb even sin itself, into himself, as acting in character, not out of the character of God. God's characteristic self-giving love expresses itself in the humility of Jesus at his baptism.

Jesus' Temptation

It is beyond our scope to examine Jesus' temptations at length. What is important for our purposes is what they reveal to us about Jesus' (thus God's) nature. In the days prior to Nicaea[11] one attempt to understand the nature of Jesus was expressed as Monophysitism—the belief that Jesus Christ had only one nature and that it was divine. By implication, he had a human body, but not a human nature; he had only a divine nature,[12] and so in his essential being Jesus Christ was not fully human. The problem with Monophysitism should become clear: if this is true, Jesus' temptations in the desert and in Gethsemane were not real, for his divine nature could not have said yes to them. It would therefore be impossible for him to sin. Monophysitism effectively denies that he "was tempted in every way as we are" (Heb 4:15). But Jesus was fully human and experienced the full force of the temptations.

So what were the desert temptations about? Jesus was tempted by Satan precisely to reveal and act on his divinity only—to favor his divine nature over his humanity, by utilizing his divine power to meet his human needs. Satan repeatedly badgers him. If you are the Son of God, prove it.

---

11. And after in the form of Coptic Christianity.
12. Or will, as expressed in Monothelitism.

Instead, he chooses not to act as a God could act, but limits himself by choosing obedience and submission to God over self-exaltation, and even self-preservation. Even though he was "in very nature God," Jesus did not grasp after that equality by proving himself in the desert as God. Rather, he entered into the experiences of those who cannot grasp even a dignified humanity of their own, because they have been stripped of it. It is Jesus' willing and humble obedience in the desert that leads to "obedience to death, even death on a cross" (Phil 2:8), and reveals a God humble enough to be crucified.

The Cross

On the night that Jesus was betrayed, he took a towel and basin and washed his disciples' feet. The writer of the Gospel interjects that in doing so, he showed them "the full extent of his love" (John 13:1). We know that Jesus took the position of a slave in this act. Often this description is used to highlight the servanthood of Jesus. And as Peter's question to Jesus suggests (John 13:6), this act of humility is supposedly not appropriate for a Messiah. Nevertheless, it is this act of humility that bridges foot washing to the submission at Gethsemane, to the trial, to the cross. Jesus could have lorded it over his disciples, said no in the garden, pleaded his case at trial, fought back at his scourging, and rejected the cross. But Jesus dies. Jesus the fully divine and fully human one dies a real human death.

We have rejected theories that say only Jesus' human body dies, just as we have rejected theories that Jesus only appeared to have a human body (Docetism). This is not simply about Jesus Christ dying with the two other persons of the Trinity simply "sad" about it. Moltmann affirms "the Father who abandons [the Son] and delivers him up suffers the death of the Son in the infinite grief of love."[13] This is not simply about God dying, but about death being taken up into God, as said in chapter 6. "The Son suffers dying, the Father suffers the death of the Son, the grief of the Father here is just as important as the death of the Son."[14] It is in this way we affirm that the event of Golgotha was a triune event of loving humility for the sake of creation. In the incarnation, climaxed in the passion narrative, the will of the First Person of the Trinity and the will of the Son by the power of the Spirit are united. "This deep community of will between Jesus and his God and Father is now expressed precisely at the point of their deepest separations, in the godforsakenness and accursed death of Jesus on the cross . . . In the cross,

---

13. Moltmann, *Crucified God,* 243.
14. Moltmann, *Crucified God,* 243.

Father and Son are most deeply separated in forsakenness and at the same time most inwardly one in their surrender."[15] There is great significance in the fact that Jesus the Human One, with deep and pervasive humility, underwent the totality of the human experience through to its end. This was the truest expression of the extent of his love, that Jesus emptied himself, laid down his life for his friends, and was entombed. Moreover, it must not be forgotten that he died on a cross—the most graphic and elucidatory symbol of guilt and shame in that culture. He died the most humiliating death imaginable.

He was willing to die *for our sake*, not just for sinners, but also for the sinned-against. In his humiliation, he died for the humiliated. He allowed himself to be beaten, to empathize with the beaten. He submitted himself to excruciating pain, rejected any analgesic, to empathize with those in pain. He allowed himself to be victimized to empathize with victims of all sorts. Many victims of violence and abuse are lingering between life and death—literally perhaps; surely psychically, emotionally, spiritually. For many, their most existential question is "For God's sake, where is God?" To be clear: the cross is the means of salvation for the sinner. But it is also the most important revelation of the empathetic capacity of a God who stands in solidarity with those who suffer and die at the hands of others.

But we must go further. We have an empathetic God, but we also have a guilty God to deal with. How does the affirmation of an all-loving and essentially humble God help us? First of all, we affirm that out of love, God allows Godself to be *vulnerable* to our indictment. And so we acknowledge in God a capacity *to receive* protest and lament and a God capable of receiving every expression of "this should not be!" This is a God willing to be accursed and accused by us.

But we would also like to stress that back-side theology moves beyond protest theology by being open to the reality that the godforsaken can find new levels of healing by forgiving God. It is a theology open to the idea that there are victims of God. It is a theology open to the reality that victims of all kinds can confront, but also *forgive* God. If God was a God interested in saving face, or maintaining God's own innocence at all cost, or preserving God's own reputation, we might have a cross, but only the kind of cross that appeases God's wrath. But we affirm that God, who is essentially loving and humble, is willing to save and "*be saved,*" to reconcile and *be reconciled,* by creating space for our therapeutic need to forgive God.

In Romans 9, Paul says something remarkable: "I speak the truth in Christ—I am not lying, my conscience confirms it through the Holy

---

15. Moltmann, *Crucified God,* 243–44.

Spirit—I have great sorrow and unceasing anguish in my heart. For I could wish that I myself were cursed and cut off from Christ for the sake of my people" (Rom 9:1–3). The biblical idea that love is laying down one's life for one's friends is familiar to us. But Paul is saying more. He is saying that he is willing not only to give up his life, he is willing to be cursed and cut off from the source of his eternal salvation. Remarkable. If a human is capable of such love, how much more is the God of love capable and willing to be cursed? To extend this we might ask: is there a place where God experiences God's own abandonment, a place where God takes God's guilt into Godself, a place where God can even indict God's own self? Is there a place where sin is atoned for, *even the sins of God?* We recognize the "heresy" of what we say here. Perhaps it is helpful to mitigate the implications of a sinning God, by asserting again that we are emphasizing that God fails to stop the innocent from experiencing evil, rather than God causing the evil to occur. But even in this allowance of evil, God participates in the breaking of relationship by permitting persons to experience godforsakenness like Jesus.

Our back-side atonement theory, then, is offered in faith that God will allow us to forgive God explicitly through the kenotic act of the crucified one. Most simply put, the cross represents Jesus the Christ's deep solidarity with the victim as he allows himself to be victimized; *but* it is also the place where God repents of God's inaction in the lives of those who suffer.[16] It opens up to us the opportunity for us not only to cry out in blaming lament, but also to truly forgive God (which may take time). We are reconciled to God, and God is reconciled to us. In this way our sense of abandonment can turn from despair to hope. Jesus hangs with us on the hook of innocent blame; there we experience an intimate presence. But also, in Jesus' bearing of guilt, the First Person hangs on the hook as well; God takes blame and shame upon God's own self. God gave up Jesus unto death as a kind of apology to those who suffer. Jesus did not die in order to appease the wrath of an angry God; he died in order to appease, or conciliate, or soothe *us* in our suffering, by becoming the God of the abandoned and godforsaken, and by becoming a God with blood on God's hands. In a very real sense, our God is restored to *us* as we forgive divine neglect. Jesus is God's sacrifice to *us*, not in a juridical way, but certainly in a relational sense. Jesus is our mediator in our protest against God, and our means of forgiving God. In this sense, Jesus is the high priest in the order of Melchizedek, our healer precisely when he hangs on the cross. God dies. Dare we say, God dies with

---

16. God's repentance has biblical precedence. Consider, for example, God's repentance for destroying humanity in the flood.

godly sorrow, and repents for the unrepentable, for creating this "best of all possible worlds" where horror can still exist?

It is crucial that we state that God remains the guilty one, perpetually. In other words, forgiving God is not a theodicy to get God off the hook. The concept of the crucified God in the way we are using it is *not* intended to say—and this is key—that our abuse and abandonment must be covered over, taken less seriously, or forgotten. Also, it is *not* as if our forgiving God brings God into the clear. But this is not God's concern. We are. Our forgiving God opens *us* up to new freedom, new healing, new birth. It is with deep and empathetic compassion that we here suggest that such forgiveness breaks open the possibility of hope for a new future, found precisely in the resurrection of Jesus Christ. To that resurrection we now turn.

CHAPTER 9

Resurrection for the Sinned-Against

The week had been more horrific than her worst nightmare. Her Lord, her Master, her friend—the person she trusted more than anyone on earth, the man who had changed her life and set her free, the one who had spoken of a kingdom that would never end, was dead. She watched him die. The disciples fled in fear for their lives. But she had no life apart from the life he had given to her, and so she stood at the foot of a cross and gazed up at the torture he suffered. Her Lord, her life, dying before her very eyes. If only it had been just a nightmare. In the sleepless hours of that black Sabbath she remembered back to her life before she met him. It was a life filled with deep emptiness; some called her demon-possessed. Her life had no direction, no purpose. She found nothing to satisfy her soul. Why live a moral life and try to follow Jewish customs when they were so far above her and did nothing to fill the emptiness? But despite her attempts to numb her life in any way she could, her despair only grew, and she despised who she had become. But she convinced herself that she deserved no better life. She was enslaved by her own choices, and by a stigma cast on her by those who watched. She had lost her very self. And they called her demon-possessed.

She had no real life of her own. Until she met Jesus. The demons fled. Her openness to evil was swallowed up by his goodness. Her life had been radically different ever since. He replaced her shame with dignity. Her loneliness with love. Her aimlessness with purpose. He offered words of truth beyond her highest hopes. He gave her life. But something had gone terribly wrong. He was crucified and she watched him die. With him all her hopes died too. What in the world would she do now? Was he, after all, another false prophet? Was any of it true? Were his words of forgiveness also dead? But whatever had gone wrong, she could not deny that she loved him, deeply.

And so early in the morning she went to the garden, to his tomb. To mourn, to weep, to anoint his body as one last act of love and devotion. But when she got there, her broken heart shattered. Someone had taken his body. Couldn't they just leave him alone? Why would they take him? Why? They had stolen his life from him. Did they have to steal his dead body as well? She ran and told the disciples. "They have taken the Lord out of the tomb, and we don't know where they have put him." They ran to the tomb with her. Examined the evidence and then went back to their homes, scratching their heads. She stayed. Bewildered. Confused. And broken. She stayed. Where else would she go? Where else could she go? He had given her everything. They had taken everything away from her. She looked into the tomb again. And there she saw two angels. Her grief must have blinded her to their identity. They asked her a simple question. "Why are you crying?" How could she explain the reason behind her tears? "Why are you crying?" How could she express all the pain of this unforgettable week? "Why are you crying?" She couldn't tell them all that was in her heart, and so her immediate concern comes from her lips: "They have taken my Lord away, and I don't know where they have put him."

A third person enters the scene. And he asks her the same question. "Why are you crying?" She doesn't answer him, because there seems to be a moment of hope that she can rectify this desperate situation. Perhaps this gardener knows, so she asks "Sir, if you have carried him away, tell me where you have put him, and I will get him."

He responded gently: "Mary." And with that one word, her life was given back to her. With that one word the heartache was lifted. With that one word, her life was secure again. He's risen. He's alive. She's risen. She's alive again.[1]

The cross is most certainly an act of divine love, where God in Christ most fully enters into the pain and suffering of human persons. The First Person allowed the Son, and the Son allowed himself to be killed by those who sinfully pursued his death. At the very heart of the Christian message is a self-emptying God, who has experienced all of human life with us, and has the capacity not just to sympathize with our pain, but to empathize fully with our brokenness. Indeed, God died. In the last chapter, we boldly but humbly suggest that victims of violence, abuse, and abandonment have the opportunity to forgive God for the hell on earth that even now seems to win the day, as God waits for God knows what; and to forgive God for allowing the circumstances that harmed us as we believe God had the power to do so. We affirmed that the heart of God will go that far to love us, to receive our lament, and anger, and grief, and to allow us to beat God's chest in pain. God receives it all, as well as our need to forgive even the guilt of God. And yet, there is even more to say.

There is more to say than God has great capacity for empathy, as important as that is. There is more to say than God experienced victimization at the hands of others, as true as that is. And there is even more to say than God makes Godself vulnerable to our accusations and to our forgiveness. Something else happened to Jesus that potentially takes the *eternal* anguish out of suffering, and the *lasting* sting out of death. The resurrection of Jesus offers power and hope for those on the back side. The resurrection of Jesus is

---

1. Based on Mark 5:21–34.

God's declaration that unjust evil, violence, abandonment, and abuse do not get the final eternal word. Just as persons have a Christ who has died with them, they too can be raised in hope and power to live a new life, beyond the disempowerment they have endured. This indeed is central to back-side theology.

In a sense, it would be easier to end with Christ's suffering and a dead God who remains so in perpetuity. It would be easier, because it would explain why suffering continues today: death must not have been conquered. It would be easier to thus make God impotent, and therefore innocent of the reality of the atrocities that have occurred, and that continue to occur, by keeping God in a grave. It might even make our own sympathies for sufferers more necessary and more compelling, because we only have each other. The final death of God might more easily get us somewhere, as Nietzsche has implied.[2] But although it might be easier, it would not be Christian. It is the resurrection that calls from beyond the metaphorical graves of living victims and offers Christian hope.

It should be evident that this book has been influenced by the theology of Jürgen Moltmann. He wrote *The Crucified God* in part as a response to those who read his book *A Theology of Hope*. Moltmann saw that the powerful read his *Hope* as a justification for them to remain powerful, failing to see how this Christian hope calls, woos, invites, and even implores those who fully embrace it to be compassionately present to the oppressed and marginalized. *The Crucified God* is intended to stand as a grand critique of those who remain abusive, or wholly apathetic to the suffering of others. But Moltmann himself would certainly say that he wrote them in the wrong theological order. By that we mean that a full recognition of the consequences of evil is necessary if we are to fully comprehend the significance of the resurrection.

Hopefully this has been shown by our book's resistance to move too quickly from the cross to the empty tomb. It is too tempting to go from Palm Sunday to Easter Sunday, and cut out Good Friday altogether. And we certainly do not want to imply that saying "resurrection" with a snap of the fingers makes all things immediately better for the sufferer. Christian hope is very different from Pollyannaish optimism, or a proclamation that "you should get over it because of what is coming." One can never hurry the process toward healing. We need to be careful with our words here. We

---

2. See Nietzsche, *Gay Science*, 181–82. Nietzsche proposed that the world no longer needs God as an explanation for anything. We have outgrown our need for God. This is picked up and modified by theologians of the "death of God" movement in the latter part of the twentieth century.

affirm that suffering and hope can coexist. Cross and resurrection are not opposed to each other.

The cross and the resurrection are inextricably linked, as are faith and hope. Moltmann clarifies.

> Cross and resurrection mutually interpret one another; only if we return to the former can we properly comprehend the significance of the latter. Just as a person of faith sees beyond the cross to the resurrection promise of reconciliation, so a person of hope must see beyond or "back to" the presence of God in the cross... Only in the light of his resurrection from the dead does his death gain that special, unique saving significance which it cannot achieve otherwise, even in the light of the life [Jesus] lived.[3]

If the cross is emphasized over the resurrection, or if the resurrection is emphasized over the cross, the perfect paradoxical contradiction is nullified, and each loses its truest significance. It is not as if the cross shows God's empathy and the resurrection shows God's power. Both reveal the full nature of God's love. The resurrection shows that this God of love is *able to raise the dead*, especially those who have figuratively and literally died at the hands of others. Holding the cross and resurrection in dialectical tension best reveals the nature of God, especially for the sinned-against. Alan Lewis writes powerfully on this point:

> Would there be a Christian gospel were it not true that God is self-unveiled only *sub contrario*, that is, in the very opposite of Godness, hidden amid the outcasts of the earth who, very often in the name of God and of the church, are rejected and despised, and who, by the standards of the world, count for nothing, except to live and die that the powerful might become more powerful still? The triumph of God over the grave of Jesus would truly be—as has all too often been assumed—permission for followers of Jesus to flaunt their plumage of superiority in the face of others, were it not that God in humility ineffable has triumphed through the grave, for its many dis-graced, defeated victims and in the form of one of them. That form, seen first in a cradle, later on a cross, and finally as a corpse, is the shape of the resurrection, and there is no other.[4]

We want to honor the sufferer, and not say what we say without the deepest respect of the difficulty of the journey toward healing. Nor do we

3. Moltmann, *Crucified God*, 182.
4. Lewis, *Between Cross and Resurrection*, 90–91.

want to take the heartache, put it in a box, then wrap it pretty, and tie a bow around it. Yet Christian hope has as its foundation the message that *God is able*. God is able to save and redeem, because God has died and been resurrected. It is the resurrection that can take victims and make them survivors, to use recovery language. Open wounds can be made redeemed scars. Dis-ease can be healed. Brokenness can be mended. All because we live in a world where God is the God of the cross and the resurrection. The resurrection of Christ then, and the full resurrection and restoration that we hope for in the eschaton,[5] break into life in the here and now. There is new life, now, even if we see it in our existential situation only dimly, or only as sheer hope. But to be Christian, in faith we must proclaim that our suffering is not all there is. The potential of resurrection life is real, and it not only touches our bodies, it touches us holistically. Every part of our being can experience resurrection life and strength.

For those on the back side of the cross this is the hope of the gospel. There is hope beyond victimization, and the woundedness that it causes. There is real hope of genuine healing. And in this, the saving message of the cross becomes just as powerful for the sinned-against as it is for the sinner. New birth is offered to all. The resurrection does not undo the death of Jesus, just as it does not undo spiritual, psychological, and emotional "deaths" of the sinned-against. But the resurrection does offer new life and redemption as the declarative Word over sin, pain, violence, and abuse.

As such, the power of the resurrection also speaks declarative words of liberation to those who are oppressed and marginalized by acts and systems of injustice. In this sense, the resurrection speaks beyond just personal salvation. There is a cosmic declaration of the end of death *and* injustice; the resurrection is an invitation to recover from the lingering visages of abuse, but also an invitation to participate in the further inbreaking of the kingdom of God, in the hope of ending injustice itself. In the hope of the resurrection, the church is called to participate in the now and coming kingdom of God by embracing love and refusing to cooperate in the mechanisms that perpetuate acts of violence and abuse. The following sections, then, will probe both personal "salvation" for the sinned-against, and the cosmic liberation offered through a resurrected Christ.

---

5. Moltmann writes, "The proclamation of the Easter witnesses that God has 'raised' this dead Jesus 'from the dead' amounts to nothing less than the claim that this future of the new world of the righteousness and presence of God has already dawned in this one person in the midst of our history of death. All who hear and believe this, move from a distant expectation of an uncertain future to a sure hope in a near future of God which has already dawned in that one person." *Crucified God*, 171.

The Resurrection Verifies and Illuminates[6]

The resurrection of Jesus is not what made Jesus divine, but it confirmed that indeed God was *in Christ* reconciling the world to God.[7] The resurrection confirmed that Jesus was the Messiah, the Savior of the world. Not only so, it confirmed that God was ultimately faithful to Christ, and trustworthy in the end. The resurrection, then, becomes the foundation by which we can say resolutely that Jesus Christ fully revealed the reality and nature of the triune God, by laying down his life on the cross. As the Apostle Paul states in 1 Corinthians 15, if Christ was not raised then there would be cause for great doubt about whether Jesus was God and spoke the truth about God. Anyone can make bold claims and be martyred, but only the One who is born of God and is raised by the Spirit of God is truly the Christ. Moltmann notes that Jesus' death challenged Jesus' teaching and divinity. "The true critique of Jesus' preaching is the outcome of his life and his end upon the cross."[8] If he had not been raised, we could count him as perhaps a prophet with good ethical teaching. Therefore, it is the resurrection of Jesus that verifies Jesus' divinity and preaching. It also verifies that God is faithful in the end. In many ways, the resurrection shines back upon the entire incarnation, and specifically the passion as a revelation of who God is and how salvation and redemption come. Moltmann notes, "Jesus is not recognizable as the Son of

---

6. It is beyond our scope here to examine the modern debate regarding the historicity of the resurrection. There are those for whom the factual, historical reality of the resurrection is paramount and nonnegotiable. Wolfhart Pannenberg has based his entire systematic theology on the conceptualization of the resurrection as historical fact. In good Hegelian style, Pannenberg seeks to make the resurrection significant not only for Christian theology, but for universal history. He seeks to remove its reality from the merely subjective realm of faith and place it in the objective realm of history and science. To do so, he must therefore "prove" its reality historically and scientifically. While Moltmann and Pannenberg's "theologies of hope" are often linked, they differ significantly on their understanding of the resurrection. "Moltmann is quite clear that the resurrection of Jesus was a real event . . . but refuses to follow Pannenberg in regarding it as therefore accessible to the historian *qua* historian. The problem is that the resurrection calls in question the very concept of history which modern historical method presupposes: that of the fundamental similarity of all experience" (Bauckham, "Moltmann's Theology of Hope Revisited," 210–11). Moltmann himself states: "[The resurrection] is removed from what in modern times is understood as a factual historical proof. The resurrection of Jesus from the dead by God does not speak the 'language of facts,' but only the language of faith and hope, that is the language of promise. I have therefore denoted the proleptic structure of the proclamation of Jesus and the Christian resurrection faith by the word 'promise.' In the sphere of speech this expresses the very anticipation which for Pannenberg lies in the fact itself" (*Crucified God*, 173).

7. 2 Cor 5:19.

8. Moltmann, *Crucified God*, 123.

God until his death on the cross and his resurrection; in the order of being, he is the Son of God before this history takes place."[9] In other words, while the Son has always been divine, it is the resurrection that fully confirms that testimony.

The Resurrection Announces the End of Death

In the resurrection, God defeats death. This is the main thrust of the *Christus Victor* theory of the atonement. "We know that since Christ was raised from the dead, he cannot die again; death no longer has mastery over him. The death he died, he died to sin once for all; but the life he lives, he lives to God. In the same way, count yourselves dead to sin but alive to God in Christ Jesus" (Rom 6:9–11). We often read Paul's words in Romans chapters 6 through 8 as addressed to sinners. Certainly he declares there that sin should have no mastery over us, in the sense that we are called to allow the Spirit of God to bring us from the "death" of our transgressions to the "life" of holiness. But if we can interpret these chapters from the perspective of the sinned-against, the message is just as powerful. The God who defeated death in the raising of the Son seeks to defeat the metaphorical and literal deaths we have suffered at the hands of others, and bring us to new life. God enters into these deaths, such as victimization, in order to sit in communion with us. But God purposes to lead us up out of the communion of suffering into a communion of power and hope, and of new life through the resurrection.[10] The resurrection of the dead, then, is not simply a continuation of life after death for the deceased, but a present hope of healing that shows, again, that our "deaths" are not the last word. The resurrection is the eschatological irruption and firstfruits of the new creation. The resurrection declares and speaks God's power over death as the center and source of healing and salvation. Therefore, the resurrection verifies the saving significance of the cross.[11] "In that one man [Jesus Christ] the future of the new world of life has already gained power over this unredeemed world of death and has condemned it to become a world that passes away."[12]

In the resurrection of the dead, then, literally and figuratively, as inaugurated in Jesus Christ, death itself—as a purposeless void, as a despairing abyss, and as an uncompromising master—faces its demise. It is this confidence and hope of the resurrection of death that comes from the future and

---

9. Moltmann, *Crucified God*, 91.
10. This is part of the transformative aspects of the sacrament of baptism.
11. Moltmann, *Crucified God*, 182.
12. Moltmann, *Crucified God*, 171.

invades what might seem an uncertain present. The curse of death has been abolished. The sting of the death has been soothed. Death itself is ultimately defeated. This is a key aspect of Christian hope.

The Resurrection Liberates

As the resurrection announces the end of death, injustice retreats. So much of Christian thought has focused on the justice of God in the crucifixion throughout the centuries, as in *God's* need for justice in offering forgiveness to us. It has only been in the last few decades that justice has been addressed from the perspective of the oppressed; they need justice. Christian justice no longer refers only to a wrathful God who needs compensation. It now focuses on the need for justice for the marginalized. Many people who have been victimized and brutalized by powerful abusers not only see Jesus Christ as a fellow sufferer who has also been abused, but in his death, and then resurrection, Christ as liberator; this should be a primary lens for interpreting the atonement.

Xodus Christology emerges from the African American Christian tradition that also sees the atonement of Jesus as one of liberation. As many persons of the African American tradition have experienced unjust suffering, Xodus Christology is clear that injustice is not to be celebrated, even the injustice done to Jesus. What is celebrated is the love of Jesus to help overturn structures of oppression and bring new hope and possibilities to the marginalized. To find the unjust violence against Jesus as salvific would be to endorse it, which is the actual root of the problem. In the Xodus tradition, while Jesus is one who also suffers unjustly, there is nothing salvific in being brutalized. The atonement is about liberation and offering new hope in places of despair. What is salvific is that Christ lays down his life in love to help liberate the oppressed. Karen Baker-Fletcher notes that Christ's life, death, and resurrection is the location and inbreaking of new hope and possibilities for humanity. Christ now makes possible for "peace to be made between formerly warring peoples (Eph 2:11–22), and for genuine reconciliation to occur. Christians ought to be joyful about *these things,* not the suffering, pain, torture, and death of Jesus on a cross!"[13]

In their essay "For God So Loved the World?," Joanne Carlson Brown and Rebecca Parker suggest that in thinking about healing and redemption, Christianity should focus on justice for the oppressed, radical love to all, especially to those for whom it has been refused, and liberation from systems and situations that perpetuate abuse and victimization. In talking

---

13. Baker-Fletcher, *My Sister, My Brother,* 188.

about salvation in the Christ story, they state that his death was an "unjust act, done by humans who chose to reject his way of life and sought to silence him through death," which "is not redeemed by the resurrection ... Suffering is never redemptive, and suffering cannot be redeemed." Death is overthrown when "the threat of death is refused and choice is made for justice, radical love and liberation."[14] For Brown and Parker, the gift and power of salvation is not that an unjust evil occurred or was made good. The killing of Christ will always continue to be evil. Salvation is about the call for justice and refusal to accept the victimization of any other person. They conclude their essay by asserting, "Resurrection means that death is overcome in those precise instances when human beings choose life, refusing the threat of death. Jesus climbed out of the grave in the Garden of Gethsemane when he refused to abandon his commitment to the truth even though enemies threatened him with death."[15] The resurrection is power and invitation to those who have been marginalized and mistreated to no longer be defined by what was done to them. Moreover, the resurrection is the source of the power for all to be advocates for justice and liberation for everyone. The resurrection of Jesus Christ is not only a gift, or hope and power over death, but also a calling.

The Resurrection and Reviving Grace

There are many instances in the Gospels where Jesus says that someone's faith has saved them. The same Greek word, *sozo*, can be interpreted as salvation, but also as to heal or to cure. "Your faith has made you well," Jesus tells the grateful leper (Luke 17:19, NIV). We limit the effectiveness of the atonement when we see it as some transactional and mechanical method of God forgiving the sin that would damn us. The atonement has much more breadth and depth than that. Salvation involves much more than forgiveness of sin. If we interpret salvation as healing or "therapeutic healing," in the paradigm of John Wesley, doors open for victims of all kinds.[16] We again want to be careful here. Victims of violence, abandonment, and abuse need holistic treatment by trained clinicians in a variety of fields. What we offer is a theological reflection on how God intersects victims' lives. We are *not* advocating for a form of spiritualizing that says healing only comes directly from God. Such thinking can be abusive in and of itself. But we do want

---

14. Weaver, *Nonviolent Atonement*, 159, drawing upon Joanne Carlson and Rebecca Parker, "For God So Loved the World?," 27–28.

15. Brown and Parker, "For God So Loved the World?," 27–28.

16. See Maddox, *Responsible Grace*, 144.

to say that the resurrecting God is active in "reviving" those touched by the death-sting of violence, abandonment, and abuse. God's reviving grace is active in mending, adopting, and bringing wholeheartedness to those in need of resurrection life.

The Resurrection and Mending

Violence violates victims. We might spend time debating whether all violence is evil by examining ideologies such as the "just war" theory or arguments for pacifism. Are there instances when the use of force is necessary and therefore a good? Or, would the assassination of Hitler been God's will, for example? Or, should we approve of the death penalty? But no matter where one comes down on these somewhat speculative queries, no one would say that violence, even for a good cause, is not without grave negative effects. Violence (even against the "deserving") inflicts physical pain, suffering, and sometimes death. Physical violence violates. Emotional violence violates. Sexual violence violates. Spiritual violence violates. Violence fractures the hope of a fully integrated self.

The cross and resurrection both reveal and expose the evil of violence. Violence must be resisted. How does the life, death, and especially the resurrection of Jesus Christ inform us? As discussed at length in chapter 5, there is a huge difference between saying the crucifixion of Jesus has the powerful outcome of salvation (inclusively defined), and saying that the violence and death of Jesus were good. It is theologically important to say this with precision. In the same way, we must never imply that because there is power for new life in the resurrection, that violence itself is redeemed. It is too simple to use language that erases the significance of experiences with pain by covering them up with quick, rather mechanistic, optimism. No matter the degree, victims of violence need physical, psychological, and spiritual mending. Besides broken bones, bruises, and wounds, they often suffer from debilitating forms of PTSD. It is appropriate to note in a book like this that there are victims of religious or spiritual abuse that need a very deep healing. Persons who have been abused by spiritual authorities, or manipulated into skewed forms of toxic spirituality through coercion, or indoctrinated into false images of God and graceless demands for legalistic behavior, have suffered violence at the hands of others in the name of Christ. Bad theology abuses real people. All forms of violence outwardly or inwardly disfigure its victims.

Various therapies can be helpful if accessible. From combat war veterans, to those who have been assaulted, to children who have been beaten by their own parents, to witnesses of murder, to victims of toxic faith—the trauma is incalculable. A world filled with violence of innumerable kinds and proportions needs a *mending* that can only be matched by a God with the power to raise the dead. Resurrection hope can begin to offer such mending now, in the lives of individuals, in our continued resistance against systems and mechanisms of violence, and in the hope of the promise that finally violence will be conquered and vanquished from the earth, which begins eschatologically in the death and resurrection of Jesus.

The Resurrection and Adoption

Abandonment comes in many forms. Children are physically or emotionally neglected, or abandoned by their parents and end up in the foster care system. Or children suffer from emotional and psychological abandonment issues when their parents are too busy to meet their needs. Spouses are abandoned through various kinds of domestic abuse or divorce. The elderly can be abandoned to nursing care facilities when family members do not want to be inconvenienced, or when the elder one is alone in the world. These are only a few instances of neglect and abandonment in our society. The circumstances vary widely and can be much more private than what we can perceive, but all forms of abandonment have harmful consequences.

One of the results of the *sozo* (salvation or healing) of God, that finds its source in the atonement, is the biblical assurance of our adoption as children of God. "For those who are led by the Spirit of God are the children of God. The Spirit you received does not make you slaves, so that you live in fear again; rather, the Spirit you received brought about your adoption to sonship. And by him we cry, 'Abba, Father.' The Spirit himself testifies with our spirit that we are God's children" (Rom 8:14–16, NIV). The primary wounds of abandonment and neglect, at the time or years later, include a sense of isolation, of being alone in the world, of never knowing themselves as cherished, and of real damage to their ability to trust. Persons tend to compensate in extreme reactions. They either cut themselves off from relationships, or become addicted to them in unhealthy ways, desperately trying to meet their needs and fill their hole. Personality disorders can arise. Abandonment and neglect teach the abandoned that the world is not trustworthy, that their needs do not matter, and that they are not worthy of love. Abandonment and neglect cause deep relational wounds, and the abandoned are often, yes, estranged from healthy relationships with others, but also estranged from their truest selves.

God's reviving grace comes to the abandoned in the form of adoption. God is not a cold, distant parent who only serves as judge or disciplinarian. God is an intimate presence, who receives us as we are with the deepest of affection and love. God is devoted, gentle, and patient, filled with loving kindness and comforting tenderness. God adopts us as God's own. We are siblings of Jesus, and co-heirs with him of all that is to come. As the Spirit testifies to our spirit that we are God's children, we cry out "Abba"—a very intimate and affectionate term for "parent."

It is common in the life of the church and liturgical practice to believe that God can be the parent we might not have had. God can recapitulate our difficult childhood experiences in re-parenting us. This can be a very powerful image. The problem with it is that in many churches even today, this re-parenting has only been imagined as fathering. In this book we have been extremely careful to avoid calling God "Father" even when it would have added more clarity, specifically around the roles of the Trinity at the crucifixion. Technically, of course, God refers to all three *personae*. Distinguishing God from the First Person of the Trinity is important theologically. Since the crucifixion is the crucifixion of the Son, using parent language seems most appropriate. We decided not to go in that direction. But a discussion of God's parental role is crucial here when speaking to the emotionally orphaned.

The very word *father* must be recognized as a powerful symbol. Unfortunately for many, it is a symbol of cruelty of the most horrific kind. This can cause strong triggering reactions in the abused and abandoned who have been wronged by their fathers or father figures. When we limit our imaginations in practice and worship and name God singularly as father, we can block victims from a safe space among us. Unfortunately the church has often said "get over it" precisely at this point. Or, it has immediately offered God as a replacement father who will make it all right again. While this may indeed be helpful to some in time, we cannot assume that it will be helpful to everyone. If every prayer begins with the word "Father" many are cut off from that prayer, for it can produce a PTSD reaction that shuts the person down psychically as well as spiritually. Beyond the word *father*, our conceptualization of God as male in general can be problematic. This is not a new argument. Feminist theologians have been alerting us to the difficulties for decades. Mother language has been suggested as an alternative.[17] The problem is, mothers can also neglect, abandon, and abuse. If one has been

---

17. Examples of feminist theology's use of maternal images are numerous. One of the most fascinating comes from Jewish scholar Melissa Raphael, who uses the maternal God as a retrospective symbol to help deal with the theological ramifications of the Holocaust. See Raphael, *Female Face of God in Auschwitz*.

abused by a female, making God into a mother has all the same difficulties as claiming God is father for those who have been abused by men.

What seems appropriate and necessary is to recognize and teach that God is genderless while still invoking parenting language. God's adoption is a helpful biblical metaphor worth preserving and utilizing. What is perhaps most necessary is to clarify precisely what kind of parent God is. It is also very important to see the church not only as the body of Christ, intricately interdependent between its parts, but also as the family of God, intricately connected as siblings who are safe, loving, and trustworthy. God's adoption, and the church's supportive environment, accesses the reviving grace of the resurrected Christ.

Those within the adoption community are now alerting us to be very careful with our language. For too long we have unthinkingly used the idea that an adopted child is so lucky to have found parents willing to take them in, almost as if the child has done something wrong in being orphaned, and are now redeemed by adoption. This idea has caused some to change the language around adoption to state that the adopting parents are the lucky ones to have been blessed with this child. What this does is create space for the child to feel that she or he is a gift to the family, that he or she has something to give and to offer to them. In the same way the church should have this view of such things—the abused are not people to be tolerated in our midst, nor are they are blessed to have us to care for them, but should be seen as true gifts to the church precisely because of their experiences and perspective; indeed, they should be cherished in our fellowship. The abandoned are adopted by God, and should be adopted fully into the life of the church.

The Resurrection and Wholeheartedness

Although we would never rate the severity of the consequences of violence, abandonment, or sexual abuse, those who have been sexually violated can experience a breaking of a uniquely acidic and erosive kind. Effects can include depression and anxiety disorders, personality disorders, dissociative disorders, deviant behavior, and any number of other difficulties. Terese A. Hall reviews and summarizes some of the research available:

> Finkelhor and Browne (1985) postulate four dynamics concerning the traumatic impact of abuse: (a) traumatic sexualization, the dysfunctional shaping of sexual feelings and attitudes; (b) betrayal, the violation of trust which occurs when one on whom the child depends causes harm; (c) powerlessness, the process

by which the child's will and sense of efficacy are continually contravened; and (d) stigmatization, the sense of shame and guilt which become incorporated into the child's self-image. That conceptualization was substantially corroborated in a study by Edwards and Donaldson (1988) of 104 adult female incest survivors in outpatient treatment. Their study showed seven "stress response themes," as follows: (a) vulnerability and isolation, (b) fear and anxiety, (c) guilt and shame, (d) anger and betrayal, (e) angry reaction to the abuser, (f) sadness and loss, and (g) powerlessness.[18]

What Hall adds is a study of the effects of sexual abuse on the spirituality of Christian women. Hall shows that the spiritual effects have been infrequently studied. Hall does reference these, and specifically highlights two studies that used the Spiritual Well-Being Scale—"an instrument designed to measure a subjective sense of religious and existential well-being, found significantly lower scores for abuse victims (Papania, 1988; Rodriguez, 1989)."[19] Hall's own study measured three groups: 1. women in outpatient treatment who were sexually abused; 2. women in outpatient treatment who had not been sexually abused; and 3. a control group of non-abused women, not in treatment. They completed the Religious Status Inventory (RSI), a 160-item questionnaire, which was designed to measure religious functioning along eight dimensions.

> The eight dimensions of the RSI are as follows: 1. Awareness of God—a balanced dependence on God, and the use of prayer and worship to maintain a close relationship with God. 2. Acceptance of God's Grace and Steadfast Love—a subjective sense of being unconditionally loved and forgiven by God, trust in God's goodness, and an understanding of the role of suffering in the life of the Christian. 3. Being Repentant and Responsible—a balanced acceptance of personal responsibility and imperfections, and an ability to deal with interpersonal conflict in a responsible way. 4. Knowing God's Leadership and Direction—an active trust in God's leadership and purpose, balanced by a sense of personal responsibility in living out that purpose. 5. Involvement in Organized Religion—active involvement in religious worship, prayer, study, and service. 6. Experiencing Fellowship—a sense of community with others, both believers and nonbelievers. 7. Being Ethical—a balance of commitment to and flexibility in governing ethical principles. 8. Affirming

18. Hall, "Spiritual Effects," 129.
19. Hall, "Spiritual Effects," 130.

Openness in Faith—a tolerance for the beliefs of others and a willingness to remain open to change and growth.[20]

Hall reaches the following conclusions:

> The results of this study show significantly lower religious functioning in Christian women who were sexually abused as children as compared to those women who were not abused. The greatest differences were on Subscale 2, Acceptance of God's Grace and Steadfast Love, and Subscale 4, Knowing God's Leadership and Direction. On both subscales, the abused group differed significantly from both the nonabused clinical group and the nonclinical group. These two dimensions concern one's relationship with God and can be conceptualized in broad terms as relating to one's experience of being loved and accepted by God, trusting in God's providential care for the future, and finding meaning in suffering. Thus it would appear that early experiences of sexual abuse have a highly significant relationship with later ability to trust in God's love and provision, as well as with the ability to put painful experiences into a meaningful framework for one's life.[21]

Our focus here is not to suggest therapies to address these difficulties. However, some theological reflection may still prove "therapeutic." What victims of sexual abuse need is spiritual wholeheartedness that comes in the form of true personhood. We are not suggesting that such wholeness as a theological category is something found easily; indeed it may take an entire lifetime, perhaps even after death, for us to experience the completion of healing in God. The level of "sanctification" achievable in this life is certainly debated by various theological traditions. For now, we posit that "progressive sanctification"—defined here as growing, therapeutic spiritual healing—is available in this life. We also connect such healing to the reviving grace of the resurrected Christ. Indeed "sanctification" has been called the process by which we become truly human, implying some amount of realized personhood. Personhood is exactly what sexual abuse threatens, and exactly what becomes elusive in the healing process. Victims have been dis-integrated, pulled apart, with aspects of their humanity amputated from their experiences. Taking Hall's study as a cue, we will address wholeheartedness from the perspective of accepting God's love, trusting God in the future, and finding a meaningful and thriving life that is forthcoming in spite of one's suffering.

20. Hall, "Spiritual Effects," 130–31.
21. Hall, "Spiritual Effects," 131.

The image of God in humans has been interpreted in many different ways through the centuries. One definition is the capacity to love and be loved. We were created for loving relationships—with God, with ourselves, with other humans, and with the earth. Sexual abuse results in a relational fracturing, or a distortion of the *imago Dei* as God intends it to be. A common way to speak of this distortion in general theologically is to speak of a "depravity" in humanity as the result of sin, usually imagined as the sin of selfishness.[22] But the distortion can also come, and this is key, from being *sinned against*, as long as we divorce it from this definition of an overinflated ego. To return to one of this book's main themes, too often Christianity has focused on the effects of sin on the sinner (personal and original sin) and defined salvation as forgiveness of sin for that sinner. More Eastern and Wesleyan theology emphasize sanctification of the sinner as the renewal of the image of God. But salvation can also be imagined as the renewal of the *imago Dei* in those who have been victimized at no fault of their own. In other words, the sinned-against may participate in a grace that revives and renews their capacity to love and be loved, in healing and healthy ways. And reviving grace offers authentic, integrated personhood for those who have been fractured by others. Foremost in this is to know themselves loved by God in a truly transforming way. Because of the resurrection, God's reviving grace comes in the form of a potential for spiritual wholeheartedness as accepting the love of God.

A second aspect of spiritual healing is trusting God with the future. This seems like an insurmountable hurdle. If God has failed a victim in the past by allowing for the abuse to occur, not stopping it even though possessing the power to do so, why would she or he trust God with the future? This is an extremely legitimate question. It is not something easily overcome. Perhaps it would be helpful to return to Job for a moment. In the end, Job did not receive an answer to the question of why God allowed such awful things to occur in his life. It would be more than reasonable for Job to turn his back on God and walk away, or to curse God and die. But he does neither of these reasonable things. In the end he shockingly says this: even if you slay me God, yet will I trust you. He was able to do so, we believe, not in his own power or insight. We believe that God steps into the scene and gives Job the ability to do what he could not do for himself. And this is salvation.

Humanly speaking, it makes no logical sense to trust a God who has failed us. Humanly speaking, it might be beyond our capacity. But because God is able to raise the dead, God can revive in us an ability to trust over time. God is not just the God who forsook Jesus so that the First Person

---

22. See footnote 5 in chapter 2.

could become the God of the godforsaken. God is also the God of the resurrection because we cannot raise ourselves. The gospel is that God does for us what we are incapable of doing for ourselves. We cannot save ourselves from our mistrust of God. But the process of forgiving God as outlined in the last chapter, and the reviving grace of God that comes from the resurrection, can resurrect us to new life. That new life can renew us to a faith beyond sight.

And finally, spiritual wholeheartedness and revived personhood for the sexually abused can be experienced as finding meaning in spite of suffering. We recognize the audacity of such a claim. In previous chapters we have even said so ourselves, averring that trying to find meaning out of the absurdity of some suffering can do violence against the sufferer. And so we do not say this lightly. But another part of the saving gospel is that God can redeem our wounds, and give them retrospective meaning. Jesus' wounds are just that, horrific wounds that tell a horrific story of violence and abuse done to him. But his wounds become the very source of our healing because of the resurrection. God's reviving grace also offers us a redeeming reinterpretation of our woundedness in our search for meaning.

Viktor Frankl was a Jewish survivor of Auschwitz during the Holocaust. Out of his experiences he developed a type of therapy known as "logotherapy." Frankl believes that humanity's deepest need is to find meaning in life. He constructs his ideas out of his own suffering. He came to believe that searching for and finding meaning, even in the absurdity of his life in the concentration camp, helped him survive. He believed this perspective helped him endure until his release, when even (physically) stronger people died from hopeless resignation. Some gave up living by either killing themselves, or by succumbing to apathy and despair and allowing guards to kill them. Searching for meaning kept him alive.

His *Man's Search for Meaning* is both biographical and theoretical.[23] Its narrative and its advice have been extraordinarily helpful to many. Frankl describes the realities of what he experienced, and what he learned from them. He does not shy away from existential or spiritual questions, unlike some well-known psychologists. The search for meaning is both an existential and religious question. The book was first published in German in 1946, just a year after his release from a concentration camp. It was first translated into English in 1959. It is recognized as an extremely influential book of the twentieth century. The book is perhaps most known for this idea: even when imprisoned and far from freedom, a person still has the freedom to choose how to respond to her or his circumstances. This freedom is the

---

23. Frankl, *Man's Search for Meaning*.

path to meaning. In 1984, Frankl added a postscript to his book entitled "The Case for Tragic Optimism." Although the other two sections of the book—"Experiences in a Concentration Camp" and "Logotherapy in a Nutshell"—are both moving and helpful, it is perhaps his postscript that is most relevant here.

In it he advocates saying yes to life in spite of everything, even in the face of inscrutable suffering. "Tragic optimism" is his idea that a person can be genuinely optimistic even in the face of extreme affliction. Logotherapy speaks of a "tragic triad" that consists of pain, guilt, and death. Each element of the tragic triad can produce immense grief, even paralyzing hopelessness. But they can be resisted. They can also be an opportunity for growth and change. To say this to a person in the midst of the darkness of their suffering could certainly be detrimental. We must be very, very careful when we ascribe agency to victims, because there is a high possibility that they are not free to choose another way of being because of the captivity they have endured. But hopefully there comes a point, through progressive healing and the prevenient grace of God, when a person can reject pain, guilt, and death, and move toward new life. Better language for us may be to substitute "tragic optimism" with Christian hope. Christian hope keeps us alive, by also providing opportunity for finding meaning in spite of our pain. But we are not the source of Christian hope, as if we must conjure it up and try harder to see a half-full glass, or try to create our own meaning *ex nihilo* (out of nothing). The resurrection of Jesus for us, is an act of God, the originator of our hope. Hope, put simply, is not something we conjure up. It is a gift from God.

The question of the meaning of suffering is before us. The question plumbs the depths of human experience, and will never find a complete answer. But there are places we can journey that perhaps give us glimpses. Henri Nouwen has popularized the concept of the "wounded healer."[24] He writes profoundly on this point: God's grace and love works through us most strongly, not out of some realized perfection, but out of our brokenness; not out of our soundness, but out of our wounds; not out of our strength, but out of our weakness. "Nobody escapes being wounded. We are all wounded people, whether physically, emotionally, mentally, or spiritually. The main question is not, 'How can we hide our wounds' so we don't have to be embarrassed, but 'How can we put our woundedness to the service of others?' When our wounds cease to be a source of shame, and become a source of healing, we have become wounded healers."[25]

---

24. Nouwen, *Wounded Healer*.
25. Nouwen, *Bread for the Journey*, entry for July 8.

To be clear, God does not cause us to be victimized. Suffering of this magnitude is truly absurd and meaningless. But the redeeming God, in the aftermath, can use our wounds as a source of comfort, even healing, in the life of another as we offer them in empathy; such offering also heals us as we progress in the mending journey.[26] As we have seen from Jesus himself on the cross in his extension of his grace to the convict next to him, we must not underestimate the restorative power of true empathy. There is healing in the simple but profound words, "I understand." When we do this, the blood from Christ's wounds mingles with the blood from our wounds, which mingles with the blood of other victim's wounds. And in this, we usher them into the very presence of God. It is not accidental that this image can be understood eucharistically, as well as practically. Consequently, yet not insignificantly, such redemption extends back to us as our wounds are "recycled" (waste made useful) in the economy of God. The sinned-against can stand as a eucharistic symbol for us all. It would do us well to remember the gospel is for all the wounded, both for the sinners and sinned-against. Dorothee Soelle says: "Christianity exists for slaves. It is the religion of the oppressed, of those marked with affliction. It concerns itself with their needs. People are pronounced blessed not because of their achievements or their behavior, but with regard to their needs. Blessed are the poor, the suffering, the persecuted, the hungry."[27] The needs and wounds of the afflicted can be redeemed as they spill out as empathy for fellow sufferers. This by no means justifies their wounding! But empathy is healing for those who *give* and for those who *receive* such love. Absurd wounds find meaning when they find their way to others as instruments of grace. We are reintegrated into fuller personhood in such an offering. And we experience deeper wells of the unlimited resource of resurrection hope, in "communion-ty."

---

26 Just a reminder here—a powerful verse affirming this is also a verse that can often be used in terrible ways. Romans 8:28 is not suggesting that God causes all things that happen to us. God does not cause evil nor need evil to work good. Part of God's healing activity is that God can invite us into new levels of healing out of our pain and evil.

27. Soelle, *Suffering*, 159.

CHAPTER 10

Forgiveness from the Back Side

By
Diane Leclerc and Julie Schmidt

My father sexually abused me. He allowed others in my family to abuse me. The feelings of abandonment I experienced as a child along with the abuse created a belief that the laws of safety, love, security, and value didn't apply to me. God's love is certainly enough for others, but [God's love is] not for me—because the rules are different for me. When my dad beat my mom to a pulp to the point of hospitalization, the deacons of the church met together and came to an "official decision" that my dad had acted in "righteous indignation." Can you believe that? Righteous indignation. I've been taught that forgiving this man was the key to my spiritual maturity. I have worked toward forgiving him so that I can feel close to God. The problem is that throughout my life, forgiveness for him feels most like indifference. And this feels like a great service to him. It lifts some of the judgment I feel toward him and I let God take care of him. But I'm told forgiveness

> *means feeling a sense of warmth, compassion, love, and kindness . . . all those warm emotions toward him. I can't ever get there. Therefore I continue to beat myself up and be "beaten up" by my church leaders—like I'm not good enough spiritually. It's one more thing I have to do when I've been holding the burden of this abuse my whole life. It's one more thing I can't get right.*
>
> —*A real client*[1]

We come to one of the most important chapters in this book. It is important because its topic is so misunderstood, and careless presumptions and presentations around the issues have revictimized victims. The topic: *The forgiveness of the abuser by the abused.* It is the elephant in the room, partly because the perspective of the abused has been ignored altogether. To push the metaphor, whenever the topic of forgiveness is brought up, the sinned-against can become so distant and so left out of the conversation as we miss the mark that we might as well be talking about a giraffe in the room, when they clearly still see the elephant.

It should be obvious from the previous chapters that we strongly believe that there is hope for healing in the life journeys of the sinned-against. Unfortunately Christians sometimes introduce the idea of forgiving others as *the* litmus test of whether we are where we should be spiritually. No matter what kind of healing has occurred, no matter how much progress has been made, the sinned-against must face the lesson or the sermon that pops up from time to time and suggests, quite explicitly, that if they have not forgiven, they in turn sin themselves (Matt 6:14–15), or worse, that God will not forgive them. Messages are given that imply that forgiveness is a decision, and a decision is a matter of the will, and thus in their control. Sometimes it is added that if they still feel negatively toward that person then they have not forgiven and have failed in their duty to do so. And so, such messages add to a victim's undeserved shame (that resulted from being victimized), undeserved guilt as well, that results from not being able to do what is demanded of them. And guilt and shame are compounded. Not only has the perpetrator blamed the victim, as is so often the case, the

---

1. The narratives of several clients are offered throughout this chapter. Names and, at times, specific details have been changed to maintain their anonymity.

church comes along and blames them for not getting over it quickly enough through forgiveness, which is most often presented as a mechanical, even stoic decision, that supposedly and ironically results in warm feelings toward the perpetrator. To overgeneralize, the church has most often missed the horrific absurdity of some types of human suffering by offering a trite conceptualization of forgiveness. As we have tried to convey throughout this entire project, suffering violence, abuse, and abandonment results in peculiarly deep levels of personal fracturing. On top of its naivete, apathy, or outright practices of inhospitality, there are multiple definitions of forgiveness swirling in the church that can confound the sinned-against. They know the demand to forgive, but the church is seldom clear on what that even means.

The purpose of this book has been to talk about the "other side of sin" that we so often neglect, and to strongly suggest that the atonement offered through the death and resurrection of Jesus can be redemptive for the sinned-against (with a broadened definition of redemption). The first nine chapters have "recapitulated" and "transfigured" traditional atonement theories by presenting victims' unique voices and a theology that undergirds their experiences. We have suggested that we do not need another atonement narrative apart from Christ in order to include those who have suffered at the hands of others through abuse of all kinds. The cross is just as potent theologically with a different interpretation that can bring mending and healing to the victimized. But when it comes to the topic of forgiving abusers, it is not an extension of traditional theology that we need. What is called for is a complete rewrite of the Christian script that is so often invoked. Christians of all kinds, even victims themselves, have been told, and continue to declare theological assumptions about forgiveness that are not only damaging, but simply untrue as contortions of the biblical message. This chapter attempts to expose these wrong messages regarding forgiveness, and offer healing alternatives. Diane Leclerc has written this chapter with Julie Schmidt, as a clinician trained in trauma, who sees persons in therapy whose tragic and horrific stories of abuse and abandonment reveal the need for a new rendering of forgiveness on the basis of back-side theology.

In this chapter we will examine what forgiveness means and what it does not mean; consider insight from what the trauma-informed community now understands about the brain; offer a trauma-informed theology of repentance, suggest a reinterpretation of the parable of the unmerciful servant; and examine the relevance and power of Christ's new creation for the sinned-against. Prior to these subsections, we wrestle with a historical instance of mass abuse and suffering.

In the backdrop of back-side theology we have utilized stories from the holocaust in previous chapters. The first chapter intimated that back-side theology is more akin to Jewish protest theology than it is to process theology at the opposite extreme. The issue of the forgiveness of perpetrators by those who have been unspeakably abused was obviously relevant to the Jews post-Holocaust (continuing to today). We turn now to a book written by Simon Wiesenthal, who spent the latter part of his life pursuing Nazi war criminals and bringing them to justice.

The Sunflower: A Real Parable

Simon Wiesenthal was a Jew who live through World War II. He wrote a book entitled *The Sunflower: On the Possibilities and Limits of Forgiveness*, which was published in German in 1969, and in English in 1976. He begins by explaining the origin of the title. While in concentration camps, Jewish prisoners would sometimes be marched to work sites outside the camp. He records an incident that happened to him as he himself marched to a military hospital one day to dispose of medical waste.

> Our column suddenly came to a halt at a crossroads. I could see nothing that might be holding us up but I noticed on the left of the street there was a military cemetery . . . And on each grave there was planted a sunflower, as straight as a soldier on parade. I stared spellbound . . . [B]utterflies fluttered from flower to flower. Were they carrying messages from grave to grave? Were they whispering something to each flower to pass on to the soldier below? Yes, this was just what they were doing; the dead were receiving light and messages. Suddenly I envied the dead soldiers. Each had a sunflower to connect him with the living world, and butterflies to visit his grave. For me there would be no sunflower. I would be buried in a mass grave, where corpses would be piled on top of me. No sunflower would ever bring light into my darkness, and no butterflies would dance above my dreadful tomb.[2]

After marching by the sunflowered graveyard and reaching the hospital, Wiesenthal is randomly pulled out of formation by a nurse (a nun), taken to a room, and forced to hear the deathbed confessions of a Nazi soldier for hours. Ironically, the hospital used to house the very high school Wiesenthal had attended, and the room happened to be the office of the dean while he was there. This adds to the surreality of his experience. The soldier,

2. Wiesenthal, *Sunflower*, 14–15.

seeking to unburden himself from his guilt, states that any Jew would do to serve his purposes—"I do not know who you are, I only know that you are a Jew and that is enough."[3] Earlier, Wiesenthal states, "I didn't know what he wanted to confess, but I knew that after his death a sunflower would grow on his grave . . . It would accompany him to the cemetery, stand on his grave, and sustain his connection with life. And this I envied him."[4] The sunflower becomes a symbol for Wiesenthal of the privilege and power of the "super-race" that declared Jews were subhuman. Wiesenthal desperately desired to be released from the soldier's gruesome grip during the hours of listening to his life story, but whenever he tried to remove his hand, the soldier tightened his hold. Patricia Patterson observes in Wiesenthal's narrative a "contrasting decency" that "reveals itself in simple acts—he brushes a fly from the soldier's bandages, picks up his dropped letter, listens to and apprehends the soldier as a distinct human person, and bothers to discern his true repentance."[5] The soldier tells the story of his participation in burning dozens of Russian Jews alive, including children. Soon after he was badly wounded, taken to the hospital, where he died the day after this encounter. Here he is begging for forgiveness. What would Wiesenthal do in this situation? He asks his readers, what would you do? After hours of hearing the soldier's story, and after he pleads for this random Jew's absolution, in the end Wiesenthal leaves without saying a word.

Taken back to the camp, again marching past the sunflowered graveyard, he reflects that night on the experience. "I have failed to carry out the last wish of a dying man. I gave him no answer to his final question."[6] Earlier, "[The soldier had said] 'I know that what I have told you is terrible. In the long nights while I have been waiting for death, time and time again I have longed to talk about it to a Jew and beg forgiveness from him. Only I didn't know whether there were any Jews left . . . I know that what I am asking is almost too much for you, but without your answer I cannot die in peace."[7] Wiesenthal recounted the events back in camp to his friends, and tells them, "at last, I made up my mind and without a word I left the room."[8] His friends tell him he has certainly done the right thing.

While he wrestles for years about his decision, he finally comes to peace with leaving a dying if repentant man without granting him forgiveness. But

---

3. Wiesenthal, *Sunflower*, 54.
4. Wiesenthal, *Sunflower*, 30–31.
5. Patterson "Book Review," 476.
6. Wiesenthal, *Sunflower*, 66.
7. Wiesenthal, *Sunflower*, 54.
8. Wiesenthal, *Sunflower*, 55.

in an act born of intense curiosity about the soldier, and of some semblance of compassion, he visits the soldier's mother years later. He does not tell her about the real encounter, only that he had met her son. After hearing the details of the soldier's early life that he had longed to hear to make some sense of his experience with him in the hospital, he leaves the mother without destroying her image of her good boy. He does not tell her about Russia, and what her son had become capable of doing. Wiesenthal again leaves "in silence."

In the second edition of the book (1996), dozens of voices are added to the conversation about forgiveness as theologians (Christian and Jewish), philosophers, literary writers, political scientists, religious leaders, and persons who went through other more contemporary genocides, reflect on Wiesenthal's actions. Each wrestles with the morality of what Wiesenthal decided as he refused the Nazi soldier any absolution for his crimes. There is a wide range of responses, from disagreement to alliance with his decision; all offer great compassion for Wiesenthal's dilemma. It presents a reverence from the essayists for the depth of the ethical anguish he faced. In the face of such atrocities as the Holocaust, and in this gruesome encounter between Jewish victim and murdering soldier, what is there to say that is adequate to address the insanity of it all? More than fifty respondents attempt to say something.

Different essayists take up different points. Certainly one aspect to consider is whether the grievous amount of suffering matters. Is forgiving mass murders the same as forgiving a lie? There is unanimous agreement that the Holocaust, and other horrific examples of inflicting immeasurable suffering, require a different measurement in considering forgiveness as an option, proportionate to the damage done. Eugene Fisher (Catholic bishop, and author who holds a doctorate in Hebrew Studies) writes:

> I believe it is the height of arrogance for Christians to ask Jews to forgive them. On what grounds? We can, as established by evidence of changed teaching and changed behavior, repent and work toward mutual reconciliation with Jews. But we have no right to put Jewish survivors in the impossible moral position of offering forgiveness, implicitly, in the name of the six million . . . Placing a Jew in this anguished position further victimizes him or her. This, in my reading, was the final sin of the dying Nazi.[9]

Some essayists extend this reflection in their retelling of some of the story—it is impossible to forgive someone vicariously on behalf of others. Many of them affirm (echoing one of Wiesenthal's friends in camp) that it

---

9. Wiesenthal, *Sunflower*, 133.

would even be wrong to give the soldier what he sought, for the soldier had wronged others. That Wiesenthal was a representative Jew means nothing. The soldier wronged those he killed in the fire; only they could forgive him, but they were dead. Other essayists focus on the moral obligation to forgive a truly repentant person. Still others challenge the soldier's sincerity in his repentance, since he continues to objectify this Jew as one of any "who will do."

Eva Fleischner (professor, advisory board member of the council of Catholic-Jewish relations, and author of two books on the Holocaust) offers this insight: "[The soldier's] own suffering completely blinds him to the suffering of the Jews—not of the Jews in whose murder he participated and who continue to haunt him—but of those still alive in the camps and ghettos, also of Simon." Indeed, he seems oblivious to the fact that if Simon was discovered away from duty, he would have been shot. Fleischner continues: "While this is understandable, humanly, given his deathbed agony, I am left with the question: Could Karl have done something to ameliorate their fate, or the fate of at least a few Jews, by speaking to his fellow SS instead of summoning a poor, helpless, doomed Jew to his bedside? Would such an act perhaps have constituted Atonement?"[10]

While there are some Christian essayists who push that Wiesenthal had a moral obligation to forgive strictly on the basis of the soldier's repentance (which is assumed on the basis that there was indeed repentance), there are others who deny that he was thus obligated. Robert McAfee Brown (esteemed Christian theologian and author) insightfully resists forgiveness as the obligatory outcome.

> That we must never forget is perhaps the clearest lesson of the Holocaust. For if we forget, a time will come when even worse atrocities will be committed against Jews, and any others whom those with power wish to destroy. That we must never forgive would seem to follow from the same stern logic. For if we forgive, it will be a sign to those in the future that they can act without fear of punishment, and that the universe has a moral escape valve labeled "forgiveness" that permits evil not only to survive but to thrive. On this reading, forgiveness becomes a "weak" virtue, one that Christians seem particularly prone to champion, and one that always carries the possibility of condoning, rather than constricting the spread of evil.[11]

---

10. Wiesenthal, *Sunflower*, 143.
11. Wiesenthal, *Sunflower*, 121.

McAfee continues to tell in more detail how the atrocities of the Holocaust tear into the very moral fabric of the universe, reinforcing how easy and cheap Christians have made forgiveness. Yet, in the end, he maintains that forgiveness must remain a possibility in Christian ethics.

> Perhaps there are situations where sacrificial love, with forgiveness at the heart of it, can make a difference, and can even empower. One thinks of Nelson Mandela, released after twenty-seven years in jail, patently entitled to wreak vengeance on his tormentors, and who responds by forgiving his jailers. Or one thinks of Tomas Borge, a Nicaraguan Sandinista fighter, captured by the Contras and brutally tortured, confronting his torturer after the war ended. The court entitled him to name the punishment appropriate for his torturer. Borge responded, "My punishment is to forgive you." Such instances build up a moral capital on which the rest of us can draw: supposing, just supposing, that an act of forgiveness on our part could tip the scales toward compassion rather than brutality [in the world].[12]

Our point in highlighting *The Sunflower* here is to show that forgiveness is a complex issue that we tend to oversimplify. In that oversimplification, Christians have often abused the abused; indeed, we have further victimized them by making demands for forgiveness. We fail to understand that there are particular consequences that come from the level of objectification they have received. Just as the Jews were treated as less than human, abuse and abandonment dehumanize victims. We are not denying the power that forgiveness can have, but we must avoid careless practices and messages that further objectify those most in need of compassion. It is important to expose these careless practices for what they are.

Careless Practices of Forgiveness

It is not as if Christians have intended to do damage as they talk about the need to forgive abusers for the ways in which the victimized are harmed in this life. The intentions, we would hope, are to help persons grow in their relationship with God and move on to greater and greater maturity in Christ. The rather traditional message that we are to forgive those who trespass against us—which, of course, was originally spoken by Christ himself while teaching his disciples—points us in the direction of a theology of forgiveness in general. The problem is that many theologically untenable

12. Wiesenthal, *Sunflower*, 122–23.

assumptions have augmented the words of Jesus, and such additions have become damaging and toxic, theologically, yes, but also "clinically."

Valparaiso University professor Mark Schwehn taught an honor's seminar of Christian students from various denominational affiliations, and introduced a unit on forgiveness. Despite their theological differences, Schwehn remarks,

> They seemed to agree with one another completely about certain basic features of forgiveness. Whatever it was, they all said, it had to be offered unconditionally and unilaterally to those who had wrongly offended or otherwise injured them. It did not matter whether the offender was repentant or contrite. Nor did it even matter whether the offender knew that he or she had been forgiven by the victim. Forgiveness, whatever it was exactly, was something undertaken primarily, sometimes exclusively, for the sake of the forgiver. Forgiveness relieved the offended party from feelings of revenge or resentment so that he or she could "move on."[13]

These sentiments should not surprise us. They are representative of generically Christian ideas common today (and are shared by non-Christians as well). Again, in passing on such messages about forgiveness we believe that no one is intending to be *cruel* to the sinned-against, and so a different word is appropriate. The effects of the messages may be unintentional, but such ideas can be extremely damaging. The words *careless theology* are utilized in the attempt to name what has gone wrong. The following pages will identify the issues of such a theology. We hope to offer a *careful* reading of the stories of the sinned-against as a source for a better theological interpretation of what forgiveness really means.

Careless Definitions of Forgiveness

Sometimes the best way to define something is to describe what it is *not*. We will very briefly consider the implications of a type of "forgiveness *theologia negativa*." Attempting to discern the difficulty of forgiveness for the sinned-against requires consideration of the following misunderstandings. And so, we want to press that forgiveness is not: 1. unilateral and unconditional; 2. absolution; 3. instantaneous; 4. forgetting; 5. a demand for reconciliation; or 6. a decision of the will alone.

    1. Forgiveness is not unilateral and unconditional.

13. Schwehn, "Human Conditions."

Forgiveness as unilateral and unconditional, despite what some Christians think (including Mark Schwehn's class mentioned above), is assumed to be biblical. But true biblical forgiveness most often *necessarily* requires repentance on the part of the offender, which is then either accepted or rejected by the offended. More generally, forgiveness is a relational transaction between two people with the possibility of reconciliation in some cases. To say that forgiveness can be unconditional, i.e., not based on repentance, is simply oxymoronic. To say that forgiveness is a solitary choice of the heart done unilaterally by the one wounded, is simply untrue. We are not saying that persons who have been abused or abandoned may not need to move past the power of the experience through a type of "radical acceptance"[14] of its effects and a reclamation of their truest selves. But this is not technically forgiveness. Dietrich Bonhoeffer, for example, in his much-quoted opening to *The Cost of Discipleship*, critiques unconditional forgiveness dispensed by the church as being at the very heart of what he means by cheap grace. "Cheap grace is the preaching of forgiveness without requiring repentance, baptism without church discipline, Communion without confession, absolution without personal confession."[15] At the center of Bonhoeffer's focus is the consent of the German church to Hitler's actions, its belief in its own righteousness, and its refusal to take responsibility for the fate of millions of Jews. Forgiving someone without requiring anything of them, namely confession and repentance, allows them to continue evil behavior unchecked. It minimizes the *cost* with which the abused or abandoned have had to live. As Bonhoeffer so aptly says, grace is a free gift particularly of God to us. But it must never be seen as cheap, in light of Christ's sacrifice. Or as the writer of Hebrews implies, sinners who are not repentant "are crucifying the Son of God all over again and subjecting him to public disgrace" (Heb 6:6). In a similar fashion, requiring the wounded to forgive in the face of the reality of an unrepentant abuser is also disgraceful—dis-graceful to the abused. We tend to offer more grace to the unrepentant than we do to the victims themselves.

---

14. Radical acceptance is a clinical term, utilized by Dialectical Behavioral Therapy, that states a deep, heartfelt acceptance of the circumstances of one's life, past and present, can decrease a person's suffering. It is a movement that progresses beyond a stage of resistance that (rightly) declares "this should not be!" to the acknowledgment that this is my reality. Implied is a level of self-acceptance and love, that I have done what I needed to survive.

15. Bonhoeffer, *Cost of Discipleship*, 47.

> Julie: *I worked with a young man whose mother perpetrated various types of abuse and abandonment throughout his life. As a young adult, he made the choice to distance himself from his mother for his own safety and mental health. For several years his mother has attempted to contact him in order to reconnect. Her message to him is, "Why are you so mad at me? Why can't we have a relationship?" She tries to use guilt and manipulation to get him to be part of her life. But there has never been any acknowledgment by the mother of how her actions hurt her son. This young man choosing to be part of his mother's life would not be forgiveness—particularly since she has never apologized for it. It would be a continuation of the power and control dynamic that has always been if he invited her back into his life without a willingness to change on her part.*

Forgiveness, then, is transactional. It requires true repentance on the part of the abuser. True repentance can only be trusted when it is accompanied by real and consistent change. After a repentance is offered, the one abused has more of what she or he needs to forgive. But even then, it can still require a process, and should not be demanded. Most worrisome for the abused is forgiving the person only to be re-abused because the repentance was temporary. While Jesus tells us to forgive someone seventy times seven, he does not imply that this should be done unilaterally, without repentance. We might suggest that such forgiveness can only come from an already empowered position. It would not be compatible with Jesus' character or consistent with his actions for him to demand endless forgiveness from those severely oppressed by others, or to imply that they must do so regardless of whether repentance has been offered or not.

2. Forgiveness is not absolution.

The meaning of absolution is different from forgiveness. Absolution implies that a person is freed from any blame or guilt, *as if the offending event never occurred*. It also has the connotation that the guilty person be released from any consequences, penalties, or obligations. Although the word is used in Christian circles, it is primarily used to talk about God's absolution of a repentant sinner. There is certainly scriptural support for the idea that God makes a sinner white as snow (Ps 51:7), and throws her or his sins into the sea (Mic 7:10), and places the sins as far away as the east is from the west (Ps 103:12). Even if some actions are required as penance in an official confession, the promise is full release from guilt and consequences because of Christ's atoning work.

But it is questionable if forgiving the other requires this type of full release, as if pretending the event(s) never happened. While some definitions of forgiveness require that the victim releases the right for personal vengeance, forgiveness should not set aside justice on every level; it does not mean that victims must refrain from working with the law in order to achieve justice in a courtroom. But this is sometimes the message victims receive. "You aren't being a good Christian if you press charges." If they are to truly forgive they must not hold their perpetrators responsible, and not pursue action within the legal system. This implies that forgiveness and justice are mutually exclusive. It also implies that we should not hold persons accountable in any way for wrongdoing, including outright crimes. This idea only intensifies a victim's sense of powerlessness. If we take the idea of forgiveness to this extreme, we actually enable abusers to continue patterns of destructive and criminal behavior, when prosecution could stop them.

Julie: *My concern about advocating for forgiveness leading to absolution is that it is in our human nature to simplify and try to resolve complex issues. In my work with abuse survivors, there just isn't one answer when it comes to legal prosecution. I have worked with survivors whose abusers were never reported or prosecuted, to their detriment. One woman told me that she lives with fear and guilt about what her perpetrator inflicted on others later because she remained silent. She wonders if she could have saved others from what she experienced. The thoughts she has about the abuse being her fault is now doubled, because not coming forward earlier, which hurt others, stands as proof that she "deserved" treatment by the perpetrator because she is a horrible person. I have worked with other survivors whose abusers were reported and prosecuted. This also had complex consequences. These individuals and their families experienced intense scrutiny and questioning by law enforcement, prosecutors, and defense attorneys. Some were required to testify in front of their abusers in court, giving graphic details about what was done to them. They were re-traumatized by these experiences. I have worked with survivors who did report their abuse and were not believed by those in their lives or did not have enough evidence to move toward prosecution. These individuals were left to continue life without any outward justice, some in the very same environment that allowed the abuse in the first place. Each scenario involves pain and suffering for the survivor, whether prosecution takes place or not. Nonetheless, taking away the possibility for justice altogether under the guise that we should forgive and absolve the abuser is not the appropriate alternative.*

Absolution is not forgiveness if it means acting as if the events of abuse never occurred. This is particularly the case in the consideration of whether or not legal action should be taken. Neither path—prosecution or choosing not to prosecute—is without its complexities and consequences. Both options intensify and illuminate the brokenness that lingers in the wake of abuse. Each individual must choose which path to take. The bottom line is that it is *not* unchristian to hold perpetrators accountable for their actions in a court of law.

3. Forgiveness is not instantaneous.

One wayward definition of forgiveness has to do with calling the victimized to fast resolution. There is a danger in forgiveness happening too quickly, or demanding instantaneous mercy. It was striking how within forty-eight hours after the Oklahoma City bombing in April 1995, billboards all over Oklahoma City popped up offering forgiveness to the guilty. It is problematic to offer quick forgiveness when the full weight of the pain and injury have not been thoroughly realized, let alone processed or dealt with. In a way, a careless practice of quick forgiveness, as sometimes preached by the church, is a means of denying, avoiding, or covering over the pain that makes us uncomfortable. It is easier to sweep things under the rug so that we do not have to look at the underside of life than it is to face the messiness and damaging consequences of the wounded in our midst. It is evidence of our addiction to instant gratification to force the afflicted to quickly forgive and get over it. But crucial in helping others with forgiveness is to understand that it is often a long and painful journey, which we will see as this chapter progresses.

Julie: *Susan was a client who told me about how her husband would physically abuse her when he was drunk. She quickly followed up with how she does not hold it against him because he had a tough childhood and was abused himself. With more processing, however, it struck me that what she was calling forgiveness was really her need to quickly move on from the abuse as a survival technique. If Susan became angry with her husband, protected herself, or left the relationship, she put herself in even more danger. It was safer for her to forgive quickly as a means of diffusing the situation. To do this she often put the blame on herself. The dynamic of their relationship had reinforced a message to her that she deserved the abuse. Ironically, this seemed to give Susan some sense of power back. If the abuse was her fault, she thought she could somehow change to keep it from happening again. What she failed to realize was that she could not control his random acts of violence no matter how she tried to change or adapt. In her case, what looked like quick forgiveness after each explosive episode actually perpetuated her abuse.*

Forgiveness, then, should not be done too "quickly" if it essentially tries to erase the event or if it actually perpetuates abuse. There may be a conscious relief in quick forgiveness, but it is most likely that the unconscious will still hold the pain and attempt to process it in stealth-like and unhealthy ways of which the person is unaware. What is certainly true is that we should not force a person to hastily or hurriedly forgive as a communal coping mechanism to assuage *our* discomfort. There is no specified timing where one size fits all.

4. Forgiveness is not forgetting.

Occasionally the church's worship and practice, which often fails to pay attention to the real needs of those who have been sinned against, suggests and even celebrates a "forgive and forget" practice. Such a culture is actually harmful to both the sinner and the sinned-against. The admonition to "forget" can be dangerous. While forgiveness may come, it is not wise to forget abuse in such a way that someone can become hurt again. While the hope and goal is that persons can be set free from the power of the abuser and that the multilayered and pervasive effects can be mended, a "forgive and forget" culture that implies the abused should act as if nothing ever happened, can be extremely jeopardous and do greater injury. Forgetting is not a biblical concept, except for God's mysterious ability to do so. As has been said strongly before, healing is not about denying what occurred or simply glossing over the pain. The goal is that persons would no longer be defined by the events of the abuse they endured as they reclaim their lives. Forgetting is never the goal, if by that we mean denying that these events happened. If by forgetting we mean a deep healing and a new level of freedom overall, then perhaps the word is appropriate. What is important here is that the very ability to forgive will often come as a *consequence* of being self-defined by something new, something greater than victimization. Forgetting does not enable forgiveness, but can hinder it.

Julie: John was a client who had been viciously abused by his father when he was a child. He developed a keen sense of paying attention to his environment by paying attention to small, almost invisible clues as to how his father was feeling and might react. John says he would listen to how his father would rustle the newspaper as he ate breakfast in the morning. This would let John know how he should go about the day. If his father rustled the paper one way, John knew that he would most likely be ignored that day (a good thing), but if the newspaper was rustled a different way, the chances were good that John would need to be on guard so he didn't get thrown through a sliding glass door again. This survival strategy is not something that went away as John became an adult and moved out of his father's home. Even when John's environment was safe, he still lived in a constant state of hypervigilence. Later in this chapter, we will discuss how trauma can affect the brain and body, but John could no more forget to be on guard than he could forget to breathe. It was what kept him safe. If we equate forgiveness with forgetting, we ask some survivors not only to do the impossible, but to surrender their coping mechanisms, and to surrender themselves to an intolerable vulnerability.

Forgiveness, then, is not tied—perhaps, *should* not be tied—to forgetting what has occurred. There are reasons to remember, one of the most important of which is self-protection. If my dog bites me when I am eating, I might forgive the dog because I love him, but it would do me well to remember what happened the last time I ate in front of him, in order to avoid repeating what happened. It is also important to realize that coping mechanisms themselves have been ways for the abused to survive. These arise out of memories. An abuse survivor may need them less and less as they heal, but we who represent the church should not rip them from their hands. Persons need to remember what occurred, and the idea that they are to forgive and forget is anything but helpful.

5. Forgiveness is not a demand for reconciliation.

Another important caution is to recognize that although reconciliation is a very strong theme in Scripture, reconciliation is not always the appropriate goal of the forgiving process, and perhaps should never be the goal for the truly abused. We would not ask a rape victim to reconcile with her perpetrator, period. The true goal is the safety of the one who has been assaulted. If those involved were in a relationship previously, the question of reconciliation becomes more complicated. Particularly if there has been no repentance, reconciliation is dangerous. Where there is repentance and a true amending of life and behavior, trust must still be earned. This requires a great deal of time for repeated and habitual patterns of trustworthiness to be cultivated. Even under these conditions, the sinned-against may never regain trust. But the church has sometimes pushed a type of reconciliation between the abused and the abuser that actually covers over the damage done by the offense, because the church cannot easily tolerate conflict. What matters most for the abused is an internal reconciliation, if you will, where a reintegration of parts of the self becomes a reality. If relational reconciliation occurs, it is often a consequence of this inward healing.

Julie: Janice grew up with a mentally ill father and a mother who struggled with substance abuse. When she was a teenager her uncle started sexually abusing her when the family would get together for holidays. Eventually, Janice reported the abuse and the uncle was prosecuted; however, several family members held her accountable for the "breakup" of the family, believing the uncle was innocent. Many years later, Janice has a rational understanding of what leads to the environment she grew up in and does not wish her family any ill will, but she is unwilling to have her children exposed to it, and certainly not have them around this uncle. But she faces anger and resentment from her family for not "getting over" her abuse, and therefore has in fact attempted many times to spend time with certain family members. Each time she returns to that environment she is plagued by nightmares for days, sometimes weeks afterward. She cannot go to work. She cannot take care of her children. Reconciliation for her is not safe, it is not effective, it is not responsible. The family is still made up of persons she cannot, perhaps should not, trust.

Reconciliation simply cannot come without true repentance and substantial change on the part of the abuser. But even where these have taken place and been proven over time, reconciliation can be hindered by lingering "triggers" that go very deep in those who have been victimized. The potential for reconciliation does not need to be abandoned forever, however, in light of the grace of God in the process of healing and bringing new creation. But just like forgiveness cannot be rushed, neither can reconciliation. One of the virtues the church needs to bring as a gift toward the abused is patience.

6. Forgiveness is not a decision of the will alone.

In addition to the fact that Christians differ in their understanding of how the *will* operates (based on their dependence on the philosophies and ethical mechanisms of Plato or Aristotle or others), deeper understandings of the functions of the brain have more recently informed what we know about decision-making. In the careless demand on victims to forgive their perpetrators, Christians have at times implied that this is a decision fully under their control. And when victims find themselves unable to do so, the message is clearly conveyed that there is something wrong with them—usually encased in spiritual terms. In light of the discussions above, forgiveness is precisely not under their control, if we rightly mean by forgiveness a transaction between persons that can never be unilateral or unconditional, because it requires something beyond them, namely the true repentance of the offender. But beyond that, the church would do well to educate itself about the effects of trauma on the brain. Just as trauma affects more than the rational brain, more than the rational brain must be healed in order for deeper levels of forgiveness to ever transpire. Thus a section on the effects of trauma on the brain offered by Julie is in order here.

The Traumatized Brain

In order to understand how difficult forgiveness is for the sinned-against, we will be using the word *trauma* to describe what they have gone through. This includes sexual, physical, emotional, and spiritual abuse, neglect, abandonment, acts of violence, or "any event, series of events, or set of circumstances experienced by an individual as physically or emotionally harmful or life-threatening with lasting adverse effects on the individual's functioning and mental, physical, social, emotional, or spiritual well-being."[16] In light of what we know about how trauma affects persons on a psychic and physical level, forgiveness can be, perhaps even *should* be seen as a long-term and complex process. Forgiveness itself is not the goal, but only one of the possible outcomes of the process of trauma resolution. Experts in the field of neuropsychology have been attempting to explain and treat the effects of trauma for many years, and have made great strides with new technology in the last twenty years that can actually show the differences in brain development between people who have lived through traumatic experiences and those who have not.[17] Perhaps we do not always fully recognize the intricacy of such issues. Early and/or present psychological interventions focusing on one or two aspects of the trauma experience have been highly used, of course, like creating a narrative of the experience in traditional "talk" therapies. In recent trends current experts assert the importance of recognizing how the whole body is affected by trauma, and have expanded therapeutic

16. This definition of trauma comes from the Substance Abuse and Mental Health Services Administration: "SAMHSA's Concept of Trauma," 7.

17. Van der Kolk, *Body Keeps Score*, 39–47.

approaches. It seems that the Christian response to trauma (specifically abuse or neglect) is often to emphasize and focus on forgiveness, as if the suffering experienced by the abused is solely due to negative feelings toward the perpetrator, implying that their suffering will cease if they forgive. This neglects current research about the effects of trauma on the brain and body at a pre- or unconscious level, or perhaps more precisely, at the level of the limbic system that is "deeper" than conscious decision-making.[18]

Again, we make an assumption that most Christians who care about trauma survivors and want to be part of their lives, do so with good intentions. As a young clinician I (Julie) had the same good intentions with my clients but soon I realized an important reality: when it came to the individual experiences of trauma survivors in my practice, I did not know what I didn't know. I was driven to learn more when I realized this. This lack of knowledge in the church can be dangerous. This is not to cast blame, but to emphasize a sense of the sacred ground pastors especially may be treading on when a survivor shares his or her story and asks for advice or support. Many trauma therapies (trauma-focused CBT, EMDR, sensorimotor psychotherapy) recognize the need to provide survivors with psycho-education about the long-term neurological effects of these experiences. Perhaps such education would also be a good place to start for those in the church who care about them.

Karyn Purvis from Texas Christian University created an intervention for traumatized children called "Trust-Based Relational Intervention" or "TBRI."[19] In this model she explains that when children are born, the survival parts of the brain are established based on genetics. Much of the rest of the brain's development is primarily influenced by the child's interactions with her caregivers and her environment. The part of the brain that directs survival tasks such as sucking, breathing, as well as fight, flight, and freeze responses, has been coined the "downstairs" brain by Daniel J. Siegel and Tina Payne Bryson. More complex functions including complex thought, reasoning, emotion regulation, and speech are a function of the "upstairs brain." Traumatic experiences in childhood seem to create an over-functioning "downstairs" brain that is primarily focused on survival, safety, and vigilance in the environment. This can leave the "upstairs" brain underdeveloped.[20] This may end up looking like an individual who struggles with emotion regulation, with managing resources in order to achieve a goal (executive functioning), and/or with successfully navigating

---

18. Van der Kolk, *Body Keeps Score*, 60–61.
19. See Purvis et al., "Trust-Based Relational Intervention (TBRI)."
20. Siegel and Bryson, *Whole Brain Child*, 38–41.

relationships. Stripping the process of trauma recovery down to just the idea of forgiveness will not be helpful for survivors who do not understand why they cannot seem to fit and function in the world the way others can. Even if they do not feel anger and resentment toward their abuser(s), they often still feel more generalized anxiety or depression, or even a sense of isolation and anger toward themselves for a perceived failure to navigate life. They do not know that the downstairs brain is too busy protecting them to also allow the upstairs brain to go about its crucial tasks.

In addition, researchers like Bessel van der Kolk have found that there are distinct differences in how traumatic experiences are stored as memories in the brain, depending on the presence of trauma. Study participants demonstrated that memories of pleasant experiences could be talked about in story form as part of a timeline. Memories of traumatic events were experienced as vivid pictures, body sensations (smells, tastes, tension, tightness), strong emotions, and an overall sense of being stuck outside of time—and time is necessary to create narratives.[21]

Here is how I (Julie) might explain it to a client: *Let's say you and I are sitting in my office and there is a thunderstorm outside. I have never heard of or experienced a thunderstorm. My heart might start beating fast and I might feel terrified that the world is coming to an end because there is a booming sound and large streaks of light coming from the sky. Now, what if you said to me, "This is a thunderstorm. We are safe inside. It won't last forever and the rain will be good for watering the grass and cleaning the air. Oh, and a rain jacket would be helpful." My emotions would then subside and the experience would be stored in my long-term memory as data in my "upstairs" brain— Thunderstorm: normal; stay inside; wear a rain jacket outside. My mind would have no need to save the emotion or body sensations I experienced as part of the memory because the threat was resolved. But if you hadn't been sitting with me and I was not able to resolve the threat or perhaps I was injured by the thunderstorm, my "downstairs" brain would save that memory as primarily sensory experience and emotion, because my fight, flight, or freeze reaction would be most helpful for my survival if I was to experience another thunderstorm. From there anything that sounded, smelled, or looked like a thunderstorm would trigger the sensory and emotional experience I had before, without full access to the rational part of my brain to make sense of what was going on.* This is a practical example of what the brain does during a post-traumatic episode.

Individuals who experience post-traumatic stress, or are diagnosed with post-traumatic stress disorder, live with the possibility of current

---

21. Van der Kolk, *Body Keeps Score*, 177–78.

thoughts, images, body sensations, emotions, or beliefs triggering a traumatic memory and with having their "upstairs" brain hijacked by their body's fight, flight, or freeze response, even if, and this is important, they do not have any negative feelings toward their perpetrator. Marsha Linehan's *Dialectical Behavioral Therapy* model asserts that a dialectic is two opposing things being true at the same time.[22] The dialectic in this example is that a trauma survivor can be fully participating in the process of forgiveness and still experience the anger (fight), fear (flight), or shutdown (freeze) of a traumatic flashback, long after they have forgiven. To tell them that these "limbic" reactions are evidence of a lack in their resolve to forgive is simply cruel.

Further, contrary to some Christian belief, the emotion of anger can be a sign of healing as well as a motivator to stand up for oneself, reject abusive patterns, or fight injustice in the same or in other relationships. The creator of one psychotherapy model, Pat Ogden, asserts that the *body* stores in its memory systems how it responded to a traumatic event as well as how it *wanted* to respond to that event.[23] Those who have survived a physical, sexual, or even emotional threat can tell stories of how they fought or ran from their perpetrator. Others shared that they were able to survive by staying still and frozen, essentially "playing dead" to minimize the damage of the abuse.[24] Ogden teaches that these responses become "procedural memory," which is defined as memory for process and function and is seen as habitual *automatic* responses like movements, postures, gestures, and autonomic arousal patterns. In other words, individuals who have identified a habitual shutdown or freeze response in stressful situations may need to access the anger and/or movement of a more active body response to the threat in order to actually feel less triggered by an event. The emotion itself can be part of an important step in rewiring the brain.[25] This is thwarted if Christians make anger antithetical to forgiveness, or imply that if anger returns to a victim, they have not forgiven properly.

Understanding the effects of trauma on the brain can give us insight into the *non-volitional* nature of victims' responses. This is key. I (Julie) worked with a client who was an abuse survivor and was plagued with images of how she would kill her abuser. While she had no intention of acting on these thoughts, she reported feeling ashamed and scared of how angry she felt because it was not in alignment with who she wanted to be. Every

---

22. Linehan, *DBT Skills Training Manual*, 4–5.
23. Ogden et al., *Trauma and the Body*, 247–49.
24. Levine, *Waking the Tiger*, 95–97.
25. Ogden et al., *Trauma and the Body*, 22, 239.

time the images came to mind she would try to distract herself (flight) or shut down emotionally (freeze) because she saw herself as the threat. In reprocessing the memory with eye movement desensitization and reprocessing (EMDR),[26] she was able to experience her anger without shutting down and realized that she also felt incredibly sad. She said the anger felt safer, less vulnerable than the sadness underneath it.

Another aspect of trauma recovery is grief. Brené Brown, a well-known researcher of shame, recounts her understanding of forgiveness in an interview where she says, "In order for forgiveness to really happen, something has to die . . . In faith communities where forgiveness and love are easy, there isn't enough blood on the floor to make sense of that." Brown states that according to her research the two effects that are most frightening to humans are shame and grief.[27] My client's revelation about the anger she felt toward her abuser will require her to grieve the death of her childhood, who she might have been; the death of the belief that her parents would protect her and believe her story; the death of feeling safe in her own body; the death of believing that the faith she had been taught was big enough for her life experiences. That is a lot of death, a lot of grief. Trauma survivors have had power taken away from them. We would suggest that those of us who want to be supporters of the abused need to be able to sit with their anger until the survivor feels safe enough to feel vulnerable and to grieve fully. But we often short-circuit the process by implying they should hurry the process in order to be over it. The timing is their call. Not ours. Bessel van der Kolk says:

> Nobody wants to remember trauma. In that regard society is no different from victims themselves. We all want to live in a world that is safe, manageable, and predictable, and victims remind us that this is not always the case. In order to understand trauma, we have to overcome our natural reluctance to confront that reality and cultivate the courage to listen to the testimonies of survivors.[28]

---

26. See Shapiro, *Eye Movement Desensitization*. EMDR is a psychotherapy that focuses on decreasing the symptoms and emotional distress that can be the result of traumatic life experiences. A therapist will use a specific protocol to help a client identify specific disturbing memories and pay attention to specific aspects of that memory (visual, emotional, sensory). Then bilateral stimulation (moving the eyes back and forth or tapping left then right) is used to allow the brain to reprocess the memory and experience a sense of neutrality when the client remembers the incident. This treatment can be highly effective, and should be seen as a potential "means of grace" in the same category as medication and talk therapy.

27. Brown, "Brené Brown's Return to Faith."

28. Van der Kolk, *Body Keeps Score*, 196–97.

Too often we have heard survivors tell of how well-meaning friends, family, and even clergy have added to their hurt by invalidating the survivor's experiences and emotions. We can only assume that some of these responses come from an uncomfortable empathetic response that the listener cannot tolerate. The message to the survivor then becomes, "You need to _____ (forgive, move on, etc.) because your suffering makes me uncomfortable." Instead, a survivor's experiences need to be believed and her or his emotions need to be validated. Crucial for anyone in contact with the abused and abandoned is the development of "distress tolerance." This is the ability to listen to and hold carefully the pain of others without reacting out of our own need to avoid discomfort. Regardless of a listener's internal emotional response to the sharing of a survivor (which can be a mixture of strong emotions such as disgust, fear, shock, sadness, anger, judgment, etc.), the response needs to be to acknowledge what the survivor is saying accompanied by verbal and nonverbal communication that his or her difficult experiences are comfortably received with acceptance. It may be difficult, but this tolerance can be developed with practice and self-awareness.

One client told me (Julie) he had been part of a small men's group led by his pastor. After being invited to tell his story, my client shared how an abusive stepfather terrorized him and his mother throughout his life. He talked about being belittled, beaten, and shot at in order to protect his mother. The pastor was quiet when my client finished. He looked around the room at all of the men and said, "None of us will ever speak of this again." My client did not talk about it again for many years, to his detriment. Not being able to talk about a negative event most often increases the negative emotions around the event, and can result in anxiety and depression. It is an unfair and selfish expectation for the church and its clergy to expect such victims to anesthetize their suffering.

More positively, and in her own experience, Brené Brown says, "I went to church thinking it would be an epidural for my pain. . . . What I found was that faith and church were like a midwife who sat by me saying, 'Push. It's supposed to hurt.'"[29] But this requires the church to *foster patience* and walk alongside those who suffer on their sometimes long journey called the healing process. Such patience will not force forgiveness prematurely. It is often the case that as this healing process progresses, focusing on other deep issues of recovery, forgiveness becomes a possibility, almost serendipitously.

---

29. Brown, "Brené Brown's Return to Faith."

Careless Theologies of Forgiveness

Clarifying the Theology of Repentance

Above we have discussed careless *practices* of forgiveness, which certainly have theological undertones, but we move now to discuss theology proper. Preaching and teaching on forgiveness can be theologically careless in a variety of ways. We will address several points in the following discussion. We start with perhaps the most significant issue theologically, namely, the meaning of repentance and its surrounding implications. We start by examining God's forgiveness of sin and sinners.

To be blunt on this point, what one believes about receiving God's forgiveness depends heavily one one's theological tradition. If we were to draw a line on a spectrum of theological positions regarding conversion (also known by a variety of phrases, such as new birth, salvation, or "becoming a Christian"), there would be the wide extremes, and everything in between, regarding how God acts in the giving of this converting grace. To use precise theological words, how monergistically (defined as God's action apart from our participation) or synergistically (defined as God's action with our participation) does God save us? Unless one stands staunchly on the side of unconditional election and predestination (monergism), there is some sense that as we respond to God's calling, or prevenient grace, through repentance and faith, God responds to our response by offering "justification" and all of its concomitants. This is synergism. Our forgiveness is God's converting act that depends in some sense on our responses of repentance and faith. And so, unless we make "saving grace" unconditional—either from a Calvinist perspective on one side, or a universalist perspective on the other—our repentance matters in the "transaction" that occurs, even though grace is free.

There are two different kinds of repentance in the *ordo salutis* (order of salvation). The repentance that transpires at conversion can best be described as godly sorrow. There is a sense of our guilt before God that requires confession of sin, and a confession that we are unable to save ourselves from our sin and brokenness. Although there is a long historical debate about the presence of sin in the lives of Christians after conversion, repentance subsequent to our initial confession and reception of God's forgiveness also implies, beyond godly sorrow, that we will amend our lives, away from sin and toward holiness. God then responds to our ongoing repentance with forgiving and *sanctifying* grace, the free gift of God that enables our growth into the Christlikeness to which we are called. Again, there are a wide variety of theological conclusions on these points, depending on where one's tradition lands.

For our purposes here, the church has often strongly taught that anyone who has been harmed by other persons should forgive them, *whether or not* they have repented, in the first sense of feeling godly sorrow for what they have done wrong, or in the second sense of amending their lives through renouncing their harming ways. But when the church gives this message of *unconditional* forgiveness, are we not demanding more of the survivor than we, at least in some traditions, expect from God? Again, if our own salvation is *conditioned* upon our confession and repentance before God converts or forgives, how can we expect the sinned-against to live under a rule or law we do not even expect God to follow?

One of the key passages on forgiveness in the New Testament is Luke 17:14. This is the text where Jesus tells his disciples to forgive seven times, which comes in verse four. But the previous verses are absolutely crucial for a proper interpretation. Jesus said to his disciples: "Things that cause people to stumble are bound to come, but woe to anyone through whom they come. It would be better for them to be thrown into the sea with a millstone tied around their neck than to cause one of these little ones to stumble. So watch yourselves. If your brother or sister sins against you, rebuke them; and if they repent, forgive them. Even if they sin against you seven times in a day and seven times come back to you saying 'I repent,' you must forgive them." The context of Jesus' teaching on forgiveness here is fascinating. It is clear that Jesus connects his comments about forgiving others to one of the clearest texts in Scripture about the punishing fate that awaits *those who abuse* "little ones." He then immediately turns to the topic of what to do with those who sin against us. We now become the sinned-against. What should be our response? The first thing we are to do is rebuke them. We are to rebuke, which means to strongly reprimand, reproach, reprove, or scold. The English word comes from the French, *rebuchier*, which means to hack down or beat back. This is what we are to do to those who sin against us. The only condition by which we move from rebuke to forgiveness, according to this text, is "if they repent." If they say "I repent," then, and only then, are we required to forgive them. And if they continue to hurt us, we are to forgive them again, but only as they again repent—not only feeling godly sorrow, but amending their ways.

The church does not mention, does not teach, does not preach much about the rebuking stage. It thus strips the sinned-against of their right to their anger, rage, and other emotions that are a natural human response to abuse and abandonment, which should never have happened to them. From God's perspective, it would be better for abusers "to be thrown into the sea with a millstone tied around their neck than to cause one of these little ones to stumble." If they repent, feel godly sorrow, confess, and amend their ways, then forgiveness is available to them, from God, and from their victims in due course. But there is no implication whatsoever here that they are to be forgiven without owning up to what they have done.

In an article that probes the question "What Does the Bible Really Say about Forgiveness," Marla Mayo suggests:

> While Jesus is certainly an advocate of forgiveness—... he claims the authority to forgive sins on earth (Matthew 9:6; Mark 2:10; Luke 5:23) and announces his mission as one of "forgiveness of sins" (Luke 24:47)—he is far from consistent on the issue of interpersonal forgiveness. When he cries out from the cross, he does not say to his attackers, "I forgive you," or, as he has before, "Your sins are forgiven you." Instead, he prays that God might forgive them. Considering that earlier in Luke's Gospel, Jesus makes it very clear that repentance was required for forgiveness (17:3), and since no repentance is forthcoming from the men who are attacking Jesus, we might assume that forgiveness is a non-issue in this case. Indeed, nowhere does Jesus plainly state that unconditional forgiveness is a virtue or a requirement for the new covenant community. However, in the same Gospel, Jesus does instruct his followers to "bless those who curse you [and] pray for those who abuse you" (Luke 6:28), which appears to be exactly what he is doing on the cross.[30]

This is significant for the sinned-against. Mayo puts it directly: "I ruffle a lot of feathers when I suggest that Jesus might not be forgiving his attackers as he is being crucified. But this interpretation pays off for victims who are concerned about living faithfully in the aftermath of violence."[31] Mayo here displays appropriate empathy for the abused, and highlights the difficulty of forgiving the unrepentant. "Instead of a Jesus who appears to be endlessly and impossibly forgiving, here is a Jesus who is true to his teachings and also easier to imitate. Praying for one's attacker is an easier—and much safer—task than offering unconditional forgiveness and reconciling with unrepentant abusers. Requiring repentance before granting forgiveness gives victims another way to protect themselves while remaining true to the biblical text."[32] Mark Schwehn offers a similar point: "Notice that Jesus does *not* forgive those who crucified him directly; he prays that the Father should do so. So we might say, remembering that only God finally has the power to forgive sins directly or indirectly through those acting in God's stead, that

---

30. Mayo, "What Does the Bible Really Say About Forgiveness?"
31. Mayo, "What Does the Bible Really Say About Forgiveness?"
32. Mayo, "What Does the Bible Really Say About Forgiveness?"

we should ask God to unilaterally and unconditionally forgive those who have injured us even though we may well require that some conditions be met before we forgive them."[33] Suggesting prayer for their enemies in due course is far different than demanding that the sinned-against unconditionally forgive their unrepentant abusers. According to Mayo, even Jesus did not do that.

Misreading the Parable

There is much in the parable of the "Unmerciful Servant" that we often miss. It is found in Matthew 18, and is offered as a teaching, particularly to Peter, who asks, "'Lord, how many times shall I forgive my brother or sister who sins against me? Up to seven times?' Jesus answered, 'I tell you, not seven times, but seventy-seven times'" (Matt 18:21–22). The parable follows. But what comes before Peter's question is also significant. A few verses before we find this teaching of Jesus:

> If your brother or sister sins, go and point out their fault, just between the two of you. If they listen to you, you have won them over. But if they will not listen, take one or two others along, so that 'every matter may be established by the testimony of two or three witnesses.' If they still refuse to listen, tell it to the church; and if they refuse to listen even to the church, treat them as you would a pagan or a tax collector. Truly I tell you, whatever you bind on earth will be bound in heaven, and whatever you loose on earth will be loosed in heaven. (Matt 18:15 18)

Clearly Jesus speaks here *against* unconditional forgiveness. If the sinner is not willing to appropriately respond, which implies acknowledging the sin with regret, we are to treat them as those we consider enemies. He further says that we have some say about the binding and loosing of such people. Also important to the context of the parable are verses even further back in the chapter. It is precisely the same chapter of the parable where we find words that echo Luke's: "If anyone causes one of these little ones—those who believe in me—to stumble, it would be better for them to have a large millstone hung around their neck and to be drowned in the depths of the sea. Woe to the world because of the things that cause people to stumble! Such things must come, but woe to the person through whom they come!" (Matt 18:67).

---

33. Schwehn, "Human Conditions."

A close reading of the parable of the Unmerciful Servant itself guides us in the question of unconditional forgiveness. First to note is the fact that the man who owed the king did not go to the king first, but rather he was summoned. Only then does he cry for mercy. We are told that the king did in fact release him from his obligation. What we do not often see is that this release had great "social" implications, because the punishment for not being able to pay his debt was that he, his wife, and his children be sold into slavery as the way to pay it. Without a close reading, we assume that his punishment would have been imprisonment because that is where he finally ends up. Because of the merciful king, the servant's wife and children are spared from a life of slavery.

The parable then moves to the servant's encounter with someone who owes him a debt. The implication is that even though he is a "fellow servant" this second man is even lower on the social scale than he is, or is lower because of his debt. Either way, the first servant has some power over the second, just as the king had power over the first. He has enough power to throw the second servant into jail until he repays the debt. He does not consider mercy an option, even though he had just had mercy displayed to him. This lack of mercy, then, is what enrages the king, but it could also be argued that the first servant's lack of a merciful response to the repentant attitude of the second servant proves that his own repentance was not legitimate in the first place. He simply wanted to avoid punishment. At this the king revokes his mercy on the first servant. But, again, what we fail to see is that even in the king's response to him, there is grace for "the innocent." The servant is thrown into jail. His wife and children are not sold into slavery.

In the end, Jesus does say, "This is how my heavenly Father will treat each of you unless you forgive your brother or sister from your heart." But there is no reason whatsoever to interpret this parable as a command for unconditional forgiveness. Neither servant denies the debt he owes. Neither servant refuses to take responsibility for the debt, but rather promises to make it right by repaying all they owe.

In light of this, we would like to strongly suggest that the church stop calling persons to unilateral and unconditional forgiveness that lets abusers off the hook, and torments the abused with an unreasonable, and often impossible, demand. "Biblical forgiveness is *not* unconditional. It does not happen in the absence of the offender, and it is not without practical implication. The forgiveness that Jesus taught—and some say demonstrated—is not a psychological exercise, or as one scholar puts it, 'ethical bungee jumping.' It is a bilateral process that at its best includes apology, repentance and reparation. When those things are lacking, forgiveness does not take hold.

It is for this reason that when he was hanging from the cross, Jesus uttered a prayer for his attackers rather than forgiving them directly."[34]

It might be right to encourage the abused to reach the stage eventually to pray for their abusers, especially praying for others who might still be in harm's way because of them. And if an abuser does truly repent, then the possibility of forgiveness enters the picture. But as too many victims are aware, such repentance is rare. The psyche that can abuse is the same psyche that is prone to denial, self-justification, and even self-righteousness. While forgiveness of the abuser by the abused may come if repentance ever occurs, it must never be rushed and it must "never encourage passive acceptance of victimization."[35] Just as all sins are not equally destructive, some levels of abuse will require much more time and work to find the deeper healing required to forgive. According to Ruth Duck, "The call to forgive must acknowledge that coming to terms with experiences of victimization takes time in proportion to the degree of violation."[36] The church should spend more time exposing abusers and rebuking them, especially abusers who are within its walls, and calling out what has remained in the shadows for far too long, than it does putting the abused under undeserved pressure. It is in such revealing acts that the church really stands in solidarity with the sinned-against.

Forgiveness from the Back Side

The Meaning of New Creation

It is becoming more and more popular in Christian and even secular culture to talk about the positive benefits of forgiveness for the one doing the forgiving: We forgive so that we can be freed from the power of the experience; we forgive because it is good *for us*. "As recently as May 19, 2019, Tim Herrera wrote a piece for the *New York Times* entitled 'Let Go of Your Grudges! They're Doing You No Good.' During the course of his column, he cited the huge Stanford Forgiveness Project, which has conclusively shown that forgiveness reduces stress, reduces anger (as it should), improves the health of your heart, and just generally enhances your physical and psychological well-being."[37] The point underlying such an idea is essentially true, and certainly logical. But language matters greatly. We believe that the word

---

34. Mayo, "Aurora and the Question of Forgiveness."
35. Duck, "Hospitality to Victims," 175.
36. Duck, "Hospitality to Victims," 175.
37. Cited in Schwehn, "Human Conditions."

forgive in the adage above should be changed, because it could imply that forgiveness is the *only* avenue to greater freedom and goodness. We would argue strongly that it is not forgiveness that frees us. We would rather say something deeper frees us so that we are then able to forgive. Likewise, whatever the substitute words are here, it is *that* which is good for us. It is through this new reality that freedom and goodness come to us. The problem is that language is often inadequate to convey the existential reality of what we want to describe. We are going to put on, or take up, a word image as a substitute for the word *forgiveness* in the adage that forgiveness is good for us. Our point is that the ability to forgive at all comes out a deeper experiential way of being. The order of the cart and horse matters here.

In the closing pages of chapter 9, we used the words *mending, adoption,* and *wholeheartedness*—each connected with the healing of violence, abandonment, and sexual abuse respectively. As an attempt to bind up these powerful words together under one pervasive and hope-filled reality in which we can participate, we invoke a biblical image—that of *new creation*.

It is *new creation* that frees us from the power of the experience of victimization; new creation is the means by which we reclaim our lives; new creation is the means of freedom and goodness we seek; new creation offers a healing that makes forgiveness (properly understood) a possibility.

But saying this, without the following caveat, could lead us down another dangerous path. A reaffirmation of one aspect of God's nature is key here. As argued in the first chapter, God is not a sadistic god. God does not force Godself on us without "consent." God does not dominate and beat us into submission. God does not force some sovereign symbol of power down our throats, even the power of our own salvation. God asks for our consent, always for our consent. God is a God of synergism, mutuality, and even deferential love. This does not imply that God was not with the victim throughout her or his entire abusive experiences(s), or imply that God does not weep in empathy presently. And consent for God's deeper work of healing here is not one more thing the victim has to do and "get right" in order for God to act. But by invoking the word *consent*, we are attempting to convey that God does not encroach upon or take advantage of a victim's vulnerability, but sits with her as Paraclete (comforter and companion) until she is capable of the invitation toward more. The church would do well to intentionally treat victims with such respect.

The call in this chapter to stop demanding quick, decisionistic, unilateral, and unconditional forgiveness of the abuser by the abused is crucial, for the demand can seem violating and nonconsensual. But this is in no way a denial of the need and the grace-enabled potential to move beyond the often paralyzing damage of victimization when the victim is ready to receive new creation grace. Christian hope speaks loudly about healing that is possible. But forgiveness is not the means by which we do that moving beyond. Too often we put this particular cart before this particular horse. It is the healing of new creation that makes us into people of reclamation. Reclamation is the strongly intentional recultivation of a wasteland. In new creation and reclamation, the old is gone, the new has come. New creation people progress in acting differently because they are new in their inner being. Certainly this is a *process*, where incapacitated victims become empowered survivors, just as butterflies do not instantly appear but require time in a cocoon. But new creation does not come only at the end of the process in our transformation. New creation—given by the grace of God and with the victim in the beginning, calling her forth to new life—remains and sustains throughout. New creation is not reserved only for sinners, but also for, perhaps peculiarly for, the sinned-against. So how does new creation relate then to forgiveness, now that we have established that forgiveness of an abuser is not the precondition of new creation?

A key aspect of new creation theology (which might more traditionally be called a theology of sanctification, or even therapeutic healing), is that the invited presence of the Holy Spirit, the resurrection life of the New Being, Jesus Christ, and the grace of God breaks in to a person's life with such power that transformation of the inner being results. A result of this grace-enabled transformation is the development of virtue.

Without offering a full-blown discussion of virtue ethics (from Aristotle, who was "Christianized" by Thomas Aquinas), it is important to say that the development of virtue is characteristic of new creation life, indeed, the development of character itself. How, then, might transformation of our character relate to our ability to forgive?

> Christians might resolve many of the issues surrounding the concept of forgiveness by re-conceptualizing the whole matter as one of character rather than individual acts. Instead of asking what exactly an act of forgiveness entails, ask what the virtue of forgiveness involves. Such a virtue would be part of what it means to be "Christ-like," and it might be subsumed as a smaller virtue under the larger virtue of charity [or love]. Forgivingness would involve the disposition to forswear revenge and resentment . . . However, like all the other Christian virtues, *charity and forgivingness would be governed by Christian practical wisdom*, the virtue that would enable Christians to forgive in the right way at the right time for the right reasons.[38]

---

38. Schwehn, "Human Conditions."

In other words, rather than teaching and preaching forgiveness as some type of willed decision, true forgiveness comes out of a nurtured character that expresses itself as virtue, enabled by grace. This character, if you will, not only involves a healing of one's spirituality, but holistic healing that addresses the deep needs of trauma recovery as well. This perspective allows us to reject that there is a type of forgiveness formula that applies to all situations. Just as love cannot be wrangled into one definition or one expression or one appropriation, so too forgiveness requires discernment and wisdom. Forgiveness, as Schwehn rightly says, is a smaller virtue guided by the overarching Christian virtue of love. Reclamation of the wasteland in the wake of abuse is a reclamation of the image of God in us, out of which we live and breathe. The image of God is our capacity to love. The process of new creation, then, develops the inner disposition of love (and heals the wounds that distort love), which results in loving acts. In other words, forgiveness is a loving act that comes out of a heart of love. It is in this context, then, that we can properly talk about forgiveness as releasing our desire for revenge, and "moving on." In light of the grace of new creation, victims can have an optimistic posture toward new empowerment for living. In a sense they are releasing the abuser through forgiveness, and releasing themselves from the abuser's power over them. Certainly, this is good for us. But this leads us to perhaps an uncomfortable place for us all: The Christian ethic of love requires that we consider not only what is ultimately good for us (which would be wrong to completely dismiss), but what is good for our neighbors and our enemies. Only by the grace of God can we forgive our enemies. In order for this ethic of Christlike love to become embodied in us, the ongoing nurturing of new creation within us is crucial. One thing is certain. It cannot be done alone.

The Need for New Creation Community

We begin this section with a simple but profound reality. Victims were damaged relationally, and will find healing relationally. So many people have been hurt in the context of dysfunctional family systems, or abusive relationships, or neglect and abandonment by those who supposedly loved them. In God's wisdom, the church is intended to be a place for the wounded to find parental figures, new siblings, healthy relationships, and trustworthy companions along life's way, for the wounded to be reclaimed and nurtured in love. The church is intended to be a new creation community for all.

And so, for those who wish to stand in solidarity with, and act on behalf of those who suffer, those of who have not significantly suffered (although we all suffer from life to various degrees) or have not been victimized, may invoke the idea of new creation community. In the pattern of Christ's love, most powerfully expressed on the cross, we call those who wish to be compassionate to take up a cruciform life that carries the crosses of the sinned-against.

Jesus states clearly that if we seek to be his disciples we must take up our cross in order to follow him: "Whoever wants to be my disciple must deny themselves and take up their cross daily and follow me. For whoever wants to save their life will lose it, but whoever loses their life for me will save it" (Luke 9:23–24, NIV). These verses are familiar to many of us. But we have not always understood the meaning of the call to pick up our crosses and what this entails. We have interpreted it to mean that we have a cross to carry from time to time, maybe an illness to bear or some period of personal struggle. In light of our present focus on the sinned-against, it is extremely important to resist the temptation to say they are bearing crosses. This is absolutely not the case! This is where the orthodox proclamation that Jesus' sacrifice was volitional is key. Enduring something that happens to us against our will is not "taking up our crosses." Cross-bearing is a deliberate, intentional, and conscious choice. Christ volitionally died on behalf of others as a means of rescue. We take up our crosses when we suffer *on behalf of others*. The purpose of cross-bearing is to love others. Sharing in the sufferings of Christ explicitly means embracing the lengths to which love will go, and then going there. Cross-bearing lives out the (secondary) purpose of our new creation, to love our neighbors as we love ourselves. In this, following the crucified and resurrected Christ calls Christians to the wounds of the sinned-against, willing to bind them in love.

We should not underestimate the restorative potential of presence. Stanley Hauerwas wrote a book that explores the issues surrounding the problem of evil, without being seduced by the typical and inadequate answers of theodicy—*Naming the Silences*. What makes the book so compelling is his use of narrative (both fictional and real-life scenarios), to get at inexplicable suffering. He strongly suggests that the experience of isolation is profound in the face of grief and pain. He weaves several stories together, all involving the death of children. In his conclusion he arranges, to great effect, a series of quotes from Nicholas Wolterstorff's *Lament for a Son*.[39] Wolterstorff is a Christian, and his grief does not cause him to question the existence of God, although "[h]e expresses surprise that the elements of the gospel—particularly the hope of resurrection—he thought 'would console

---

39. Wolterstorff, *Lament for a Son*.

did not.'"[40] Wolterstorff writes, "Eric is gone, here and now he is gone; now I cannot talk with him, now I cannot see him, now I cannot hug him, now I cannot hear of his plans for the future. That is my sorrow."[41] Then Hauerwas concludes his book by reminding the reader that there are no truly satisfying answers to the problem of evil. He ends with the following, including a quote from *Lament for a Son*:

> Just as Wolterstorff is not interested in false or easy answers, so he is not interested in false or easy comfort. So do not tell Wolterstorff that death—the death of Eric—is "not really so bad. Because it is. Death is awful, demonic. If you think your task as comforter is to tell me that really, all things considered, it's not so bad, you do not sit with me in my grief, but place yourself off in the distance away from me. Over there, you are of no help. What I need to hear from you is that you recognize how painful it is. I need to hear from you that you are with me in my desperation. To comfort me, you have to come close. Come sit beside me on my mourning bench."[42]

We as individuals, and as the new creation community called the church, are called to precisely this kind of restorative presence. In this sense, we take up our crosses when we carry the anguish that others bear. We do not force upon them the need to deny their pain and desperation. We do not imply that their sorrow is not that bad. We do not create barriers to their authentic expression in our midst. And we certainly do not try to solve the problem of evil in front of them, talking to ourselves while they shrink back into darkness. We humbly sit with them in love on their benches. We do not force hope down their throats. We *silently* hold for them a hope in present and future resurrection, hope for new creation and freedom, until that hope becomes theirs. Such resurrection will only come as we give them the dignity of personhood stolen from them. Such resurrection will only come when we cherish them as gifts to us. Such resurrection will only come as they know themselves genuinely accepted and deeply loved, by us and by the God of reviving grace and the God of new creation. Such love will allow the wounded to say salvation is for "me too" when they have so often felt excluded. A quote from Frankl:

> The thought transfixed me: for the first time in my life I saw the truth as it is set into song by so many poets, proclaimed as

---

40. Hauerwas, *Naming the Silences*, 149.
41. Wolterstorff, *Lament for a Son*, 31.
42. Hauerwas, *Naming the Silences*, 151; internal quote, Wolterstorff, *Lament for a Son*, 34.

the final word by so many thinkers. The truth—that love is the ultimate and the highest goal to which [we] can aspire. Then I grasped the meaning of the greatest secret that human poetry and human thought and belief have to impart: The salvation of [all humanity] is through love and in love.[43]

The love of God is fully manifested on the cross, and confirmed in the resurrection. The path to full salvation and new creation—for sinners, but especially for the sinned-against—is through love and in love. In love, God creates, invites, restores, revives reclaims; in love God mends, adopts, integrates, and brings wholeness of heart and life. In love God offers the grace of new creation transformation. In love, *God is able* to do immeasurably more than we can ask or imagine. This is our hope and faith. And so we end with a prayer, especially said here for all who have been victimized, who for far too long have waited alone on their mourning benches, and stood at the *back side* of the cross wondering if Christ's sacrifice was meant for them too:

> We pray that out of God's glorious riches God may strengthen you with power through the Spirit in your inner being, so that Christ may dwell in your hearts through faith. And we pray that you, being rooted and established in love, may have power, together with all the Lord's holy people, to grasp how wide and long and high and deep is the love of Christ, and to know this love that surpasses knowledge—that you may be filled to the measure of all the fullness of God. (Eph 3:16–19)

---

43. Frankl, *Man's Search for Meaning*, 37.

PART 2

Pastoral Resources

The whole fabric of the social and cultural life of a person or congregation contributes to the understanding brought to the sermon and is involved in the meaning of salvation which the sermon brings. It is right that preachers be concerned that the Word of God not be hindered, but it is also right they understand that this hindrance may be caused not only by the mishandling of a text of Scripture but by a misreading of the situation of the congregation. Taking the congregation out of context is as much a violation of the Word of God as taking the Scripture out of context . . . [Pastors] know that even with carefully guarded study hours behind locked doors, the people stand around [their] desk[s] and whisper, "Remember me."

—Fred Craddock[44]

---

44. Craddock, *As One Without Authority*, 130, 132–33.

CHAPTER 11

Standing in the Gap of Nurture
The Minister as Child Advocate

By
Aisling Zweigle

"Can you pick me up from school today? Something happened and I don't want to go home." That was a text message I sent to my pastor and mentor, a woman who loved me even though I was a wreck, the woman who got me into counseling when I was suicidal, the woman I trusted with my life, my hurts and secrets. I crawled into her van, and with tears streaming down my face I said, "my dad assaulted me on my seventeenth birthday and I remembered him doing worse to me when I was little." And I sat there and cried as she held my hand. The police officer at school wanted me to tell my mom, so this godly woman helped me write a letter to my mom and her husband explaining everything. She stayed with me when talking with my family. My mom believed me, as did her husband, but no one knew the depth of this secret or of this shame.

When I moved across the country for college I met another woman like her, and she became my second mom. She loved me well. She checked in on me. She welcomed me to her dinner table on a weekly basis. She trusted me in ministry. She re-parented me. She was the person I confided in when I was most angry at God for the injustice of being sexually abused as a child, by the hand of my own father, for almost ten years.

All through my life, to this day, I can trace God's prevenient grace in the people he has put in my life. A neighbor who let me hang out at her house when I was young, no questions asked. That pastor who picked me up from school. A mentor who taught and reassured me of who I am in Christ. A counselor who cancelled what she had to do and sat beside me as the words, "he raped me" came out of my mouth for the first time. And friends who helped me through some of the darkest days of healing. Sometimes the church (that is, the people) need to divinely step into the lives of others and teach them that they are deserving of love, and that at the core of who they are, there is good.

—a victim

For the abandoned and the abused, all the concepts of a loving Savior, all that is spoken about the One who enters into their suffering, may ring empty and meaningless if not also spoken by someone who is radically present in their lives. Christ's resurrection that was realized in the past, and is still waiting to be fully realized in their future, may seem too distant a hope, if their wounds are too far gone. Their anguish throbs with an aching pulse that threatens to give way to death right now, today. Make no mistake about it, the things that have been done to those suffering like this do reek of death. What they cry out for is something, or someone, who will stand in between them and this "death" itself—someone who is willing to declare for them: death will not have the last word, not today, and not with this child of God.

Ministers are able to act as world changers as they stand in the gap of nurture for our world's harmed children. As they carry out their ministry, they are able to do this in key ways. The minister acts as an advocate for the abandoned, abused, and vulnerable by actively building secure relationships with children who need it the most. The minister, however, does not do this alone. Ministry leaders are acting as catalysts, or agents of influence, as others in the church observe the security-rich relationships they model. In this way, ministers may build whole teams of people working with this goal of healthy nurture in mind. Together they are able to share the love of Christ in a way that activates whole networks of nurture. This effort must be carried out in places of safety. Ministers are called to create environments that are specifically designed to keep children safe from further harm, within the church and the community. Child protection must be a top priority in these environments.

Local congregations exist in global communities around the world and down the street. Wherever the body of believers gathers is exactly the place where whole groups of people are already positioned to make the greatest difference in offering redeeming relationships. Within these groups, ministers and ministry leaders may act as child advocates on the front lines on behalf of the vulnerable. Exploring what is already known about child nurture in this chapter will help build a foundation for the ways the church may better do this work. Attachment principles powerfully inform church leaders on what it looks like to take child security seriously. These principles further inform the church's practices and programs, regardless of location.

Pastor as Child Advocate

If the church is doing things right by reaching out and opening its doors to be inclusive, often children come to church programs already hurting. In the wake of a child's hurt and harm, the minister may say with intentional care for each child they serve, "Not on my watch! You cannot harm this one!" A person who watches for darkness on the horizon of a child's life and dares to usher children into places of safety sounds more like a first responder than simply a children's pastor or youth pastor. However, if this contradicts expectations it may well be the imaginations of God's people sorely in want, for ministers are called to serve the world's vulnerable children, who are not just "out there" but in our midst. We teach them about and embody the love of a Savior who conquers death. This requires a wisdom that is both gentle in nurture and steeped in resurrection power. The hope of the resurrection empowers ministers to boldly face a child's unbridled chaos and the lies previously spoken over children-at-risk. As the minister stands in the gap of a child's harm and hurt, they can dramatically touch a child's life. Some of the world's vulnerable children already know this to be true. These children encounter the gospel as the minister provides good news with skin on it. Their stories are ultimately changed. Just as Jesus was, the minister is a child advocate. Regardless of what department or age-level ministry one serves, the need is great. Many of the world's children are experiencing unspeakable harm. Their past, and present, hurts cause real and present storms and they beg to be truly seen and recognized for what they are—children in need of a saving love.

The church has the incredible privilege of looking these children in the eyes and saying, "God is for you—and we are on your side!" Yet these words are only received in the security of genuine, mutual relationships. This requires the tireless work of women and men who dare to show up, again and again. Ministers of the gospel who dare to enter in, and stay in. This entering into the lives of the sinned-against means wading into old-creation suffering. It can be messy. It requires putting into action a good shepherd-style love, like the one described in John chapter 10. It requires clinging wholeheartedly to a new-creation hope that saves lives, daily, perhaps literally, from death's snare. This can be done in big and small ways, both personally and programmatically.

Children-at-Risk around the Globe

Of the nearly 140 million children classified as orphans in 2015, over fifteen million lost both of their parents . UNICEF unpacks these staggering numbers, noting that of these many orphans, "sixty one million reside in Asia, fifty two million in Africa, ten million in Latin America and the Caribbean, seven point three million in Eastern Europe and Central Asia."[1] More millions still have lost their most vital connections to family members due to death, natural disasters, poverty, and familial abuse and neglect. These threats do not respect cultural boundaries or country lines. Many of our world's hurting children are living disconnected from safe, secure adults who actively engage in their lives. Some of them live on the other side of the globe. Many of them live just down the street from local congregations, in the place church members call their home. Very unfortunately, church members' children can also be victims of abuse and neglect.

1. As cited in UNICEF's 2017 updated press release.

In the United States alone there are many children facing what health professionals have for two decades now have referred to as ACEs, or adverse childhood experiences.[2] These negative life experiences, including familial abuse, exposure to drugs and alcohol, or mental health disorders, correlate negatively to a substantial number of overarching child welfare statistics. As the numbers of ACEs increase in a child's life, the obstacles to child health also increase. Their risk of adult-onset disease and disorders also increases as a result.

Many children in the United States live in unsafe environments. In 2014 the United States had over six million children referred to child protection, approximately three million children were investigated in child maltreatment reports, and state agencies found over 702,000 victims of child abuse or neglect. In 2014, fifty states reported 1,546 child deaths as a result of that abuse or neglect.[3] Once again, many of these children and families have been housed in neighborhoods near our churches.

What We Already Know

The abandoned, abused, and vulnerable are seeking people who will step into the gap of their safety and provide a responsive nurture. This requires a kind of nurture that dares to enter in, or really *see the child* and recognize her or his need for security. Attachment theory research has much to bring to this conversation, at the back side of the cross, where children have lacked security.

Beginning in the mid-twentieth century attachment theorists, such as John Bowlby,[4] Mary Ainsworth,[5] and Mary Main,[6] documented extensively the process children experience upon the loss of a parent figure's security, involving confusion, grief, and possible attachment repair.[7] Their studies observed the role that a "security figure" played in helping a child who is experiencing fear maintain her *felt security*. The causes of separation initially studied included an array of life circumstances, both those inside and outside of a parent's control. Their studies included loss of a safety figure's presence due to parental death, or time away while receiving treatment in the case of disease, or separations due to seasons of war.

2. Felitti et al., "Relationship of Childhood Abuse and Household Dysfunction."
3. U.S. Department of Health and Human Services, *Child Maltreatment 2014*.
4. Bowlby, *Forty-Four Juvenile Thieves*, 1–56.
5. Bowlby and Ainsworth, *Child Care and the Growth of Love*, 1–254.
6. Main and Goldwyn, "Adult Attachment Scoring and Classification System."
7. Robertson and Robertson, "Young Children in Brief Separation."

Foundational to early attachment theory were the ways in which a child's early experiences built for them an *internal working model*. This working model created for children a framework of anticipated security in their relationships, defining for children how secure they'd expect to be (or not to be) in present and future relationships. Ultimately, these attachment studies furthered the world's understanding of how child abuse and neglect also impacts a child's ability to anticipate relational security, or insecurity, and how this affects a child in all areas of their ongoing development.

Classic attachment theorists, and modern attachment theorists after them, have defined four key parts to a child's *circle of security*.[8] This circular process begins with a parent's safe presence, understood as a *secure base*. When the child experiences a heightened sense of distress following the loss of a parent's presence, or other stimuli that leaves them feeling threatened, this activates the use of *attachment behaviors* as the child signals to the parent or caregiver their distress and desire for comfort or closeness. When the parent returns, after moments of separation, the child may enjoy a time of attachment repair known as a *safe haven* for the child. If these security figures can be counted on to be present, they remind the child of their trustworthiness and their ability to mirror the child's needs and behaviors with their availability for reconnection.

Furthermore, this circle of security allows for the child's own healthy explorations as they dare to leave the parent for moments of growth and learning away from a parent's side. If they step away, knowing that the parent's consistency in nurture can be counted on, then when the child extends him- or herself beyond what feels safe, he or she can initiate a reunification to support his or her unmet needs. One only has to consider a child's natural ability to cry out when they desire a parent to come near. In the case that a security figure is instead counted on as one that harms rather than heals, or is absent altogether in the case of extreme neglect, a child's brain development is profoundly impacted. These harsher realities also result in learned behaviors that often negatively impact the child's future relationships and potential life trajectories.

With this type of betrayal to the child's brain and body, a child experiences losses in ability to regulate her or his own stress and arousal responses. Rather than receiving comfort, as she or he reaches out for the nurture of a loved one, she or he learns that such calming by an adult cannot be consistently found. Rather than learning how to utilize her or his own agency and self-calming behaviors, the child instead struggles to connect the dots between her or his own behaviors and the consequences she or he regularly

---

8. Knabb and Emerson, "I Will Be Your God and You Will Be My People."

confronts. The parts of the brain that neuroscientists observe lit up in brain imaging studies while children receive nurture after periods of stress (that is, the limbic systems in the right hemisphere of the brain) are the same parts of the brain often found underdeveloped, or "dark," in those who have experienced abuse and neglect. These brain areas are strongly connected to children's ability to concentrate, to regulate their own moods or behaviors, or to process cause and effect sequencing such as processing the social cues of those around them with empathy.[9] In the most extreme of cases, these children may be referred to as attachment-resistant. Theirs is a state of physical and social-emotional limbo as their brain and body difference consistently interferes with their ability to attach and impacts opportunities for family permanency. Healthy attachment, and its absence, impacts people of all ages in local congregations, as experiences in childhood leave their mark on future resiliency of all adults.

Present-day neuro-regulation specialists contradict the notion that any particular set of parent-to-child behaviors are prescribed as *always* kind or *always* loving. Instead, their research makes a case for the way that security figures must flex and adapt to a child's cues, allowing for a level of responsiveness, be it in tone of voice, eye contact, or physical proximity, that is attuned with the child's present needs or changing cues.[10] In other words, there are those behaviors that are sometimes comforting, but if they do not change to mirror the child's new needs when experiencing stress, then those once-kind behaviors may now turn hurtful or intrusive—especially if they result in an increased level of arousal, stress, or pain in the life of the child.[11] If there is instead the ability to adapt or change together, as a pair, then together the caregiver and child can share an end goal, that is of mutual relationship expressed in increased security, enjoyment, and attunement. In the best of circumstances, families experience this life in abundance, safe guarded in tandem by child and security figure(s) alike.

What is understood as dramatically harmful to this dance of attachment is the presence of a security figure that is at times present and pleasant and then alternatively emerges as one who hurts or damages the child instead—surprising the child with unexpected acts of violence, be it physical, sexual, or social-emotional harm after previous moments of meeting the child's felt needs. This disorganized set of patterns in parent-to-child interaction is detrimental to the child's ability to process his or her present well-being and trust in his or her future chance of survival. There are

---

9. See Schore, "Modern Attachment Theory."
10. Meins et al., "Mind-mindedness as a Multidimensional Construct."
11. Siegel, *Developing Mind*, 117.

children experiencing these forms of insecure and disorganized attachment relationships across the globe and next door.

The Saving One as the Matching One

Together with David Cross, the research of Karyn Purvis has left a legacy of healing especially poignant for parents and caregivers who seek to make meaningful connections with children living in adoptive and foster care families. The resource *The Connected Child*, as well as *Empowered to Connect* national conferences, provide intervention strategies for children who've experienced attachment-deficit. Purvis has made the principles of connecting, correcting, and empowering behaviors all the more accessible in a free online *Created to Connect Study Guide*[12] and Bible study. These resources are a great training for congregations that are serious about coming alongside the abandoned, abused, and vulnerable and are serious about showing up and playing a meaningful part in their circles. Of particular help is understanding the role of *matching behaviors*.[13]

From the earliest of days, an infant-to-parent relationship naturally displays ongoing moments of matching. As the child cuddles and coos, the caregiver often responds with *matching behaviors* that express reciprocal warmth and presence. The child changes their facial expression and the parent matches it back. As the child ages, the parent continues to make efforts to speak on the child's level, to mirror back or match the child's changes in tone, facial expression, and demeanor. This form of evolving responsiveness becomes all the more vital a form of nurture for the harmed child with unmet needs for respect and security.

Matching may also be incredibly helpful in understanding all the more why wounded children (and adults) at the back side of the cross respond powerfully to a Savior who "mirrors" their own suffering. As Christ knows what it means to suffer violence at the hands of others, and even knows what it is to cry out to the God who has abandoned him, the wounded may see in their Saving One a security figure who enters into their world with matching tears, scars, and hurts. Yet, this One does not remain forever in the tomb. As chapter 9 has outlined, the resurrection story is one that moves and empowers the abandoned and abused child to consider the courage to hope, heal, and be brought to life again.

At the same time, a minister who stands in the midst of a child's broken story must be cautious about claiming for the child a reality of healing still

12. Purvis, *Created to Connect Study Guide*.
13. Purvis et al., *Connected Child*, 16.

beyond them, especially if they remain in hurtful circumstances. However, the minister may powerfully *match* the child's experience of loss. The child needs adults that take their losses seriously. This can be expressed in matching tones of earnest sympathy and regret. This can also spur the minister on to hope on behalf of the child, and to hold the truth that this was never what Christ intended this child to experience.

Making the Cross-Connection Count

As children are busy protecting their wounds, they struggle to regulate their states of stress, in both body and brain. This produces a hypervigilance that may keep them wary of trusting an adult who suggests they have good intentions. If a harmed child sees an adult who cares, or hears one speak, they may well struggle to recognize the voice at all, regardless of how loving a person the adult is. These children might even wrestle against this nurture—perceiving it as a threat to their vulnerability instead.

Yet, the church's people embody the Good Shepherd and speak with his voice. Loving those with broken stories is not for the faint of heart. Those serving on the front lines know full well that early on in the process of healing not all children-at-risk are found basking in the warmth of a caregiver's voice who speaks with a Good Shepherd's love. But the church is a people with the conviction that Christ's love is worth sharing at all costs. Jesus describes himself as the Good Shepherd who gives his very life to guard the sheep, both those in the pen and those not yet included in the fold. This Savior not only stands in the gap, but stretches his own body out over the entry to the sheep pen. He does this freely, willingly putting the priority of their lives before his own—willing to offer up his life and death, as means to love those in his care. Christ desires that his children be given the gift of safe pasture, abundant life, freedom from harm. The minister as child advocate is given this same calling to protect children from harm.

This increased sense of calling impacts the way ministers pray and prepare their weekly lessons and sermon messages. As their awareness of broken stories increases, locally and globally, they read Scripture texts and recognize words of hope the Savior specifically speaks over the children-at-risk in the minister's reach and care. This is all the more true for those who are actively teaching children whose past or present homes are not as safe and nurturing as the minister (or the child) would hope for them to be. Practically, this means that the children's pastor teaches about Jesus' healing work with greater sensitivity. They meet the eyes of the foster child in the front row, who has experienced abuse firsthand, and are mindful of the way that child's hurts creates a lens through which their spiritual formation must grow. The minister is filled with compassion. How gravely important it is to take great care in never conveying that this God's loving character is prone to change. How much damage could be brought in likening this One to a parent who comes in peace at one moment, and comes at the next with the intention to harm or hurt.

In addition, ministry leaders designing spiritual formation programs and volunteer teams must intentionally consider the support people needed for children who struggle to regulate their own behavior, due to past trauma and the brain changes that have resulted. These leaders see the child's needs, that interrupt the flow of classroom and worship routines, as being worth their time and energy. They respond by either planning for additional volunteers to come alongside the child, or alternatively, planning for times when other team leaders will lead in the minister's place, so that the minister her- or himself can step away from speaking or teaching roles and make that child's pressing need the priority. A minister with this unique calling will seek further training so that he or she may know better each year how to lead in a way that shows each child with words, glances, and classroom environments, that the child's well-being is well worth the time. This may be a sentiment with which the child is unfamiliar and ill-acquainted.

Oftentimes, children-at-risk are unable to count on their fingers a single adult who cares for them in this way—even as their healthy development requires its existence. Children must have at least one adult in their life that is utterly committed to their well-being. And certainly each child would benefit by having more than just one! This discussion must take into account the unfathomable worth of those who stand in this gap of relationship, and for vulnerable children everywhere. As Christ entrusts his church family with the most vulnerable, the minister is called to act as advocate to the abandoned and abused, and to lead others in doing so. Of particular importance are the ways in which ministry leaders may serve as catalysts, activating whole networks of nurture in their churches.

Fanning the Flame of Others

The role of individual leaders is also to be an agent of influence at the back side of the cross—they can, and must, multiply themselves. The numbers of children with stories that break the hearts of men and women with ears to hear, stretch the minister's abilities. These pressing needs require skill well beyond a minister's own capabilities. This can weigh heavily on those called within our churches. Indeed, even for those most called, it can be a weight beyond what can be borne. It is precisely at that breaking point, and perhaps well before it, that leaders must stop to consider their role, as ministry leaders, and leverage the potential for influencing other Sunday school teachers, age-level volunteers, and mentors in congregations. And above all, we must engage in and offer as much education about these issues as possible.

Leaders who stand in the gap of love for the vulnerable do well to recognize the profound influence they have on whole-church families who may serve as child advocates in congregations and beyond. In an individualistic Western understanding of personhood, the collective power of influence is often all too little considered. Other cultures, more collective in their understanding of relationships, speak more readily to the layers of interconnectivity that surround a child.[14] This same interconnectivity may potentially surround a pastor's every move as they serve as teacher, disciple-er, and friend. They must also connect to those outside the church who have something to offer to the conversation, or to other professional advocates of a child. A pastor's role may well serve as a catalyst for whole movements of love and healing—if only they have eyes to see their role as influencer anew.

As those on volunteer teams learn of a ministry leader's work on behalf of the vulnerable, an increased number of people may become committed to the slow healing of God's children who've been harmed. This increases the number of those safeguarding children from further wounds while on the minister's watch. This provides layers of nurture that stretch over multiple seasons of a child or young person's life—mentors who serve in moments of time. This influence can be further communicated in intentional prayer emphases, advocacy initiatives, awareness campaigns, as well as partnering with community organizations, be it foster parent support groups or school-to-church partnerships for children and families falling through the cracks.

These advocacy efforts may include fanning the flames of those who already work on behalf of community children in need of security. *Outside* the local congregation, a ministry leader can seek to build a positive relationship with an area school nearby. By meeting one-on-one with the school counselor, principal, or behavior support person, the minister expresses the church's desire to link arms with that school and community. *Inside* the local congregation, the ministry leader can communicate with existing foster parents in the church, seeking to find ways they are able to come alongside, sharing the burden of prayer or care for their foster and adopted children. These parents are often silently weary and in need of additional support. Foster parents often care for traumatized children with nearly invisible brain and body difference.

---

14. See Keller, "Autonomy and Relatedness Revisited."

As the church prays for the vulnerable and is attentive to the Spirit's prompting, it may act in ways that model for others a radical, rescuing, redeeming love for the sinned-against. These practices create contagious ripple effects that spur on additional leaders, young and old, to safeguard and serve children-at-risk. This multiplying effect helps to lift the burden off of one single minister or advocate's shoulders. It empowers ministers to also stand back and see the work of their hands and heart, carried out by many others, as the passion of their own calling inspires the gifts and graces given to their sisters and brothers, their aunts and uncles, as well as their many children and grandparents present in their faith family. This may activate the very graces of those who have been harmed themselves, as they come to divinely understand their own woundedness was never intended to be the end of their story. Their own healing gives way to the healing of others around them. In this new creation story the agency of those at the back side of the cross gets the last word, as they may also say,"yes" to loving and serving others in Christ's name.

Staying on the Lookout and Creating Safe Environments

We look at this passage in perhaps a new light:

> He called a little child to him, and placed the child among them. And he said: "Truly I tell you, unless you change and become like little children, you will never enter the kingdom of heaven. Therefore, whoever takes the lowly position of this child is the greatest in the kingdom of heaven. And whoever welcomes one such child in my name welcomes me. If anyone causes one of these little ones—those who believe in me—to stumble, it would be better for them to have a large millstone hung around their neck and to be drowned in the depths of the sea. Woe to the world because of the things that cause people to stumble! Such things must come, but woe to the person through whom they come!" (Matt 18:2–7)

Finally, in this same calling of minister as advocate, there is hardly anything to be done, in the way of healing, if the greatest care is not given to ensure that church and community environments are safe from further harm. Pastors and teachers serve as gatekeepers to those most vulnerable. The church cannot be fooled. Those thieves, seeking to steal, kill, and destroy the life right out of God's children, are not sleeping on their jobs— there are those who intend further harm even inside the church. If they can find church families blind to their intentions, then what chance does the church have in creating safe havens for the sinned-against? Instead it runs the risk of creating comfortable hiding places for those still very active in their sin. This is why child protection policies and protocols for the safety of the vulnerable (the young, old, differently abled, and the already wounded) must take priority.

The church is called to be gentle in its care but Christian nurture must also be wise to the real and present threat of predators. Like a mother bear or lioness, pastors and leaders do well to keep eyes and ears, noses and feet, alert and on the ready. The fight with evil is a cosmic one, but is also, all too often, fought on behalf of one sinned-against child at a time. Utilizing background checks for those who serve in the children's department and youth group is a good initial step. Ensuring that all volunteers regularly watch mandatory child safety videos, as means of ongoing volunteer training, is another practical step in the right direction. These trainings must remind the church that child predators are often those already known to children, those uniquely good at breaking down boundaries. Predators pride themselves on their ability to earn the trust of ministers, and parents, who serve as gatekeepers . These thieves work diligently to gain access to the church's children and youth. As ministry team members prove themselves trustworthy, ministers must never forget that any volunteer (or staff person) is potentially a wolf in sheep's clothing. All children in local congregations are worth this caution.

Holding fast to a volunteer onboarding process is also vital to child safety. This includes a volunteer's need to fill out an application, be interviewed by the minister or team leader, provide personal and professional references, and undergo a six-month waiting period before serving in a way that grants them access to children. This may look more formal or informal depending on the size and culture of the church context. But regardless of context, all of our world's children are deserving of this protection. Children in our local congregations can be better protected, despite the inconvenience it may cause those busy with ministry obligations. Inconvenience pales in comparison to the potential of a child's harm.

Adding team members who serve as greeters for child and youth spaces provides additional eyes and ears to child worship areas and classrooms. This layer of observation is critical to child environments. It is important that those filling this role feel empowered to both welcome and safeguard. Those with a propensity for noticing when an adult or child is behaving differently are best suited for this role. These greeters also need to be empowered by the pastor(s) so they may confidently state and restate boundaries without fear of being hurtful to church attendees who pressure them for leniency on child safety protocols. Regular inquiry regarding any incidents that caused a volunteer concern must be a normal part of the volunteer team and staff culture. Team members must know their contribution to their church's child safety daily matters.

The church is an interconnected family made up of many people in a variety of contexts. As children around the globe experience harm in past, and present, relationships, local congregations have the privilege of providing these children healthy, attachment-rich relationships. The minister as child advocate is powerfully positioned to stand in the gap of harm for the world's abandoned, abused, and vulnerable children. This task is not an easy one but it is worthy of the minister's calling. The minister shows up again and again in the child's life and strives to really see the child and the child's hurt. This impacts personal ministry preparation routines and programs. And they don't do this alone. The minister as child advocate is able to model for others a Good Shepherd love that seeks to radically redeem the brokenness faced by children-at-risk. The minister as child advocate serves as catalyst, potentially activating whole networks of nurture. And together, as a faith family, the greatest of care is given to provide child-safe environments that ensure children are protected from further harm.

CHAPTER 12

Sorrow in the Saving
Lament as Faith

By
John W. Nielson

> *"Eloi, Eloi, lema sabachthani?"*
> *which means, "My God, My God,*
> *why have you forsaken me."*
>
> —Mark 15:34

The cry of Jesus from the cross marks a vital reality that must not be missed as we reflect on the essence and impact of the atonement. While the results of the atonement should surely lead to a response of joy in the good news of full salvation, there is also the need to connect with the various ways that the faithful practice of lament intersects with the story of redemption. The place and purpose of the cry of Jesus from the cross has theological and soteriological significance, as this book has shown. It is certainly significant to note that in that moment, Jesus reaches back to the Psalter, to a psalm of lament, and releases this questioning, sorrowful cry from his lips: "Why have you forsaken me?" By reflecting on these words through the lens of lament, we are invited to hear a familiar cry—the cry in the darkness. It is in this moment, placed in the very heart of the atonement that we can identify with this crucified Christ the most, this "Man of Sorrows."

Mark invites us into the darkness of Jesus' agony, as if to remind us of the fullness of the incarnation—Jesus has entered all the way into our experience, one that will include not only physical death, but also the darkening despair that often comes while we still live. In Mark's account of the crucifixion, we find two moments when Jesus cries out in a loud voice. The first takes place "at three o'clock" when Jesus utters the phrase, "Eloi, Eloi, lema sabachthani?" (Mark 15:34). The second loud cry is at the moment of his death where no words are recorded (Mark 15:37). In the first cry Jesus quotes the opening lines of Psalm 22, not only to anchor his death in the fullness of messianic expectation, but to give expression to the depth of his own experience. Scholars often remind us that in quoting the first line, Jesus is intentionally calling to our attention the entirety of the psalm's message, including other phrases that powerfully mirror what is happening during these six hours. We should not, however, assume that the cry of Jesus is merely a detached reference to his messianic mission in order to identify himself. He is giving voice to his own authentic experience. In his commentary on the Gospel of Mark, R. T. France writes, "To read into these few tortured words an exegesis of the whole psalm is to turn upside down the effect which Mark has created by this powerful and enigmatic cry of agony. Six hours after he was placed on the cross, and after three hours of darkness, Jesus feels abandoned by God."[1] It is possible that this cry of lament may be of a different emotive tone from the final cry that soon follows at the moment of his death. However, as we have seen, Mark does not provide the content of these words (15:37). Even so, we should not minimize the genuine lament that bursts from the lips of Jesus. France continues:

> It would be possible to read Mark's notes of time as indicating that the darkness lifted "at the ninth hour," the time of Jesus' cry, so that that cry marked the end of the time of separation, but that is to read rather a lot between the lines. But if Mark does not tell us how long the sense of abandonment lasted, he gives us no

---

1. France, *Gospel of Mark*, 652.

grounds for supposing that it was not, at the time of Jesus' cry, utterly real and all-embracing. He leaves no room for the heroic serenity of Jesus' death in later docetic reconstruction.[2]

While the connection of the God-forsaken feeling of abandonment that the cry of Jesus suggests to the theological understanding of the atonement is important, the primary implication should not be theoretical, but rather personal and practical. We are invited to identify with Jesus, most precisely in this moment, however we describe or understand it, as this moment is one that is central to an atonement theology that lives and breathes.

Mark's real purpose here is not to posit a particular theory of the atonement, but to enter deeply into the cry that accompanied it. "He wants us to feel Jesus' agony, not to explain it."[3] Of course, we must guard against making final pronouncements on the intent of the Gospel writer, much less the inner thoughts of Jesus in these moments on the cross. Still, we return to the primary purpose for their inclusion in the passion narrative. "We have no way of knowing what the historical Jesus actually felt as he died or what his last words on the cross, if any, were. What is clear is that Mark did not portray Jesus' last words on the model of the noble death. Jesus' last words in Mark are passionate, expressing both the loneliness of intense suffering and a bold and demanding challenge addressed to God."[4] Mark highlights them as a cry of lament, which is, fundamentally, what the words themselves convey. And in so doing, we are ourselves invited to enter into the faithful practice of lamenting.

While the topic of lament is broader than the scope of this chapter, it is important to provide a basic overview of lament as we continue to explore ways that lament connects to the atonement. A basic definition of lament is a passionate expression of grief or sorrow. To lament is to express grief for or about, to mourn (to lament a death) or regret deeply; to deplore ("he lamented his thoughtless acts"); to grieve audibly, to wail, to express sorrow or regret. It can mean a feeling or an expression of grief, or a lamentation, which is a song or poem expressing deep grief or mourning. It can also be an expression of anger and a "why" to God, as found in the Psalms. The lament expressed in Scripture and the lament that is needed in the church today would include all these definitions. Lament is a missing language in much of the liturgical/doxological life of the church, and yet the narrative of Scripture models the language of lament as an integral and necessary component of our language and practice. It is necessary for praise, for prayer, for

2. France, *Gospel of Mark*, 652.
3. France, *Gospel of Mark*, 653
4. Collins and Attridge, *Mark*, 754.

proclamation, and for an authentic response to the devastating realities of the world around us.

> Lament indispensably shapes prayer, proclamation, ministry, and witness for such times . . . It is our shared conviction that lament, particularly biblical lament, provides the church with a rhetoric for prayer and reflection that befits these volatile times, a rhetoric that mourns loss, examines complicity in evil, cries for divine help, and sings and prays with hope. For indeed, what ultimately shapes biblical lament is not the need of the creature to cry its woe, but the faithfulness of the God who hears and acts.[5]

Returning to the cry of lament from Jesus on the cross, the mere presence of this cry invites us to consider a connection between atonement and the sacred sorrow of lament. This reality not only informs us about the person of Jesus, but about our own experience as people who seek to worship Christ and follow his pattern. We see that the atonement was not only about "bridging the gap" that sin had caused between us and a holy God; it was also about addressing the suffering and sorrow in our lives that the depth of sin has left behind, on sinner and sinned-against alike. Said another way, we find an affirmation of individual experience, where, in a particular context or circumstance, one offers the prayer of lament. We also discover that this voice is always joined by the voice of Christ who enters into our pain and sorrow on the very basis of his own experience here on earth, most significantly, on the cross. In a remarkable statement, Patrick Miller writes, "Jesus died for our suffering as much as our sins."[6] Therefore, when we listen to Christ's voice from the cross, we realize that our prayer of lament is not a solitary one. The lament from the cross gives permission and precedent for the full range of lament to be expressed in our own lives. As we explore some specific ways that atonement and lament intersect and intermingle, we begin with a primary response to the cross itself, and the reason the atonement was necessary at all.

Lament for the Cross

One of the essential responses to the atonement is sorrow for all that was endured by Christ on the cross. While the benefits of the atonement are the means through which we receive redemption, and we rejoice in Christ's

5. Brown and Miller, *Lament*, xix.
6. Brown and Miller, *Lament*, 21.

saving work, we also cannot help but look upon the Man of Sorrows and feel the weight of his agony. This is a type of lament. With that recognition, we are compelled to weep. We lament the cost of our redemption and that human sinfulness is linked with the agony that our Savior endured during those dark hours. As seen in the previous chapters, not only the cross but the entirety of the christological event, from the cradle to the cross, takes place for our redemption. It is in the crucifixion, however, that the apex of Christ's suffering takes place. We re-envision the moment where "sorrow and love flow mingled down"[7] and we, too, respond with the cry of lament. The hymn writers give us language to express this sorrow. In a verse that is often omitted when the hymn "At the Cross" is sung, the great hymn writer, Isaac Watts, penned these words:

> Thus might I hide my blushing face
> while his dear cross appears,
> dissolve my heart in thankfulness,
> and melt mine eyes to tears.[8]

Lament for the cross not only includes sorrow, but the question of "why?" that is also internal to lament. "Why should my Savior to Calvary go? Why should He love me so?"[9] These are but a few examples of a wide range of hymns and songs that give voice to our response of lament for the event that the atonement necessitated. This sorrow for the death of Jesus may be the most obvious connection of lament to the atonement, and the one most regularly expressed within the Christian community. Because of this, it provides a potential gateway into a wider understanding and practice of biblical lament.

One particular setting in the life of the church where lament for the cross can be expressed is through the cycle of the Christian year. The season of Lent, and especially of Holy Week, are natural times when we can be intentional about including the practices of lament in general and, particularly, this lament for the cross. These seasons can be effective opportunities for walking through patterns of lament as a corporate body, joining us to the broader church around the world and through the ages. In *Worship Seeking Understanding*, John Witvliet suggests that in the various cycles of the Christian year we find a corresponding pattern to the one found in the Psalms and to the practice of lament. "Every year, time and time again, we journey from the eschatological lament of Advent to the profound adoration

---

7. Watts, "When I Survey the Wondrous Cross," 1707.
8. Watts, "At the Cross," 1707.
9. Robert Harkness, "Why Should He Love Me So?," 1925.

of the incarnate Christ at Christmas and Epiphany, from the baptismal soul-searching of Lent to the unbridled praise of Easter morning. This yearly journey provides ready-made moments to give voices to the cries and acclamations of people at every point in the journey of faith."[10] We sing songs together and participate in acts of remembrance, so that we can fully lament all that Christ's sacrifice has accomplished for us. Songs such as those previously referenced give time and space for the community of faith to practice lament. Additionally, this can include Scripture, prayers, litanies, and a wide range of creative liturgies that allow us to express these feelings as acts of worship, thanksgiving, penance, and reflection. Special services such as Tenebrae, Good Friday, and Holy Saturday observances and vigils are all powerful opportunities for intentional, corporate lament to take place, all in response to the reality of the atonement.

Lament as Confession

The gift of atonement is simply that—a gift. It is received; it is not earned or deserved, and yet we enter into the benefits of Christ's atonement through the acceptance of faith. It is through the response of faith, made authentic through confession and repentance, that the benefits of the atonement are realized in the life of the sinner. To repent and believe requires confession. Confession of sin (and thus our need), as well as confession that Jesus is Savior and Lord, are critical components of our faith. This confession is, fundamentally, lament. It is sorrow for sin. Where the church has often failed is proclaiming that confession and repentance are only owed to God. This has allowed many to feel secure in their faith, without ever having confessed to those they have hurt. Victimization happens within the church, but too often it is covered up and hidden from view. Christians abuse other Christians, but power differentials are often preserved. Certainly confession to God is necessary, but it is not enough. Jesus speaks just as strongly about our relationships with others as he does about our relationship with God. With that said, confession in the context of worship is more than appropriate, albeit uncomfortable.

Beyond the broader patterns of the yearly cycle already referenced, it is partly through confession that lament can enter into the weekly practices of worship. We can find time and space to reflect confessional lament in how our weekly worship is structured. While the thrust of the lament cycle is tied to confession (and the classical prayer, *kyrie eleison*) and the praise component (and the classical prayer, *gloria in excelsis Deo*), there is a helpful

10. Witvliet, *Worship Seeking Understanding*, 50.

framework in which to shape and form worship to include space for this range of expressions, lament and praise.[11] While there are other dimensions of lament that need to be incorporated into the regular worshiping life of the church, to view confession as a form of lament gives us one way to recognize that there are people present whenever we gather who need to express sorrow, not just for sin, but for the broken places in their lives. There is confession not only for sin, but confession for our need for God's broader healing. In a day when corporate worship leans heavily on the one note of celebration, being intentional about including the lament of the confession of need broadens the emotive palette, thereby making room for people on a greater range of the spectrum of life. We must take seriously the reality that on any given Sunday the church "includes people of praise and people of lament—people whose silence and pain crave release and people whose joy seeks resonance in community."[12]

The challenge is that in many contexts today, by and large, practices of lament are neglected. This tendency is present broadly in American contexts, with a hyper-individualism that resists sharing any personal weakness or deficiency, and even more specifically in many traditions with an aversion to acknowledging confession as an ongoing and necessary practice.

> Why call on God for help when we think we don't really need any help? The absence of an ongoing practice of lament and confession in the church exacerbates its grandiose assumptions of exceptionalism rather than evoking the necessary humility. Why engage in humble confession when we assume we have nothing to confess? The reality check that confession demands is absent, leading to the perpetuation of sinful attitudes and values.[13]

Coinciding with the need to rediscover lament as a regular, faithful, corporate practice, we must make room again in our worship for the confession of sin, of need, and of brokenness. The function of lament as confession must include confession that extends beyond lament for personal sin and failure. We must also confess the broader factors of corporate failure and systemic injustice. When we lament tragedies and injustices, we are called not only to express sorrow but to confess the ways that we have willingly and unwittingly participated in these realities. This is part of a larger category of corporate lament where, in the words of a song by Michael Card and a book by Kathleen O'Connor, we "weep the tears of the world." O'Connor's

11. Witvliet, *Worship Seeking Understanding*, 56.
12. Witvliet, *Worship Seeking Understanding*, 57.
13. Cannon, *Forgive Us*, 27.

commentary on Lamentations explores five poems of sorrow and helps us connect their place and purpose with current practice in response to the brokenness of our world. She makes a powerful case that lament allows us to enter fully into the reality of our own sorrow and suffering, which then allows us to enter into the sorrow and suffering of those around us.[14]

> The voices of Lamentations urge readers to face suffering, to speak of it, to be dangerous proclaimers of the truths that nations, families, and individuals prefer to repress. They invite us to honor the pain muffled in our hearts, overlooked in our society, and crying for our attention in other parts of the world. In this way Lamentations can shelter the tears of the world.[15]

While the corporate work of such confessional lament is challenging and forces us to look fully into the mirror of our own culpability, it is a necessary expression not only of lament but of authentic worship as well.

This commitment to corporate confession and lament is a direct impact of the totality of the atonement, the purpose of which is not only to reconcile the individual to God but to redeem all things. "For in him all the fullness of God was pleased to dwell, and through him God was pleased to reconcile to himself all things, whether on earth or in heaven, by making peace through the blood of his cross" (Col 1:19–20, NRSV).

The practice of lament-confession also leads us to an eschatological longing, which is at the core of all true lament. We not only express the sorrow, pain, anger, etc. for things that have happened in the past, or which we are experiencing in the present, but we also look forward to the day of deliverance. We long for things to be different, to be better. In the biblical practice of lament, this is not mere wishful thinking or sentimentality, it is a faith-filled expectancy, anchored in Christian hope. It is taking our sorrow, pain, anger, doubts, fears, and questions to the very One who is the final hope for all that we are facing. Even when we lament with Jesus, "My God, why have you forsaken me?," we do so believing somewhere deep within us that our only hope is that God will, in fact, not forsake us in the end, and that even though it seems like God is far away, God is indeed present to hear my questioning of God's absence. It is this hope-filled longing that inhabits

---

14. O'Connor's work suggests that faithful practice of lament personally is what enables us to express lament corporately and for the sake of others. This is an insightful sequence. However, there may be validity in some cases to the pathway into lament working in the opposite direction. Sometimes we may first "weep the tears of the world," or for someone around us who has entered deep sorrow, and find that this awakens a personal need, allowing us the permission to express lament for things and experiences in our own lives.

15. O'Connor, *Lamentations and the Tears of the World*, 95.

biblical lament that is necessary if our lament is to be faithful to the biblical pattern.[16]

Lament as Gift

Accepting our lament is a gift from the God who is not interested in resisting our accusations. Perhaps one of the most significant connection points between the atonement and lament is that included in the benefits of the atonement is a deepened intimacy with God that is now possible through Christ's reconciling, redeeming, and healing work. This intimacy allows our honest expression to God. Of course, we must remember and affirm that lament was a long-standing practice of the people of God even before the atonement of Jesus. Still, if the language of lament was practiced and encouraged by the psalmists and by the prophets under the old covenant, how much more should lament be permissible and practiced with the gift of the new relationship that the atonement provides? Why would we fail to express the sacred sorrow that we feel when we know that Christ understands our sense of godforsakenness, and has shared our cry?

This gift of lament is offered to the individual and needs to be expressed in significant ways to the community of faith. Before we look at the corporate expressions of lament, an area that the church has often failed to fully practice, it is important for us to reflect on the ways that lament is a gift to the individual. This gift is offered to us in the midst of personal loss and in the sorrows and griefs that we experience, not only in death or disaster, but in the multitude of ways that we experience the pain of brokenness in a fallen world. This gift of sacred sorrow is especially extended to the sinned-against. Like the psalmist and like Jesus, the suffering servant, we are invited to cry out in our pain and in our suffering, to question even God's presence when enemies surround us, seemingly on every hand. When we have experienced violence or vengeance, persecution or prejudice, betrayal or brokenness, abandonment or abuse—we find solidarity with the psalmist

---

16. Another important element of biblical lament that has not been included here is the commitment to future trust and praise. Claus Westermann points out the internal transition in the psalms of lament, a move from lamentation toward trust and praise. "There is not a single Psalm of lament that stops with lamentation. Lamentation has no meaning in and of itself. That it functions as an appeal is evident in its structure. What the lament is concerned with is not a description of one's own sufferings or self-pity, but the removal of the suffering itself. The lament appeals to the one who can remove suffering" (Westermann, *Praise and Lament in the Psalms*, 266). Westermann points out that this transition is often indicated by a "but" (*wĀẇ*) that introduces some form of statement of trust. Thus, most laments conclude with a vow of praise. Despite Westermann's claim above, most scholars point to Psalm 88 as the single exception to the rule.

who cries out, "How long shall my enemy be exalted over me?"[17] We identify with the feelings expressed in Psalm 69:4, "More in number than the hairs of my head are those who hate me without cause; many are those who would destroy me, my enemies who accuse me falsely. What I did not steal must I now restore?" The psalms of lament frequently question God's presence and seeming inactivity in the face of injustice and unwarranted treatment.[18]

When we are on the receiving end of the sins of others, the power of lament is offered as a primary response. We feel pain and suffering that is not of our making. We are left with the consequences of the actions of others who have sinned against us. We live with the pain, suffering, and even trauma of the violence of others. Where can we go with the pain, the anger, the anxiety, the loss, the broken pieces of our shattered souls? We cry out from the depths to the God who seems not only absent, but indifferent. We weep for what we have lost, for what, perhaps, can never be restored. We question why it happened. We suffer in the darkness, begging for the light to be restored. We wonder where God was when it happened and where, in the midst of our chaos, God is now. All of this is contained in the language of lament. It is finding the mustard seed of faith that finds a way to believe that somehow out of the depths, God loves us infinitely, and death is conquered ultimately. This lament of the injured is also an invitation to consider Jesus, the suffering servant whose experience of betrayal and abuse, of violence and mocking, and of cruelty and punishment, enables God's empathetic response. It is in remembering the one who was wrongfully accused and unjustly executed that we can most fully enter into the realities of the lengths to which love will go. In the same Psalm (22) that Jesus quotes from the cross, we find these words:

> But I am a worm, and not human;
> scorned by others, and despised by the people.
> All who see me mock at me;
> they make mouths at me, they shake their heads;
> "Commit your cause to the Lord; let him deliver—
> let him rescue the one in whom he delights!" . . .
>
> I am poured out like water,
> and all my bones are out of joint;
> my heart is like wax;
> it is melted within my breast;

---

17. Psalm 13:2.

18. A great example of this specific type of lament is found in Psalm 10. This psalm powerful expresses both the questions and complaints, but also the vivid description of the experience of one who is facing unjust suffering.

> my mouth is dried up like a potsherd,
>> and my tongue sticks to my jaws;
>> you lay me in the dust of death.
>
> For dogs are all around me;
>> a company of evildoers encircles me.
> My hands and feet have shriveled;
>
> I can count all my bones.
> They stare and gloat over me;
> they divide my clothes among themselves,
>> and for my clothing they cast lots.

For the one who is suffering, whatever the context or cause, our practice of lament invites us to remember that Jesus joins us in our pain and grief. Jesus laments before us, and for us, and, most importantly, with us. As Jürgen Moltmann writes, "[W]hen we feel pain we participate in his pain, and when we grieve we share his grief . . . People who believe in the God who suffers with us, recognize their suffering in God, and God in their suffering."[19] Lament allows us to meet Jesus on the back side of the cross. We find Jesus as a fellow traveler on the road of suffering. As our circumstance intersects with his atonement, we can come to know and even understand Jesus in new and deepening ways. We might wish that it would not require suffering to come to this knowledge, however, it is often only in the midst of deep sorrow that we find the opportunity of seeing Jesus as never before. In a helpful article in *The Table*[20] entitled *The Suffering God: How Jesus Meets Us in Pain*, Danielle Cummings writes,

> Though we are inclined, when privilege allows, to follow the crucified Christ without identification with suffering, there comes a point when we are confronted by utter brokenness. And at this crossroads, though the pain is strong, lies an opportunity for greater solidarity with Jesus and deeper enjoyment of his love. As our suffering joins with his, we find there is indeed nowhere we can go away from his love. Our experience of suffering pushes us to the margins of our theology, and we find that his story does not leave us alone. His suffering presents a salve and trajectory to our own which we would otherwise want; his cross questions the surprise with which we first meet pain.

---

19. Moltmann, *Crucified God*, 45–46.
20. *The Table* is a publication of the Biola University's Center for Christian Thought.

Suffering is the retrofitting to any discipleship foundation, the gap between program and practice. The suffering God can help. We find him at our side, mending our story with His anew and deepening our devotion to a crucified and risen Messiah.[21]

While it is beyond the scope of this chapter to fully explore all of the ways that lament can be practiced faithfully (especially corporately, in the life of the people of God), we can explore some basic principles that can guide the individual or local communities of faith in the journey of rediscovering lament as a regular practice for the church. Given the challenges of this process, it is certain that intentional planning is necessary.

Congregational Lament

A congregational plan to introduce or expand the practices of lament should begin with knowledge and education. The theme of lament needs to be addressed by the pastor. This can take place through a sermon or, better still, a series of sermons. Preaching on lament could certainly be done at any time, however, as has already been stated, it may be especially appropriate during certain seasons of the church year, such as Advent or Lent, or it might be preached in response to times of tragedy or loss either on a local, national, or global level. Another helpful way to introduce lament is as part of a larger preaching series on the Psalms, demonstrating that lament is a significant literary form in the Psalter. An introductory sermon could be followed up with a more focused series on lament.

Another facet of the knowledge and education plan could include a study of lament within a small group structure. A Sunday school class or other discipleship group opportunity can be a wonderful way to have people engage with lament at a much deeper level. There are some wonderful small group resources that can be used to help inform and educate a congregation.[22] Providing such an opportunity for further study is a great way to offer follow-up to a sermon or series of sermons on lament.

The next layer of a congregational plan could focus on bringing lament into pastoral care. This can happen in several ways. First, the language of lament can be brought more intentionally into pastoral conversation and prayer with people who are going through difficult times. During hospital visitation, care during times of loss, or other conversations, the pastor can

---

21. Cummings, "Suffering God."

22. One great example is the book and experience guide by Michael Card, *Sacred Sorrow*, published by NavPress. Additional small group resources can be found at www.sacredsorrow.com.

encourage the practice of lament by acknowledging and modeling it. This can include asking the kinds of questions included in the psalms of lament, such as, "How long, O Lord?" (i.e., Psalm 13), or acknowledging the perception that God seems distant. It is affirming tears and even doubt; it is confessing our confusion, pain, anger, and fear. It is using the full biblical model and then coming to "the turn." "But, we are trusting in you, Lord. We are going to continue to thank you and praise you." We do so even though we may not see the answer yet. This phrase must only be said with great pastoral discernment about where a person is on their journey.

It is also important to expand our understanding of lament to include areas other than the loss associated with death. Pastors must realize and respect the broad range of issues over which their people may need to lament. This would include broken relationships, barrenness, miscarriage, divorce, the loss of a pet, the declines associated with aging, the loss of a job, children who are away from God, addictions, abuse, the loss of a dream, and so on. Acknowledging this need for lament, giving people the freedom to grieve, and helping them be able to express their sorrow is a tremendous pastoral gift.

A second pastoral care focus on lament revolves around the funeral. The pastor who is serious about encouraging lament needs to be intentional about bringing lament into the funeral itself. While this might seem like something that would happen automatically, there is a tendency among many Christians to assume that true faith means portraying a form of spiritual stoicism that views tears and grief as inappropriate or something for which a person needs to apologize. This attitude may be manifested in a variety of ways. For example, a person may say, "We don't want to have a funeral; this needs to be a celebration." Now certainly for the Christian we do not "sorrow as those who have no hope" (1 Thess 4:13), but neither do we hope as those who have no sorrow. We understand what it means to be able to celebrate a life well-lived when death invades our ranks but these are times we also need to truly grieve the loss that we have experienced. We may even hear someone say, as one pastor shared, "I don't want any tears at this funeral." The pastor instead may need to be the one to ensure that there is a place for lament when people are facing death and that the voice of lament is heard in the funeral service and message.

A related pastoral care issue for shaping lament into a local congregation is to challenge many of the theologically inappropriate words that are often said to people in times of loss. I am thinking of phrases such as, "God needed another angel," "It must be God's will," "God knew what he was doing," or "There's a reason for everything; we just can't understand it." These responses are hurtful, unhelpful, and even harmful. They reflect bad theology and run counter to the more biblically sound alternative, which is to lament. Pastors can challenge their people to avoid saying these types of platitudes, and also teach them how to respond appropriately with lament. To help their people know that the best thing we can do when people are grieving is to be physically and emotional present and to join them in their sorrow, is part of the process of lament.

Another step in a congregational plan to introduce or expand lament is through a dedicated service of lament. While not limited to certain seasons, this service can be introduced very effectively during Advent or Lent. A service of lament gives people the opportunity to remember loved ones lost in recent or even long past days. This service of memoirs might include music, reading of names, lighting of candles, Scripture and other readings, etc. An Advent or Christmas lament service can be a valuable introduction to lament but once such a service is incorporated, it would be important to expand it further to include broader categories of lament. As has been noted, in addition to death, we lament any of the broken places where we experience loss and brokenness. Whether in Advent or Lent, or another time altogether, some form of lament service can be a wonderful yearly addition to the worship life of the local parish.

A final step in a congregational plan to introduce or expand lament would focus on ways to bring lament into the regular, ongoing worship life of the church. Including elements of lament through music, prayer, Scripture, litanies, etc. in corporate worship acknowledges the reality that on any given week when the church gathers, there are people who are grieving some real or perceived loss, and they need to lament. While these regular practices of lament might not be included every week (though a sensitivity to this need would always be in order), certainly including them on a regular, perhaps monthly, basis would be an effective way to encourage lament in the lives of the people of God. These standard practices of lament must go beyond prayer time each week. While these times of pastoral prayer can be infused with elements of lament, it will not happen automatically; there must be intentional focus in assisting the practice of lament. And yet, it is this aspect of corporate lament that can be the most challenging, though it is also most needed. Additionally, it is also here where the fewest resources are available. Although they can be obtained, it requires diligent searching of a wide range of sources.[23]

September 11, 2001, the tsunami of 2004, Hurricane Katrina in 2005, the 2011 tornado in Joplin, Missouri, the Sandy Hook Elementary School

---

23. For a site that seeks to collect and curate a variety of lament resources, visit www.sacredsorrow.com.

shootings in 2012, the 2017 Los Vegas shooting, devastating hurricanes in the Caribbean, racial tensions, increased violence and terror in our nation and throughout the world—these represent just some of the tragic events that life can bring. Add to that personal tragedies, the deaths of the young and the old, divorce, the death of dreams, financial hardships, broken relationships, and the adverse effects of addictions and abuse upon so many families. These and countless other realities are faced by our people each and every day. What do we do in response to these realities? What do we say when there are no answers? How do we respond to their questions, hurt, anger, or doubt? Do we pray? Absolutely! Do we seek to bring relief? Of course. But one significant response has been missing far too often. What we desperately need is to lament. This biblical pattern, this theological gift, this language of sorrow, is one that is lacking in the lives of many people and in many churches. The lost language of lament must be recovered. If we do not learn to lament we are doing a disservice to the faith we profess. We must remember again the words of Michael Card, "Until we learn to lament, we have nothing to say to most of the world."[24]

Woven through the fabric of the doctrine of the atonement is this recurring theme of lament. From the cry of Jesus on the cross, to the tears that we weep for his suffering. From the sorrow we feel for our sin, to the tears that we weep for the world. For the questions that come in the journey, to the longing we feel for the kingdom that is yet to come. All through the atonement and the ways that the atonement is realized in the lives of those who respond to this most gracious gift, there is this blending of joy and sorrow. And through it all, we remember that because of the work Christ accomplished, we are able to express the deepest sorrows of our hearts to the One who is fully acquainted with our grief. When we feel forsaken, he has felt forsaken too. Yes, there truly is sorrow in the saving—and lament, like the atonement that provides for it, is a gift of grace.

---

24. Card, *Sacred Sorrow*, Kindle location 399.

CHAPTER 13

Re-Envisioning the Table
Eucharist as Therapeutic Healing

When she heard him preach by the sea, she felt love for the first time in a long time. She felt that she could be worthy of love and forgiveness. Her liturgies of shame and guilt were being replaced by hope and healing. She saw how he loved those who most of the Pharisees scorned and repudiated. She heard him two weeks earlier and she wanted to find him and simply show him how she loved him and desired this grace and hope of which he spoke. He was supposed to be eating at the home of a religious leader. She grabbed some perfume, it was the only thing of value she had. She knocked on the door of a home she knew would reject her, but she hoped he would welcome her and receive her gift. The servant at the door tried to keep her out but she persisted. Then she heard his voice. She was filled with emotion as she ran toward him, bursting past the servant. She dove to his feet, grasping and kissing them. She was overwhelmed. Her gratitude for him and the message of hope he offered came flooding out. She was sobbing, but these were not tears from places of guilt and pain, but of faith and promise. She used her hair to dry the tears that were falling from her face to his feet. She then poured perfume on them. While Jesus' eyes were welcoming, the religious leader became indignant. He began yelling at her that she needed to leave. She was making a spectacle of herself, bringing shame and dishonor into the house. He also told Jesus that he should not allow such a sinful woman to be touching him and making him impure. Did Jesus want shame to fall on him? What would happen next? It is true she was not worthy to even be touching and washing his feet. Her past had soiled her from deserving any love. Yet Jesus looked at her and began to tell a story. He told a story about forgiveness and debts and how those who have large debts forgiven are more thankful than those who are forgiven smaller ones. Jesus then called the owner of the house by name and said that she had shown him more love and hospitality than he, the host of the party. He then looked at her and said, "Know your sins are forgiven. Go and sin no more." It was a moment that began a new life of living into the dignity he had shown her. It was a meal of forgiveness, an encounter of transformation, a meal of hope for this one thankful woman, brave enough to break through her social confinements and go to the source of all true blessing.[1]

This chapter explores both theologically and practically how the eucharistic table can be a means of grace for the sinner and the sinned-against. While primary attention will be given to how pastors can care for those who come to the table from the back side of the cross, this must not be disconnected to those who come predominantly as sinners. In fact, by paying attention *to* and caring *for* those who have been sinned against, the Eucharist is an opportunity for a needed penance for those who have hurt and offended others. It is the main thesis of this chapter that the Lord's Supper is to be a meal of hope, renewal, and promise for both the sinner and sinned-against. While it is a meal of thanksgiving and forgiving grace, it

---

1. Based on Luke 7:36–50.

can also be a meal where persons who come with anger and lament toward others and God can also experience the grace of healing as a therapeutic sacrament.

Specifically, this chapter will explore how the Lord's Supper is a meal of divine transformation. In light of this grace-filled encounter, this chapter will consider both theological affirmations and practical practices of hospitality. It will explore the issues of God's *presence* and *accessibility* (who may come to the table). Then the conversation will note how this is a meal of resurrection power and eschatological hope, which invites healing without a quick "forgive-and-forget" demand for the abused and abandoned. It will also consider how this can be a meal where the public naming of hurts and pains can become the mending balm for sinners and the sinned-against. Finally, this chapter concludes with a *prayer for the people* and eucharistic liturgies that follow the major rhythms of sacramental prayers through the centuries. These prayers offer specific grammar and attention to the ways in which this meal can be a place of confession for sinners and laments for the sinned-against, while offering healing in all its mysterious complexity. The emphasis of this chapter is not to deny that the table is a place for sinners, but how it can also be reimagined for those who have been victimized.

Jesus' Table Fellowship: Meals of Healing and Transformation

From Jesus' meals at Simon's house, to eating with Matthew and Zacchaeus, with his disciples in the upper room, and at the seashore, what is clear is that meals with Jesus are invitations to transformation. The Lord's Supper is an immediate encounter with Christ who was born, crucified, resurrected, and is now dynamically present by the Spirit. Some imagine the Lord's Supper as a meal of remembrance, as if that remembrance is an attempt to mentally memorialize events that Scripture narrates of Jesus long ago. However, the remembrance (*anamnesis* in Greek) of the Lord's Supper is not simply pointing back as sentimental recall, it is very much a present, relational experience. What those on the back side of the cross often need is to be present to Christ, especially if they are still in the midst of the pain and evil. From Adam and Eve, to Abraham and Sarah, Moses, Hannah, Elijah, Paul, and to us, a *present encounter* with God invites the beginning of healing and transformation.

Transformational Encounter

While there is no space here to enter into the larger conversation of various theories regarding the meaning and dynamics of the Lord's Supper, it is our recommendation that we fully support and affirm that Jesus Christ is powerfully present at the table. Often neglected within the debates over Christ's presence in the meal is that Christ's presence is not the only presence of concern. As is true in many eucharistic liturgies in the Christian faith, not only does the church pray to the First Person that Christ be present by the Spirit, the church also prays that the "First Person would send the Spirit *on us* and on these gifts of bread and wine."[2] At the table, the First Person helps make both Christ and Christians present to each other by the Spirit. This *presence* encountered there is the center of the grace and transformation found there.

This spiritual encounter is also sacrificial. As the rite represents (or becomes) the body and blood of Jesus, it reveals his sacrifice for us. Also, in the spirit of Romans 12:1–2, Christians present themselves at the altar as their spiritual act of worship. This offering of ourselves as a living sacrifice can be both an offering of praise (oblation) and/or an offering of lament. Both praise and lament are appropriate ways of offering ourselves before God. The eucharistic invitation is that we come however we are, in our praise, in our hurt, in our hope, in our anger and pain, seeking for God to forgive, but also to heal and transform our brokenness; it may also be a means to see God's willingness to be forgiven (see chapter 8).

All have sinned. All need forgiveness. But as has been said earlier in this conversation, many on the back side also need to come and find the God who has entered into solidarity with their pain. It may be helpful for those on the back side of the cross to consider how the Christ who was crucified is present to them. Just as this theology from the back side is resolutely not a theodicy, getting God *off* the hook for the evil God allowed to happen, in many ways the Lord's Supper can be a uniquely healing place for those who have been sinned against, precisely because they encounter the God who stays *on* the hook, and who desires to be present to them in their suffering. Moreover, this fellowship in Christ's sufferings may be to join in Christ's lament on the cross, "My God, my God, why have you forsaken Me?!" Perhaps it is this kind of kindred encounter with the fellow Sufferer and Lamenter that can be a key therapeutic step for those on the *back side of the cross*. This unique mysterious meal can be the pathway that leads them to move front and center, and see the suffering Christ face-to-face. For both the sinner and sinned-against, then, it is crucial this meal be seen as a present encounter

---

2. See the eucharistic liturgy at the end of the chapter. Emphasis ours. This prayer is part of what is called the *epiclesis*, which literally means "call upon."

with the One who was born, crucified, and resurrected. It is the power of Christ's resurrection that provides the presence of hope and power to both the sinner and sinned-against.

"Profanity" and Hospitality at the Table

Some Jewish religious leaders detested Jesus' table fellowship with tax collectors, prostitutes, and sinners. It is striking in Luke 7 (the opening story of this chapter) that a meal with such a sinner occurs in the home of a Pharisee, likely Simon. Jesus' association, especially at meals, with sinners violated many Levitical laws that Pharisees felt were crucial to being holy. Meals were times to practice holiness by staying away from people and things that were deemed impure and could contaminate. This impurity could come from both the foods eaten and people present.

Yet Jesus' table fellowship provides a model for Christians that a meal can become a place where sinners and the sinned-against can come and be welcomed. The irony is that Simon, the host, failed to see that he was also deeply a sinner (perhaps even more so), who had failed to love and show hospitality both to this woman and to Christ. By looking at Scripture, we see that it is essential to eradicate all theological notions that God's purity and holiness can be tainted by the presence of sinners. God's holiness *cannot* be corrupted by associating with sinners. All of Scripture describes a God who continually seeks to redeem and restore those who have sinned and been sinned against. God's presence always invites and seeks healing; this can be a meal of reconciliation and restoration. That God seeks to woo, pursue, and seek after the lost, should guide the conversation regarding who can come to the table. This leads to the question of what is known as the accessibility of a *closed* or *open* table.

A Closed or Open Table?

The conversation about a closed or open table also deserves more space than will be allotted; however, some historical and ecclesial context may be helpful. The ecclesial issue concerning open or closed communion is also known as *fencing the table*, a rather unfortunate metaphor. For the Orthodox, Roman Catholic, some Lutheran traditions, and a few others, persons are invited to the table only if they have been baptized and/or confirmed *in that tradition*. Other denominations invite *all* Christians who are baptized—whether they are members of those specific denominations or not—to the table; this offers the first layer of open communion. But, thinking it to be a meal of covenant, still only those already in the covenant through baptism are invited. The second layer of an open table would be the practice of some traditions that do not even require persons to be baptized before they come to the table. There are others, however, who look to the meal practice of Christ in the New Testament and see Jesus continually having table fellowship with "outsiders" and inviting them to be healed and transformed, and question whether the table should be "fenced" at all. While some may be quick to suggest only Jesus' Last Supper with his disciples should be seen as eucharistic, there is room, we believe, to look more broadly at Jesus' ministry. Fencing at all seems incorrect, specifically in light of the Gospel of John. It is noteworthy that John does not record Jesus' institution of the Lord's Supper during Passover. Rather, the Eucharist is instituted in John 6 in the feeding of the five thousand narrative. The classic eucharistic actions of Jesus—taking, blessing, breaking, and giving—mark that passage as thoroughly eucharistic. These persons were seeking after Christ, albeit naively at this point. But by the end of the narrative, Jesus questioned their motivation as a means of calling any who followed him into deeper levels of commitment. But he still fed them. It does seem reasonable from the juxtaposition that the feeding with Jesus' eucharistic language in John 6, for us to see the Lord's Supper as a meal where *all* who are hungry and thirsty for God are invited to partake and begin to follow after him. This has led at least one tradition (following John Wesley) to say that Eucharist can be a *converting ordinance*; that in coming to the table they take their first step of faith.

    I (Brent) had the privilege of participating in a global theology conference in South Africa. These conversations were rich and deep. As a sacramental theologian, I was especially anticipating our conversation on the sacraments and specifically the Lord's Supper. Although I had heard of this before in my own context in a limited way, I was completely blown away when I heard that the common practice in Africa was that *most* people do not partake of the Lord's Supper in my denomination. They have been led to fear ever taking Communion because they dreaded the possibility of taking it "unworthily." This led people, faithful people in congregations, to actually feel unworthy, and they believed others would deem them as unworthy as well. The passage of 1 Corinthians 11 had caused many not to come to the table at all because they understood that if anyone had any sin in their life and they participated anyway, they would be eating and drinking *unworthily*, which was a horrible offense and one that would harm them physically. Some churches were even reported to have a "white line" to sit behind unless they were holy enough to participate. Who would be bold enough to find themselves worthy enough in such circumstances? While the caution in the text to not eat or drink unworthily should not be ignored, it would be wrong to understand that Paul is suggesting that only those without sin are worthy to partake. No one is worthy to receive the gracious transforming presence of Christ. The invitation to the table is all about gift and grace, undeserved and unmerited.

John Wesley noted this same concern in the eighteenth century. Wesley was dumbfounded by the masses who feared God and chose not to commune. Wesley observed that many had not communed because they were worried about eating and drinking unworthily. Wesley suggested their fears should be reoriented. "How much greater the danger is when they do not eat or drink at all."[3] Rather than being fearful of eating because one has sin and is not pure enough, persons should fear because God provided a means of grace at the table and they refused to come. Further, Wesley encouraged passionate and regular participation at the table as God provides opportunity. All should see themselves as hungry and thirsty. To deny themselves food and drink is to deny themselves the nourishment they need for spiritual growth and health.

> We must neglect no occasion which the good providence of God affords us for this purpose. This is the true rule—so often are we to receive as God gives us opportunity. Whoever therefore does not receive, but goes from the holy table when all things are prepared, either does not understand his duty or does not care for the dying command of his Saviour, the forgiveness of his sins, the strengthening of his soul, and the refreshing it with the hope of glory.[4]

What does this have to contribute to our conversation regarding the sinned-against? With Wesley's eucharistic exuberance and optimism about spiritual healing, the pastor would be wise to recognize that for many on the *back side* the layers of *undeserved* shame and guilt are so thick that coming to the table is a sheer impossibility. Love, care, and encouragement should be offered to *all* those who do not feel worthy, or feel excluded from God's forgiveness. But we should be even more in tune with those who have been sinned-against. They sit among us in shambles and in shackles, unable to move toward the healing meal because we have failed to invite them in ways they can hear us. Moreover, some may have so much anger at God that they may also believe this makes them inappropriate candidates to partake. This presupposes that lament and anger at God is sinful, which it is not, as the lament psalms teach us. Both public and private pastoral teaching

---

3. Wesley, "Sermon 101," 147.

4. Wesley, "Sermon 101," 148. This sermon was adapted largely from the Non-Juror Robert Nelson's 1707 Sermon, "The Great Duty of Frequenting the Christian Sacrifice."

and encouragement should offer a loving hospitality and fitting invitation *especially* to those who have been sinned against to come to the symbols of God's own brokenness and forsakenness and receive them as healing food.

It is also noteworthy that what Paul is dealing with within the Corinthian church was, in fact, a matter of social justice. The rich were exploiting the poor by failing to be hospitable to them, failing to share from the bounty of the table. It, therefore, is not out of place at all to see this passage through the lens from *the back side of the cross*. To use our language, those from the front side of the cross were not leaving space and resources for those on the back side. Paul's anger is at the powerful, not the poor. His point actually calls for more inclusion of the oppressed, not less.

A Table of Resurrection Hope and Healing

Part of the healing of the Lord's Supper for those on the back side of the cross is certainly the association of Christ's wounds with theirs. But the Eucharist also participates in the power of the resurrection. As Paul writes so well in 1 Corinthians 15, if Christ has not been raised all of our faith is in vain. Likewise, there would be no power at the table without the power, promise, and hope of the resurrection. As explored earlier, it is in the resurrection that the full power of God over sin and death is embodied. Jesus Christ's resurrection is then firstfruits, a beginning of the new creation, for which all of creation desires and groans, awaiting its redemption.[5] Although it is easy to miss, this power of the resurrection is the center of the hope in the encounter at the Lord's Table, for both the sinner and sinned-against, for the resurrection confirms all accomplished on the cross, spilled out as grace upon grace before us.

The celebration of the Eucharist celebrates a divine-human encounter with the very One who laid down his life and was slain, yet who was raised from the dead; thus it is an eschatological feast with Christ and all he saves is offered, as a promise for wiped-away tears and an end to suffering. For those on the *back side* this is part of the hope of the eucharistic meal.

Early theology affirmed that after the celebration of the Eucharist communicants left the church strengthened in their resolve to resist the violence and exploitation of the principalities and power of the world. It is just as appropriate to see the table as the means of such a strengthening power for the sinned-against, who depart to wrestle with disempowerment itself, brought on by human devils of all kinds. They depart from the table strengthened to continue to resist and to heal. What about those who want

5. Rom 8:19–24.

to stand in solidarity with them? May it be a meal that strengthens us in our resolve to truly see them, eat with them, and live with them as vital parts of our communities of new creation. The affirmation of Christ's presence in the eucharistic meal assures us that he is now alive by the resurrecting power of God and with us by the immanence of the Spirit, binding us all together in perfect love.

Pastoral Suggestions for Healing at the Table for Those on the Back Side

We now turn to offer some practical helps to those who minister to those on the back side of the cross.

Welcoming All

As suggested earlier, the idea of an open table should be considered as an expression of pastoral hospitality. If one's tradition prevents this by stating the communicants must be a part of a denomination, or must be baptized, it is still possible to show sensitivities to those victimized who are part of said tradition. It is important to note that acknowledging those on the back side is not simply a nice gesture by pastors and churches who wish to appear more inclusive. It is a theological and pastoral imperative. It is the case that in almost every local congregation there are those gathered who have been, or are being, abused and victimized, who feel excluded from open and honest fellowship because they have absorbed the message that their peculiar kind of pain is not welcome in such a sacred gathering. They also feel excluded from the table because of the unresolved and undeserved shame they carry, particularly if we give the message that the Lord's Supper is for the righteous and saintly who have it all together, or the opposite, for the worst of sinners to find absolution (apart from confession to those they have harmed).

Central to Christian hope is the conviction that the kingdom is here and coming more fully each day. Therefore, it is the local church's responsibility and calling to recognize and appropriately care for those on the back side. This requires that we specifically call both the sinner and the sinned-against to the table. The hard part is knowing how to do this, especially since victims are probably not going to reveal themselves in a sacramental setting. Since many victims hide in our midst, the church must practice a radical hospitality to all. And since many have left the church precisely for its resistance to issues of suffering and injustice, great, great care must be taken here to be inclusive without placing a scarlet V (for victim) on their chests. It is just as dangerous to "out them" as it is to forget and ignore them. Pastors must walk a very thin line indeed, but this is absolutely necessary. And so, the language that we use to invite persons to the table must change. There is an example of such an invitation below.

Naming Injustices and Violations

If the communion table is impossible to use because of certain fencing, another way the to care for the sinned-against is to provide a special service as a space for the public naming of the injustices we commit or remain complicit in, and/or a space for victims to publicly tell their stories. This seems counter to what was just said. But there are some cases where naming the violation aloud can be part of the healing process for those who have suffered under it. For too many on the back side of the cross, both their lives and the abuse they endured have stayed in the dark recesses and the dusty corners of the church. While this is very real and disempowering to the abused, often the abusers, and the larger Christian culture as a whole, suppress truth-telling of the devastating depths of pain and isolation those on the back side have endured. Preparation for such truth-telling will of course be crucial. But a public naming of injustices in which individuals and the church have participated can wake the entire community to hear and see the extent of the pain of violating sins done to the vulnerable. Ruth Duck affirms, "Such naming is a sacred trust and must be treated with utmost care and confidentiality."[6] Indeed, a special service such as this requires great care and discernment on the part of the pastor, and ample and appropriate planning. Depending on the liturgy and the practices of confession and vulnerability offered in this context, it is crucial that all persons, especially the abused from the back side, are given clear instructions and assurances so that it might be a space where all feel safe. This safety is not only good pastoral care, but such safety allows deeper vulnerability to occur. Duck affirms again that for those on the back side of the cross, "The church can best respond by welcoming the voices of victims of injustice, removing injustice from its own life, and working for justice in society."[7] It might be appropriate to have victims write out their stories, leaving them anonymous to be read by someone else. It could be a creative aspect of the preparation to answer

---

6. Duck, "Hospitality to Victims," 175.

7. Duck, "Hospitality to Victims," 175.

the stories with "stanzas" of sorrow and confession from the church as a whole, that steps in as representatives of appropriate apologies.

On the other hand, if a particular worship service is focused on lamenting the pain of the victimized, it may be helpful to omit some prayers of confession from such services. Too often the corporate call to confession focuses on what each person has done wrong. It has been said often in this conversation that some on the *back side* have coped with their pain by thinking and imagining the abuse they received was somehow their own fault. In a desperate attempt to regain some sense of power, they can blame and shame themselves. Hence, prayers of confession need to be thoughtful and instructive on these points. "Liturgy that is hospitable to victims must be spacious enough to accommodate the breadth of their feelings in the presence of God and patient enough to let the Spirit work slowly to bring the healing that makes genuine forgiveness possible."[8] If confessions are offered, it may be wise to include places of lament that serve as confessions, not of sin, but of a need for healing from pain and anger.

Clearly some local churches and pastors will be new to the perspectives of this book. But if a pastor is willing to venture into this new territory, the Holy Spirit can draw persons and the church into deeper healing and unity. Teaching, preaching, and dialogue with all parts of the church will be important. The key is to see how a local church's worship, and especially the sacrament of the Lord's Supper, can be a meal of grace both for the sinner and the sinned-against. This chapter is far from exhaustive. There are many other facets for pastors and leaders to consider, such as how and where people can receive the elements. What is the physical space saying theologically? How can the rest of the service, or services without the sacraments support those on the back side? How does music and other prayers support this intention and care? Encouragement is given to experiment with great care. Mistakes may be made along the way, but staying in communication is important, especially with those who come to pastors as victims. A pastor must never reveal what they are told, of course, under the obligation of pastoral confidentiality! But truly listening to such narratives will certainly help shape all the ministries of the church, including worship and holy communion. The question, then, is how do we create safe places where the sinned-against can move to trusting us with their suffering? With love, grace, and the Holy Spirit, times of communal worship and times at the table can be life-giving for all.

The example below is a eucharistic liturgy that is inclusive and hospitable to the sinned-against. It follows a traditional rhythm that first includes

---

8. Duck, "Hospitality to Victims," 176.

The Prayers of the People. We hope it is evident that special attention is given to those who come and join in Christ's lament from the cross. This liturgy will need to be tweaked and adjusted based on context, or even completely rewritten. The point is to not remain seemingly oblivious to the needs of the sinned-against in worship. We can no longer be silent, or silence them. We hope that what follows can offer some creative ideas on how our praying and practicing can be re-envisioned to more fully care for those *on the back side of the cross*.

A Liturgy

The Prayers of the People

(You are invited to stand, kneel, sit, or come to the altar as we pray. All are encouraged to add your own prayers to these, silently or aloud. Those who would like to be anointed may go to the altar on your right, where a pastor will pray for you and anoint you for physical, emotional, or spiritual healing.)

Minister: Let us pray for the church and the world: Loving God, we pray for your church throughout the world; grant that our divisions may cease, that we may be one, and that we may be found without fault at the day of your coming. We, as the church, confess to the ways in which persons have hurt and abused individuals, and we fully recognize that we have sometimes been complicit or apathetic to their pain. Those who have been hurt and abused have not been allowed to name their experiences of their suffering in our midst. We confess the ways in which the church has silenced victims of abuse and have denied them their story, or even covered up and lied about their pain. Help your church to be open to your Spirit's power to bring to light those things that have been kept hidden in the dark.

(Please add your own requests, either silently or aloud.)

Minister: Lord, in your recreating love and infinite mercy,

People: Hear our prayer.

Minister: We pray for the poor, the persecuted, the sick, and all who suffer at the hands of others; for refugees, prisoners, and all who are in danger; that they may be relieved and comforted. We pray for those who have been hurt on the basis of their differences, for those who have received injury from racism, sexism, classicism, or ableism. For those who have experienced physical, emotional, or spiritual violence this week or in the past, we lift them to you. Hear our cries. We pray especially today for the sinned-against, for those who have been victims of sin. We join today in their pleas and cries for help, and join them in their lament and even anger at you, God, for not intervening. It makes no sense to us, and so we cry "why have you forsaken us?"

(Please add your own requests, either silently or added aloud.)

Minister: Lord, in your recreating love and infinite mercy,

People: Hear our prayer.

Minister: We pray for those we or others have injured or offended. Help us go to them in humility and grace. We pray for those who have heard the demands to forgive and forget their abuse too quickly; we confess that they have been inflicted with new layers of injury through our uneasiness. May you grant us patience, keep us from setting the timetable for when and how forgiveness may come, give us the endurance to continue to walk with them, never to leave their side. Grant them your peace, and enable us to be peacemakers.

(Please add your own intentions, silently or added aloud.)

Minister: Lord, in your recreating love and infinite mercy,

People: Hear our prayer.

Minister: We pray for this congregation, that we might show forth your reviving strength in all that we do; and we pray for those among us who have need of our prayers, including those who are sick, those who grieve, those who struggle in the circumstances of their lives, those who have been sinned against that they would begin to find hope and healing from their places of undeserved shame. We pray especially for these here seeking anointing. We pray for your mending at the very deepest parts of their being. Grant that all of those for which we pray may be freed to live in your wholeness and transformation. Help your church to faithfully live into the power of the Holy Spirit that we might reflect the love of our suffering Savior and Resurrected Lord.

(Please add your own intentions, silently or added aloud.)

Minister: Lord, in your recreating love and infinite mercy,

People: Hear our prayer.

Minister: We bless your holy name for the thanksgiving of your people, including these:

(Please add your own praises, either silently or aloud)

We thank you for those in every generation in whom Christ has been rightly honored and reflected. Give us grace to follow their good examples, that with them we may be partakers of your heavenly kingdom. We also pray that you break the cycles of the sins for our forbearers by teaching us new ways to live. We thank you for our redemption from sin and for offering new life to those who have been damaged by sin. We thank you for all that you have done for us, all that you are to us, and for where you will lead us as we seek to be your faithful people.

Minister: Lord, in your recreating love and infinite mercy,

People: Hear our prayer.

Preparation for Holy Communion (the people sitting):

(The Invitation) Minister: The Lord's Supper was ordained by God to be a means of conveying grace according to the needs of each person. Those for whom it was ordained are all those who know and feel that they want the grace of God, to restrain them from sin, or to forgive their sins, or to assure them of pardon, or to renew their souls in the image of God, or to find deeper healing from the wounds they bear. All those who want to enter into the holy presence of God in communion through the Spirit should hear that no preparation is indispensably necessary, other than a desire to receive whatsoever grace God pleases to give. No fitness or church membership is required at the time of communicating, other than a sense of our state, of our sinfulness or our woundedness apart from Christ. Therefore, if you want such grace as God pleases to give to you, draw near with faith, and as you prepare to receive this holy sacrament to your comfort and strength, make your sincere confession of sins to God, or your sincere declaration of your need of God to bring deeper healing in body, soul, and spirit.

People: We confess the ways we have sinned against you and others and pray you will allow us the opportunity to seek their forgiveness in a spirit of repentance and sorrow. We also pray along with those who come to the table and are broken and in pain because of abuse done by others. We here lament for all the ways this world is not as it should be. We pray in solidarity with those seeking healing to replace unspeakable sorrow and unmerited shame. Within our confession of sin, our confession of need, and our expression of lament, we ground our prayer in praise to you who bore our shame and became sin for us on the cross. We also praise you for the gift of hope and new creation afforded to us in his resurrection.

Minister: The Lord be with you.

People: And also with you.

Minister: Lift up your hearts.

People: We lift them up to the Lord.

Minister: Let us give thanks to the Lord our God.

People: It is right to give our thanks and praise.

Minister: It is right, always and everywhere to give thanks to you, God, creator of heaven and earth, and of humanity, created in your loving image. Although we marred that image and thwarted your purposes, you did not leave us on our own. Despite our brokenness, you loved us by sending your Son. We praise you for the sacrifice that he offered as an act of love to you and on our behalf; on the cross he took away the sins of the world. And he takes away the sin we bear, those we have committed and those we have received. We thank you now for inviting us to your table, just as you invited the weak and the outcasts to eat with you while on earth. We thank you for offering forgiveness to the sinner. We thank you also that your Son allowed himself to be abused and mistreated so that God would be present to those abused and mistreated. As both the sinner and the sinned-against, we thank you for making us a part of your new creation. Help to make your church one in hope and peace. We are invited to the table to live into this transforming and resurrecting grace. And so, with all your people on earth and all the company of heaven, we praise your name and join their unending hymn:

(Sanctus) All: Holy, holy, holy Lord, heaven and earth are full of your glory, Hosanna in the highest. Blessed is he who comes in the name of the Lord. Hosanna in the highest.

Holy, holy, holy Christ. You are risen! You are risen indeed! Hallelujah!

Holy, holy, Holy Spirit. God of comfort, comfort we your people! Praise to your name!

Minister: Holy are you our God, and blessed is your Son Jesus Christ. Your Spirit anointed him to preach good news to the poor, to proclaim release to the captives and recovery of sight to the blind, to set at liberty those who are oppressed, and to announce that the time had come when you would save your people. He healed the sick, fed the hungry, and ate with sinners. By the baptism of his suffering, death, and resurrection you gave birth to your church, delivered us from slavery to sin and death, and made with us a new covenant by water and the spirit.

(Institution Narrative) On the night in which he gave himself up for us and entered into solidarity with those who have been victimized by sin, Our Lord Jesus took bread, gave thanks to you, broke the bread gave it to his disciples, and said:

"Take, eat; this is my body which is given for you. Do this in remembrance of me." Likewise, when the supper was over, he took the cup, gave thanks to you, gave it to his disciples, and said: "Drink from this, all of you, this is my blood of the new covenant, poured out for you and for many for the forgiveness of sins. Do this, as often as you drink it, in remembrance of me."

And so, in remembrance of these your mighty acts in Jesus Christ,

ALL: we offer ourselves in praise and thanksgiving as a holy and living offering, in union with Christ's offering for us, as we proclaim the mystery of faith: *Christ has died; Christ is risen; Christ will come again.*

(Epiclesis) Pour out your Holy Spirit on us gathered here, and on these gifts of bread and the cup. Make them be for us the body and blood of Christ, that we may be for the world the body of Christ, redeemed by his blood, healed through his grace.

By your Spirit make us one with Christ, provide healing to both the sinner and sinned-against. May persons at the table who come in lament, abused and broken, hear a word of your sorrow and a word of your hope as they are in need of your presence. Help your church to find unity with each other, as one in ministry to all the world, until Christ comes in final victory and we feast at his heavenly banquet. Through your Son Jesus Christ, with your Holy Spirit in your holy church, all honor and glory is yours, all loving God, now and forever. Amen.

Bibliography

Alison, James. "God's Self-Substitution and Sacrificial Inversion." In *Stricken by God? Nonviolent Identification and the Victory of Christ*, edited by Brad Jersak and Michael Hardin, 166–79. Grand Rapids: Eerdmans, 2007.
Aquinas, Thomas. *Summa Theologiae* Prima Pars, Q. 14 and 19 and *Summa contra Gentiles*, bk. I, chs. 72–88 and *Quaestiones disputatae* De malo.
Aulén, Gustaf. *Christus Victor*. New York: MacMillian, 1967.
Baker-Fletcher, Karen. *My Sister, My Brother: Womanist and Xodus God-Talk*. Bishop Henry McNeal Turner/Sojourner Truth Series in Black Religion 12. Maryknoll, NY: Orbis, 1997.
Barth, Karl. *Church Dogmatics III/3, The Doctrine of Creation*. Translated by G. T Thomson et al. Edinburgh: T. & T. Clark, 1936.
Batten, Alicia J. "Honor and Shame in the New Testament." http://bibleodyssey.org/tools/ask-a-scholar/honor-and-shame-in-the-new-testament.
Bauckham, Richard. "Moltmann's Theology of Hope Revisited." *Scottish Journal of Theology* 42 (1989) 199–214.
Beck, Richard. *Unclean: Meditations on Purity, Hospitality, and Morality*. Eugene, OR: Cascade, 2011.
Blumenthal, David R. *Facing the Abusing God: A Theology of Protest*. Louisville, KY: Westminster John Knox, 1993.
Bonhoeffer, Dietrich. *The Cost of Discipleship*. New York: Simon and Schuster, 1995.
Bowlby, John. *Forty-Four Juvenile Thieves: Their Characters and Home-Life*. London: Tindall and Cox, 1947.
Bowlby, John, and Mary Ainsworth. *Child Care and the Growth of Love*. New York: Penguin, 1965.
Boyd, Greg. "The 'Christus Victor' View of the Atonement." https://reknew.org/2018/11/the-christus-victor-view-of-the-atonement/.
Brondos, David A. *Paul on the Cross: Reconstructing the Apostle's Story of Redemption*. Minneapolis: Fortress, 2006.
Brown, Brené. "Brené Brown's Return to Faith." Prayer and Poutine (podcast). https://prayerandpoutine.wordpress.com/2016/10/27/brene-browns-return-to-faith-jesus-wept/amp.
Brown, Peter. "Sexuality and Society in the Fifth Century AD: Augustine and Julian of Eclanum." In *Biblioteca Di Athenaeum 1: Tria Corda, Scritti in onore di Arnaldo Momigliano*, edited by E. Gabba, 49–70. Como, Italy: Edizioni New Press, 1983.
Brown, Sally, and Patrick Miller. *Lament*. Louisville, KY: Westminster John Knox, 2007.

Brueggemann, Walter. "The Shrill Voice of the Wounded Party." In *The Other Side of Sin: Woundedness From the Perspective of the Sinned-Against*, edited by Andrew Sung Park and Susan L Nelson, 25–44. New York: State University of New York Press, 2001.

Caldwell, John Matthew. "Religion and Sexual Violence in Late Greco-Roman Antiquity." PhD diss., Syracuse University, 2003.

Calvin, John. "Forms of Prayer for the Church." In *Tracts and Treatises on the Doctrine and Worship of the Church* vol. 2, translated by Henry Beveridge. Grand Rapids: Eerdmans, 1958.

Cameron, Averil. "Virginity as Metaphor: Women and the Rhetoric of Early Christianity." In *History as Text: The Writing of Ancient History*, 183–208. Chapel Hill, NC: University of North Carolina Press, 1989.

Cannon, Mae Elise. *Forgive Us: Confessions of a Compromised Faith*. Grand Rapids: Zondervan, 2014.

Card, Michael. *A Sacred Sorrow: Reaching Out to God in the Lost Language of Lament*. Colorado Springs, CO: NavPress, 2005. www.sacredsorrow.com.

Carlson Brown, Joanne, and Rebecca Parker. "For God So Loved the World?" In *Christianity, Patriarchy and Abuse: A Feminist Critique*, edited by Joanne Carlson Brown and Carole R. Bohn, 1–30. New York: Pilgrim, 1989.

Chrysostom, John. *On Virginity; Against Remarriage*. Translated by Sally Rieger Shore. New York: Edwin Mellen, 1983.

Clark, Elizabeth. "Introduction." In *On Virginity; Against Remarriage, by St. John Chrysostom*, vii–xlii. Studies in Women and Religion. Lewiston, NY: Edwin Mellen, 1983.

———. "Theory and Practice in Late Ancient Asceticism: Jerome, Chrysostom, and Augustine." *Journal of Feminist Studies in Religion* 5 (1989) 25–46.

Collins, A. Y., and H. W. Attridge. *Mark: A Commentary on the Gospel of Mark*. Minneapolis: Fortress, 2007.

Cone, James. *The Cross and the Lynching Tree*. Maryknoll, NY: Orbis, 2012.

———. *God of the Oppressed*. Rev. ed. Maryknoll, NY: Orbis, 1997.

Considine, Kevin. "Han and Salvation for the Sinned Against." *New Theological Review* 26 (2013) 87–89.

———. *Salvation and the Sinned-Against: Han and Schillebeeckx in Intercultural Dialogue*. Eugene, OR: Pickwick, 2015.

Corrington, Gail Paterson. *Her Image of Salvation*. Louisville, KY: Westminster John Knox, 1992.

Craddock, Fred. *As One Without Authority*. Nashville, TN: Abingdon, 1987.

Cummings, Danielle. "The Suffering God: How Jesus Meets Us in Pain." *The Table*, 2018. https://cct.biola.edu/suffering-god-jesus-meets-us-pain/.

Davis, C. Truman. "A Physician's View of the Crucifixion of Jesus Christ." http://www1.cbn.com/medical-view-of-the-crucifixion-of-jesus-christ.

Des Pres, Terrance. *The Survivor: An Anatomy of Life in the Death Camps*. Oxford: Oxford University Press, 1976.

Duck, Ruth. "Hospitality to Victims: A Challenge to Christian Worship." In *The Other Side of Sin: Woundedness From the Perspective of the Sinned-Against*, edited by Andrew Sung Park and Susan L. Nelson, 165–80. New York: State University of New York Press, 2001.

Felitti, V. J., et al. "Relationship of Childhood Abuse and Household Dysfunction to Many of the Leading Causes of Death in Adults: Adverse Childhood Experiences (ACE) Study." *American Journal of Preventive Medicine* 14 (1998) 245–58.

Ford, David Carleton. "Misogynist or Advocate? St. John Chrysostom and His Views on Women." PhD diss., Drew University, 1989.

Fortune, Marie M. "The Conundrum of Sin, Sex, Violence, and Theodicy." In *The Other Side of Sin: Woundedness From the Perspective of the Sinned-Against*, edited by Andrew Sung Park and Susan L. Nelson, 123–42. New York: State University of New York Press, 2001.

Foucault, Michel. *Discipline and Punish: The Birth of the Prison*. Translated by Alan Sheridan. New York: Vintage, 1995.

France, R. T. *The Gospel of Mark: A Commentary on the Greek Text*. Grand Rapids: Eerdmans, 2014.

Frankl, Viktor. *Man's Search for Meaning*. Boston: Beacon, 2000.

Girard, René. *Sacrifice*. Translated by Matthew Pattillo and David Dawson. East Lansing, MI: Michigan State University Press, 2011.

———. *The Scapegoat*. Translated by Yvonne Freccero. Baltimore, MD: John Hopkins University Press, 1989.

Green, Bill. "The Crucifixion of our Lord Through the Eyes of Surgeon." http://www.crucifixion1.com/asp.php.

Gunderson, Erik. "The Ideology of the Arena." *Classical Antiquity* 15 (1996) 113–51.

Hall, Terese A. "Spiritual Effects of Childhood Sexual Abuse in Christian Women." *Journal of Psychology and Theology* 23 (1995) 129–34.

Harkness, Robert. "Why Should He Love Me So?" ©1925. Renewed 1980 Broadman Press (Admin. by Music Services, Inc.).

Hauerwas, Stanley. *Naming the Silences: God, Medicine, and Suffering*. Grand Rapids: Eerdmans, 1990.

Hays, Richard B. *The Moral Vision of the New Testament*. New York: Harper One, 1996.

Heath, Elaine. *We Are the Least of These: Reading the Bible with Survivors of Sexual Abuse*. Grand Rapids: Brazos, 2011.

Heyward, Carter. *Saving Jesus from Those Who Are Right: Rethinking What It Means to Be Christian*. Minneapolis: Fortress, 1999.

Hopkins, Julie M. *Towards a Feminist Christology: Jesus of Nazareth, European Women, and the Christological Crisis*. Grand Rapids: Eerdmans, 1995.

Irenaeus. *Against the Heresies*. In *The Ante-Nicene Fathers*. Edited by Alexander Roberts and James Donaldson, vol. 1 (1885–1887); reprint, Peabody, MA: Hendrickson, 1994.

Irigaray, Luce. "Any Theory of the 'Subject.'" In *Speculum of the Other Woman*, 133–46. Translated by Gillian Gill. Ithaca, NY: Cornell University Press, 1985.

Jenkins, Patty, dir. *Monster*. Beverly Hills, CA: Media 8 Entertainment, 2003

Jonathan (Father). "A homily by an Orthodox presbyter, Fr Jonathan." https://cost-of-discipleship.blogspot.com/search?q=waters+do+not+part.

Kallas, James. *The Satanward View: A Study in Pauline Theology*. Philadelphia: Westminster, 1966.

Keller, Heidi. "Autonomy and Relatedness Revisited: Cultural Manifestations of Universal Human Needs." *Child Development Perspectives Online Journal* 6 (2012) 12–18.

Kierkegaard, Søren. *The Sickness Unto Death*. Translated by Howard V. Hong and Edna H. Hong. Princeton, NJ: Princeton University Press, 1980.

———. *The Sickness Unto Death*. Translated by Walter Lowrie. Princeton University Press, 1954.

Knabb, Joshua J., and Matthew Y. Emerson. "I Will Be Your God and You Will Be My People: Attachment Theory and the Grand Narrative of Scripture." *Pastoral Psychology* 62 (2013) 827–41.

Leclerc, Diane. *Singleness of Heart: Gender, Sin, and Holiness in Historical Perspective*. Lanham, MD: Scarecrow, 2001.

Levine, Peter A. *Waking the Tiger: Healing Trauma*. Berkeley, CA: North Atlantic, 1997.

Lewis, Alan E. *Between Cross and Resurrection: A Theology of Holy Saturday*. Grand Rapids: Eerdmans, 2001.

Linehan, Marsha M. *DBT Skills Training Manual*. New York: Guilford, 2015.

Lyman, J. Rebecca. "Reflections on Early Christology in the Light of Elisabeth Schussler Fiorenza's Theology." Unpublished paper. Used with permission.

Maddox, Randy. *Responsible Grace: John Wesley's Practical Theology*. Nashville, TN: Abingdon, 1994.

Main, M., and R. Goldwyn. "Adult Attachment Scoring and Classification System (1985/1991)." Unpublished manuscript, University of California, Berkeley.

Mallett, Xanthe. "Women Also Sexually Abuse Children, but Their Reasons Often Differ from Men." https://theconversation.com/women-also-sexually-abuse-children-but-their-reasons-often-differ-from-mens-72572.

Mayo, Marla. "Aurora and the Question of Forgiveness." https://www.huffpost.com/entry/aurora-and-the-question-of-forgiveness_b_1693458.

———. "What Does the Bible Really Say About Forgiveness?" https://www.huffpost.com/entry/forgiveness-in-the-bible_b_911562?guccounter=_Puudn-ModhaxHXMEcfNe-P7oKCoz9DWHSo.

Meins, E., et al. "Mind-mindedness as a Multidimensional Construct: Appropriate and Non-attuned Mind-related Comments Independently Predict Infant-mother Attachment in a Socially Diverse Sample." *Infancy* 17 (2012) 393–415.

Mjaaland, Marius Timmann. "The Fractured Unity of God: Lament as a Challenge to the Very Nature of God." In *Evoking Lament*, edited by Eva Harasta and Brian Brock, 99–117. New York: T. & T. Clark International, 2009.

Moltmann, Jürgen. *The Crucified God*. Minneapolis: Fortress, 1993.

———. *Jesus Christ for Today's World*. Minneapolis: Fortress, 1994.

Moxnes, Halvor. "Honor and Shame." *Biblical Theological Bulletin* 23 (1993) 167–76.

Nam-Dong, Suh. "Towards a Theology of Han." In *Minjung Theology: People as the Subjects of History*, edited by Committee on Theological Concerns of the Christian Conference of Asia, 51–66. Rev. ed. Maryknoll, NY: Orbis, 1983.

National Association for Christian Recovery. https://www.nacr.org/abusecenter/spiritual-abuse.

Niebuhr, Reinhold. *Man's Nature and His Communities: Essays on the Dynamics and Enigmas of Man's Personal and Social Existence*. Eugene, OR: Wipf and Stock, 2012.

———. *The Nature and Destiny of Man*. Vol. 1, *Human Nature*. New York: Charles Scribner's Sons, 1964.

Nietzsche, Friedrich. *The Gay Science*. Translated by William Kaufmann. New York: Vintage, 1974.

Nightbirde. (Aka: Jane Marczewski.) "God is on the Bathroom Floor." https://www.nightbirde.co/?fbclid=IwAR2v3q1q9cHXlDn7M1eND2JB1E6oxSbV3dKYjikUwAP6VVR-75zWwgFbKzg.

Nouwen, Henri J. M. *Bread for the Journey.* New York: HarperOne, 1997.

———. *The Wounded Healer: Ministry in a Contemporary Society.* New York: Doubleday, 1972.

O'Connor, Kathleen M. *Lamentations and the Tears of the World.* Maryknoll, NY: Orbis, 2002.

Ogden, Pat, et al. *Trauma and the Body.* New York: W. W. Norton and Co., 2006.

Oord, Thomas J. *God Can't.* Grasmere, ID: SacraSage, 2019.

Oxenham, H. N. *The Catholic Doctrine of the Atonement.* London: Longman, Roberts, and Green, 1865.

Park, Andrew Sung. "The Bible and Han." In *The Other Side of Sin: Woundedness From the Perspective of the Sinned-Against,* edited by Andrew Sung Park and Susan L. Nelson, 45–60. New York: State University of New York Press, 2001.

———. *From Hurt to Healing : A Theology of the Wounded.* Nashville, TN: Abingdon, 2004.

———. *The Wounded Heart of God: The Asian Concept of Han and the Christian Doctrine of Sin.* Nashville, TN: Abingdon, 1993.

Park, Andrew Sung, and Susan L. Nelson, eds. *The Other Side of Sin: Woundedness From the Perspective of the Sinned-Against.* New York: State University of New York Press, 2001.

Park, Andrew Sung, and Susan L. Nelson. "Why Do We Need Another Book on the Subject of Sin?" In *The Other Side of Sin: Woundedness From the Perspective of the Sinned-Against,* edited by Andrew Sung Park and Susan L. Nelson, 1–24. New York: State University of New York Press, 2001.

Patterson, Patricia M., "Book Review on Simon Wiesenthal, *The Sunflower: On the Possibilities and Limits of Forgiveness.*" In *Administrative Theory & Praxis* 28 (2006) 474–78.

Perl, Gisella. *I Was a Doctor in Auschwitz.* New York: International University, 1948.

Peterson, Brent D. *Created to Worship.* Kansas City, MO: The Foundry, 2012.

Purvis, Karyn. *Created to Connect Study Guide.* https://empoweredtoconnect.org/created-to-connect-study-guide/.

Purvis, Karyn, et al. *The Connected Child, Bring Hope and Healing to Your Adoptive Family.* New York: McGraw Hill, 2007.

Purvis, Karyn B., et al. "Trust-Based Relational Intervention (TBRI): A Systemic Approach to Complex Developmental Trauma." *Child & Youth Services* 34 (2013) 360–86.

Raphael, Melissa. *The Female Face of God in Auschwitz: A Jewish Feminist Theology of the Holocaust.* New York: Routledge, 2003.

Ray, Darby Kathleen. *Deceiving the Devil: Atonement, Abuse, and Ransom.* Cleveland, OH: Pilgrim, 1998.

Riley, Stephen. "Psalm 22." *Plain Account Online Commentary.* http://www.aplainaccount.org/lent-2b-psalm/.

Robertson, James, and Joyce Robertson. "Young Children in Brief Separation: A Fresh Look." *Psychoanalytic Study of the Child* 26 (1971) 264–315.

Rondet, Henri. *Original Sin: The Patristic and Theological Background.* Staten Island, NY: Alba House, 1972.

Rusch, William G. *The Trinitarian Controversy*. Philadelphia: Fortress, 1980.
Saiving, Valerie. "The Human Situation: A Feminine View." In *Womenspirit Rising*, edited by Carol Christ and Judith Plaskow, 25–42. San Francisco: Harper and Row, 1979.
Schore, Alan N. "Modern Attachment Theory, the Enduring Impact of Early Right brain Development on Affect Regulation." (2012) 4:47/49:06, 201–64.
Schwager, Raymund. *Jesus in the Drama of Salvation*. New York: Crossroad, 1999.
Schwehn, Mark R. "Human Conditions: Defining the Terms of Forgiveness." *The Cresset: A Review of Literature, the Arts, and Public Affairs* 83 (2019) 12–17. http://www.thecresset.org/2019/Michaelmas/Schwehn_M19.html.
Shapiro, Francis. *Eye Movement Desensitization and Reprocessing (EMDR) Therapy*. New York: Guilford, 2018.
Shengold, Leonard. *Soul Murder: The Effects of Childhood Abuse and Deprivation*. New York: Ballentine, 1989.
Siegel, D. J. *The Developing Mind: How Relationships and the Brain Interact to Shape Who We Are*. New York: Guilford, 2012.
Siegel, Daniel, and Tina Payne Bryson. *The Whole Brain Child*. New York: Bantam, 2012.
Soelle, Dorothee. *Suffering*. Philadelphia: Fortress, 1975.
Son, Chan Hee. *Haan of Minjung Theology and Han of Han Philosophy: In the Paradigm of Process Philosophy and Metaphysics of Relatedness*. Lanham, MD: University of America Press, 2000.
Substance Abuse and Mental Health Services Administration. "SAMHSA's Concept of Trauma and Guidance for a Trauma-Informed Approach." July, 2014. https://ncsacw.samhsa.gov/userfiles/files/SAMHSA_Trauma.pdf.
Szalet, Leon. *Experiment "E."* Translated by Catherine Bland Williams. New York: Didier, 1945.
Tillich, Paul. *The Courage to Be*. New Haven, CT: Yale University Press, 2014.
———. *Dynamics of Faith*. New York: Harper and Row, 1957.
UNICEF. Updated press release, 2017. https://www.unicef.org/media/media_45279.html.
U.S. Department of Health and Human Services, Administration for Children and Families, Administration on Children, Youth and Families, Children's Bureau. *Child Maltreatment 2014*. http://www.acf.hhs.gov/programs/cb/research-data-technology/statistics-research/child-maltreatment.
Van der Kolk, Bessel. *The Body Keeps the Score: Brain, Mind, and Body in the Healing of Trauma*. New York: Penguin, 2015.
Volf, Miroslav. "Forgiveness, Reconciliation and Justice." In *Stricken by God? Nonviolent Identification and the Victory of Christ*, edited by Brad Jersak and Michael Hardin, 268–87. Grand Rapids: Eerdmans, 2007.
Walsh, Sylvia. "On 'Feminine' and 'Masculine' Forms of Despair." In *International Kierkegaard Commentary: The Sickness Unto Death*, edited by Robert L. Perkins, 121–34. Macon, GA: Mercer University Press, 1987.
Watts, Isaac. "At the Cross." (1707) Public Domain.
———. "When I Survey the Wondrous Cross." (1707) Public Domain.
Weaver, J. Denny. *The Nonviolent Atonement*. Grand Rapids: Eerdmans, 2001.
Weil, Simone. *Waiting for God*. New York: G. P. Putnam's Sons, 1951.
Weinstock, Eugene. *Beyond the Last Path*. Translated by Clara Ryan. New York: Boni and Gaer, 1947.

Weiss, Reska. *Journey through Hell*. London: Vallentine, Mitchell, 1961.
Welz, Claudia. "Trust and Lament: Faith in the Face of Godforsakenness." In *Evoking Lament*, edited by Eva Harasta and Brian Brock, 118–35. New York: T. & T. Clark International, 2009.
Wesley, Charles. "O For a Thousand Tongues to Sing." Public Domain.
Wesley, John. "Sermon 101, 'The Duty of Constant Communion.'" In *The Works of Rev. John Wesley 7*, edited by Thomas Jackson, 147–57. Peabody, MA: Hendrickson.
Westermann, Claus. *Praise and Lament in the Psalms*. Louisville, KY: Westminster John Knox, 1981.
Wiegman, Issac. "Divine Forgiveness and Mercy in Evolutionary Perspective." In *Connecting Faith and Science: Philosophical and Theological Inquiries*, edited by Matthew Nelson Hill and Wm. Curtis Holtzen, 183–214. Claremont, CA: Claremont, 2017.
———. "The Evolution of Retribution: Intuitions Undermined." *Pacific Philosophical Quarterly* 98 (2017) 193–218.
Wiesel, Elie. *Night*. New York: Hill and Wang, 2006.
Wiesen, David S. *St. Jerome as a Satirist: A Study in Christian Latin Thought and Letters*. Cornell Studies in Classical Philosophy 34. Ithaca, NY: Cornell University Press, 1964.
Wiesenthal, Simon. *The Sunflower: On the Possibilities and Limits of Forgiveness*. New York: Schocken, 1976.
Witvliet, John D. *Worship Seeking Understanding: Windows into Christian Practice*. Grand Rapids: Baker Academic, 2003.
Wolterstorff, Nicholas. *Lament for a Son*. Grand Rapids: Eerdmans, 1987.
Yoo, Boo-wong. *Korean Pentecostalism: Its History and Theology*. New York: Verlag Peter Lang, 1988.

www.ingramcontent.com/pod-product-compliance
Lightning Source LLC
Chambersburg PA
CBHW030822230426
43667CB00008B/1334